SHIPWRECK
AT CAPE FLORA

NORTHERN LIGHTS SERIES

Copublished with the Arctic Institute of North America
ISSN 1701-0004 (PRINT) ISSN 1925-2943 (ONLINE)

This series takes up the geographical region of the North (circumpolar regions within the zone of discontinuous permafrost) and publishes works from all areas of northern scholarship, including natural sciences, social sciences, earth sciences, and the humanities.

SHIPWRECK
AT CAPE FLORA

THE EXPEDITIONS OF BENJAMIN LEIGH SMITH,
ENGLAND'S FORGOTTEN ARCTIC EXPLORER

P.J. CAPELOTTI

UNIVERSITY OF
CALGARY
PRESS

NORTHERN LIGHTS SERIES
ISSN 1701-0004 (Print) ISSN 1925-2943 (Online)

University of Calgary Press
2500 University Drive NW
Calgary, Alberta
Canada T2N 1N4
www.uofcpress.com

LIBRARY AND ARCHIVES CANADA CATALOGUING IN PUBLICATION

Capelotti, P. J. (Peter Joseph), 1960-
    Shipwreck at Cape Flora : the expeditions of Benjamin Leigh Smith, England's forgotten Arctic explorer / P.J. Capelotti.

(Northern lights series, 1701-0004 ; 16)
Includes bibliographical references and index.
Issued also in electronic formats.
Co-published by: Arctic Institute of North America.
ISBN 978-1-55238-705-4

    1. Smith, Benjamin Leigh, 1828-1913. 2. Explorers—Great Britain—Biography. 3. Arctic regions—Discovery and exploration—British—History—19th century. I. Arctic Institute of North America II. Title. III. Series: Northern lights series ; 16

G875.S65C36 2013   910.92   C2013-900287-1

The University of Calgary Press acknowledges the support of the Government of Alberta through the Alberta Multimedia Development Fund for our publications. We acknowledge the financial support of the Government of Canada through the Canada Book Fund for our publishing activities. We acknowledge the financial support of the Canada Council for the Arts for our publishing program.

Printed and bound in Canada by Marquis
♻ This book is printed on FSC Silva Enviro paper

Cover design, page design, and typesetting by Melina Cusano

To the memory of Harry 'Red' Caughron (1922–2010) of Wood-berry Forest, Virginia, a gentle giant of a man and every bit the equal of the Appalachian mountains he introduced me to, this volume is inscribed with love, affection, and remembrance.

HIKING'S THE TOPIC! Peter Capelotti of Brockton and Harry 'Red' Caughron, former All-American at William & Mary and now head athletic Director at Woodberry Forest Prep School in Virginia, share stories about eastern mountain backpacking with students in a shelter atop Blue Ridge Mountains in the Shenandoah National Park, Va.

On Loft Mountain, Virginia, July 1976

CONTENTS

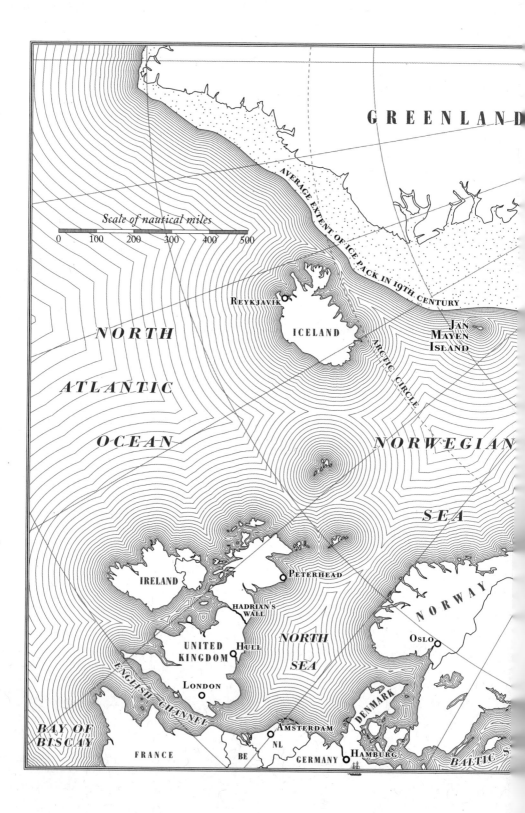

GREENLAND

Scale of nautical miles

0   100   200   300   400   500

AVERAGE EXTENT OF ICE PACK IN 19TH CENTURY

REYKJAVIK

NORTH

ICELAND

JAN
MAYEN
ISLAND

ATLANTIC

ARCTIC CIRCLE

NORWEGIAN

OCEAN

SEA

PETERHEAD

IRELAND

NORWAY

HADRIAN'S
WALL

NORTH

OSLO

UNITED
KINGDOM

HULL

SEA

LONDON

ENGLISH CHANNEL

DENMARK

*BAY OF
BISCAY*

AMSTERDAM

FRANCE

NL

BE

GERMANY

HAMBURG

BALTIC S

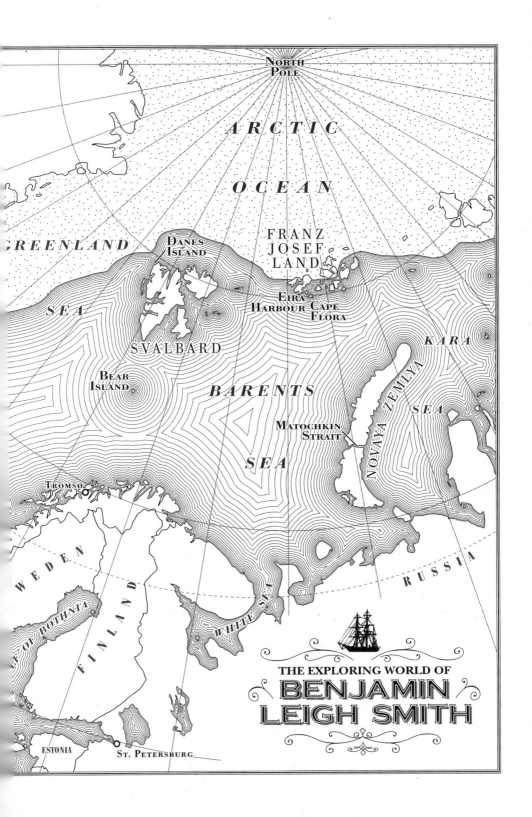

NORTH POLE

A R C T I C

O C E A N

FRANZ JOSEF LAND

GREENLAND

DANES ISLAND

EIRA HARBOUR CAPE FLORA

SEA

KARA

SVALBARD

BEAR ISLAND

BARENTS

NOVAYA ZEMLYA

SEA

MATOCHKIN STRAIT

SEA

TROMSØ

RUSSIA

SWEDEN

FINLAND

WHITE SEA

GULF OF BOTHNIA

ESTONIA

ST. PETERSBURG

THE EXPLORING WORLD OF
BENJAMIN LEIGH SMITH

LIST OF FIGURES

north and east of Bjørnøya, finally settling on an advance north along the west coast of Svalbard. Chart derived from Petermann, 1872, 'Originalkarte.'

14. Track of *Sampson* along Svalbard's west coast to Danskøya, round Hakluyt's Headland, and to Sorgfjorden (7–31 July 1871). *Sampson* then penetrated Hinlopenstretet as far as Wilhelmøya (1–31 August 1871). Tumlingodden, from where Leigh Smith and others thought they could sight 'Gile's Land' (actually Kong Karls Land), is the eastern point of Wilhelmøya. Petermann thought Gile's [Gillis] Land was actually further north and east. He was correct in believing that what Leigh Smith had seen was Kong Karls Land. Chart derived from Petermann, 1872, 'Originalkarte.'

15. The break-out from Hinlopenstretet (31 August 1871) and the flying expedition eastwards past Kapp Platen (4 September 1871), to Foynøya (5 September 1871), to Kapp Leigh Smith (6 September 1871). *Sampson* then retreated along the north coast of Nordaustlandet to the Seven Islands (Sjuøyane). There, north of Rossøya, Leigh Smith made his farthest north of lat. 81°25′ N at 11 a.m. on 11 September 1871. *Sampson* then made for Wijdefjorden where Leigh Smith charted Vestfjorden (12–16 September 1871). Chart derived from Petermann, 1872, 'Smyth' & Ulve's.'

16. Norwegian walrus-hunting *jakts* off the northern coast of Svalbard, 1880 (courtesy Hancox Archive).

17. Chart of Leigh Smith's progress from England to Jan Mayen along the edge of the polar ice to Svalbard (from Wells, 1873).

18. Chart of ocean stations conducted by *Sampson* in 1872 (from Wells, 1873).

19. Track of the *Sampson*, 1 July–29 August 1872.

20. The Moffen Island whale skeleton (from Wells 1873).

twenty-one-year-old University of Edinburgh medical student Arthur Conan Doyle (courtesy Hancox Archive).

31. Leigh Smith ashore at what appears to be Smeerenburgfjorden, Svalbard, in 1880 (courtesy Hancox Archive).

32. *Eira* working through the ice, 1880 (courtesy Hancox Archive).

33. Skinning walrus off May Island, 1880 (courtesy Hancox Archive).

34. Leigh Smith's explorations along the southern reaches of Franz Josef Land, 1880 (from Markham 1881).

35. 'Cathedral Point,' Mabel Island, 1880 (courtesy Hancox Archive).

36. *Eira*, in likely the only photograph taken in its namesake harbour. Bell Island to the left (courtesy Hancox Archive).

37. *Eira* in Franz Josef Land, 1880. This image shows the ice conditions encountered near the limits of *Eira*'s exploration of the western reaches of Franz Josef Land (courtesy Hancox Archive).

38. *Eira* aground near Hammerfest, Norway, after the 1880 expedition (courtesy Hancox Archive).

39. *Eira* at Cape Crowther. One of W. W. May's sketches to illustrate Clements Markham's talk to the RGS in 1881 (courtesy Hancox Archive).

40. *Eira* foundering, 21 August 1881, off Cape Flora, Franz Josef Land (courtesy Scott Polar Research Institute, University of Cambridge).

41. The sinking of the *Eira*, August 21, 1881 (courtesy Scott Polar Research Institute, University of Cambridge).

42. A sketch of Flora Cottage (from Markham 1883).

43. 'The Hut' (Flora Cottage), one of four pencil sketches by Benjamin Leigh Smith made during the 1881–82 expedition (courtesy Scott Polar Research Institute, University of Cambridge).

44. The crew of the *Eira* dragging their boats across the ice. Engraving by C. W. Whyllie from a sketch by Benjamin Leigh Smith made during the 1881–82 expedition (courtesy Scott Polar Research Institute, University of Cambridge).

45. Rescue of Leigh Smith and the crew in Matochkin Strait, Novaya Zemlya (courtesy Scott Polar Research Institute, University of Cambridge).

46. The estate at Glottenham, ca. 1890 (courtesy Hancox Archive).

47. Leigh Smith and his young sons at Scalands, early 1890s (courtesy Hancox Archive).

48. Charlotte Leigh Smith at Scalands, 1898 (courtesy Hancox Archive).

49. A hunting party at Scalands (Charlotte sitting in front of Leigh Smith; Richard Potter on right) (courtesy Hancox Archive).

50. Professor Julian A. Dowdeswell, PhD, Director of the Scott Polar Research Institute, in his rooms at Jesus College, Leigh Smith's alma mater at Cambridge University. A portrait of Leigh Smith, as painted by J.L. Reilly after a Stephen Pearce portrait, is in the background (courtesy Julian Dowdeswell).

51. Summer, 2009. Polar historian Huw Lewis-Jones with Leigh Smith descendant and novelist Charlotte Moore by the whale jaw brought from the Arctic to Scalands by the explorer (author).

PROLOGUE: TWILIGHT

On Christmas Eve, 1909, the British explorer Benjamin Leigh Smith was nearly eighty-two years old and increasingly confused. To his large and extended family, he was still the formidable 'Uncle Ben,' or, much more distantly, 'The Explorer,' but amid the new millennium chaos of his London surroundings, his name and fame were all but forgotten. Now he was in the middle of an inexorable slide into dementia that his family attempted to legally recognize.

The relentless contractions of his memories had distilled down to one last small icy harbor where his brain could still find firm holding ground. Everything around him that had once been familiar – even down to the names of his children – was fading from his mind, but his life as an explorer endured as the one firm spot on his mental map. A man born into wealth, he had personally financed and led five expeditions to the Arctic that defined the geographic limits of two major Arctic archipelagoes. He had discovered dozens of new islands and named them after expedition companions, favored relatives, and some of the major visionaries of British science in the nineteenth century. He had pioneered deep-ocean research in Arctic waters and, in true Victorian fashion, had returned from his voyages with the holds of his ships groaning with carefully preserved specimens of birds, fossils, and rocks, and even a live polar bear or two.

Perversely, his personal deterioration was occurring at the very moment in history when other explorers were claiming to have completed the work he once believed might crown his own life: the attainment of the North Pole. Just outside the windows of his London townhome, newspaper barkers filled that entire fall and winter with hyperventilated arguments over suddenly momentous issues of polar priority – whether either,

Fig. 1. Benjamin Leigh Smith at the end of his life; oil painting by Reginald Eves, ca. 1911 (courtesy Scott Polar Research Institute, University of Cambridge).

neither, or both of the Americans Robert Peary or Frederick Cook, had, in fact, reached the North Pole; whether the Anglo-Irish Ernest Shackleton would return to finish his work at the South Pole or would he be superseded by British naval officer Robert Falcon Scott; whether or where the Norwegians Fridtjof Nansen or Roald Amundsen would return to the field; would any of the cast of lesser international lights such as Evelyn Briggs Baldwin, Walter Wellman, Ejnar Mikkelsen, Jean-Baptiste Charcot, Douglas Mawson, or Ernest de Koven Leffingwell steal the spotlight.

In such an environment of bitter personal rivalries and screaming national intensities, amplified each day by a new and rapidly expanding era of newspaper hype, Benjamin Leigh Smith was very much an antique from a long-vanished boutique of gentleman explorers. A relic. Yet nearly forty years earlier, serious observers had suggested that Benjamin Leigh Smith would be the first human being to stand at the North Pole. He himself was so confident of it that he had sent a brief note to his favorite niece, Amy, the eleven-year-old daughter of his brother Willy.[1] It is a profound and beautiful letter, a kind of illustrated prose poem, written from the Arctic port of Tromsø, Norway. In it, Leigh Smith describes his first experiences with the sense-altering summer environment of northern Norway, where the endless daylight plays tricks on the body clocks of all visitors from more southerly latitudes.

Tromsø
June 9th

Dear Amy

Here I am in a place where the sun never goes to bed in the summer, and I am writing to you by daylight or rather nightlight at midnight. The sun looks rather stupid about this time as if it has made a mistake and felt ashamed of himself. It has been snowing today so the summer is a sort of winter. As I came here we passed through a place where we had a sunset and a sunrise all at once and yet there was only one sun. Next Monday we are going to sail round the North Pole and then hoist a flag on the top of it.

At the end of the note, Leigh Smith sketched the Earth with a line drawn straight through it from South Pole to North Pole. There, at the top of the world, next to a St. George's Ensign planted in the ice, stood Uncle Ben, The Explorer. From that mysterious point he waved ecstatically to Amy, who stood off to the south and west, astride England and Ireland. Given a choice of whom he would rather meet should he return triumphantly from the North Pole in the fall of 1871, a choice between, say, his favorite niece Amy on the one hand and on the other hand Her Majesty Victoria, by the Grace of God, of the United Kingdom of Great Britain and Ireland Queen, Defender of the Faith, Empress of India, it seems clear who The Explorer would have preferred.

Now, with all of the optimistic gleams of his exploring years long past, Benjamin Leigh Smith awaited with an irritable dread as a doctor arrived who would administer a competency examination on behalf of his family. They were increasingly anxious over control of his considerable money and property. He had inherited a fortune in both from his father, which he then controlled with a rigidity that was in direct contrast to the flexibility with which he had taught himself to explore the Arctic. A half of a century of tightly-wound control over his family's legacy, over the many lives that depended on his properties and finances, over every servant and crop, gander and swine, tree and twig, had now led him inevitably into family confrontations over money, property and status, and these were all now accelerated by the legal urgencies of his encroaching senility.

Preoccupied by managing his inherited estates and accounts and then for more than a decade by his polar explorations, he had delayed a domestic life until it was all but too late. He finally married a beautiful French woman by the name of Charlotte Sellers in 1887 when he was fifty-nine and her an impossible forty years younger. His young wife was as vigorously Catholic as he was almost foppishly sexual. By 1909, they had lived apart for years, arguing over allowances. His two boys, born when Leigh Smith was already in his sixties and then coming of age when The Explorer was in his mid-seventies, were now as distant from him in temperament as they were in age. There are hints that one of the boys tended towards a form of high-functioning autism (though it would not have been possible even to recognize such a condition for another half century) that perhaps led him to be sent down from Cambridge, while the other boy's artistic aspirations led to curt dismissals by his father almost as if he not had been his at all.

If his family had long since drifted from his orbit, the public that once took note of the restrained celebrations of his work as a polar explorer, or his generosity toward expeditions both at their start and in their times of peril, had by 1909 moved into another galaxy altogether. What is almost certain, as he neared the end of his earthly life, is that this fact hardly troubled Leigh Smith, if he thought of it at all. He had never desired, much less needed a public persona. As a man of inherited wealth whose shrewd investing had only made him richer, he never possessed a need for the publicity that virtually all later explorers of the Heroic Era of Polar Exploration would absolutely require in order to finance their expeditions.

Comfortable finances were not the only reason Leigh Smith avoided publicity. He was descended from a family of political radicals, a heritage carried on by his famous sister Barbara Bodichon. His other siblings added to the cacophony of challenging personalities. Then there was Leigh Smith himself, a middle-aged man with a fascination if not a fetish for much younger women. The blazing scrutiny later directed at explorers like Peary, Cook, Scott, and Shackleton could have made for Leigh Smith an unwelcome level of discomfort in the polite, rigidly structured, and highly mannered society Victoria's subjects had created for themselves and in which tightly-regulated circles Leigh Smith moved. Either of these situations – his wealth and family and its burdens or his array of women and their temptations – would have been enough on their own for someone to think it in his best interests to avoid public recognition and the potential inspection that might have attached to it.

Whether from one or some combination of these factors, Benjamin Leigh Smith wrote virtually nothing of his often brilliant Arctic adventures. He left behind no books or articles and always let others keep his logbooks, draw his charts, and deliver his results to scientific societies. When it came time to accept the occasional medal for his achievements, either from a foreign government or before one of the great geographical societies of the age, he always begged off, sending someone else in his place. When the Swedish King wanted to honor his effort to save the Swedish polar explorer Adolf Erik Nordenskiöld's expedition in Spitsbergen in 1873, the decoration had to be sent to Leigh Smith in the mail.

No trip to Stockholm for him. Even members of his own family had to root out and circulate second-hand accounts in order to keep up with his adventures. He once told his brother-in-law that if Queen Victoria herself asked to see his Arctic photographs, he would send his expedition photographer around to the palace with them.

If his inherited wealth allowed Benjamin Leigh Smith both the freedom and immunity from such bourgeois notions as publicity and fame, there is nevertheless no record of any energetic disputation of his place as a pioneer of polar exploration. During his 1873 expedition, when he would save from a horrible fate the expedition of the much more experienced Nordenskiöld, the *Saturday Review* noted that "it seems pretty clear that a successful exploration of the polar mystery can be only a question of time. Possibly the prize may fall to the lot of some bold adventurer, such as Mr. Leigh Smith, who is now running similar risks on his own responsibility."[2]

It was thirty-six years later, on the morning of Christmas Eve, 1909, with such promise and hope long vanished, that the doctor arrived. The morning's newspapers were filled with the exploits of a new generation of explorers, each of whom – quite unlike Benjamin Leigh Smith – grabbed hungrily at publicity wherever and whenever it could be found. These were media celebrities who readily posed in Neanderthal-like furs in photographic studios filled with fake polar scenery and stuffed Arctic polar bears jumbled together with Antarctic penguins all for the entertainment of a stupefied public that believed they were all fighting over a place of permanent ice and snow inhabited by Sinterklass, Santa Claus, Saint Nicholas, and Father Christmas.

The doctor was an ingenious and widely-respected man by the name of Norman Moore. In a remarkable turn of fate, Moore was about to assess the mental competency of an elderly polar explorer who nearly forty years earlier had done his level best to destroy the doctor's prospects. As a promising young physician, but without title or capital or promise of inheritance, Moore had unwittingly set a collision course with Leigh Smith over Amy, the same favored niece to whom Leigh Smith had written his poem from the Arctic. Amy was now sixteen, determined and lovely. Moore, a brilliant, driven man and multi-disciplinary scholar of the highest order, had conquered every challenge set before him. Already at the age of twenty-seven he had earned the post of Warden at St. Bartholomew's

Hospital Medical College in London, at a time when the hospital treated over 100,000 patients a year. Despite his deep spirituality, he became both friends and a medical advisor to Charles Darwin (converting to Roman Catholicism only after Darwin's death); despite his broken family and absent father he rose in his field to become President of the Royal College of Physicians; and his lack of political connections was no barrier to being made a baronet in 1919. He was the prototype of a man who would have risen to the top in any kind of meritocracy one cared to design.

Leigh Smith came to despise him. For all his gifts, Norman Moore at the time he met Amy was not gentry, landed or otherwise. So when Moore forthrightly made his intentions clear, Leigh Smith's reaction was little short of volcanic. The novelist and essayist Charlotte Moore is Leigh Smith's great-great-grandniece and great-granddaughter of Norman and Amy. As she delicately and correctly writes, Leigh Smith's "devotion to his pretty niece might nowadays be seen as unwholesome."[3]

Leigh Smith's place as the eldest son of inherited wealth in Victorian England made both his position and his proclivities virtually unassailable. It was largely through Leigh Smith's furious reaction to Norman Moore's courtship that Moore and Amy were kept apart for five full years before they were eventually allowed to marry. In the interim they could neither see nor even correspond with one another, a separation Moore had marked with an unposted letter to Amy every day. Moore had learned the price to be paid for encroaching on territory to which The Explorer had already staked a claim.

The couple reunited and married as soon as Amy turned twenty-one in 1880. Benjamin Leigh Smith celebrated the union by sailing to a part of the Arctic so remote no one had ever seen it before. But the marriage survived and thrived until Amy's early death twenty-one years later. Only then did her ill health soften Leigh Smith's resentments towards her, if not towards Norman Moore.

After Amy's death, in a twist so bizarre it was all but predictable, Moore married another of Leigh Smith's nieces, though by this time Leigh Smith was in his seventies and had his own young wife and small children to worry over. Perhaps by then Leigh Smith could also see, grindingly, grudgingly, what had long been evident to almost every other observer:

that Norman Moore was well on his way to his eventual position as one of the pre-eminent physicians in England.

It was against this backdrop of the most public of international polar spectacles and the most intensely personal of family rivalries, that Dr. Norman Moore arrived at the rooms of Benjamin Leigh Smith at 37 Bury Street in St. James, halfway between Green Park and Piccadilly. There is no reason whatever to suppose that Moore's errand was conducted in anything but a professional manner, just as there is no evidence to suggest that Moore, despite the ill treatment he had suffered from Leigh Smith, had ever held a reciprocal grudge.

Leigh Smith's wife Charlotte, who in 1909 was a still-young woman of forty-one, had asked the courts for control over The Explorer's finances. She maintained that he could no longer competently look after them. Norman Moore, with both his impeccable reputation yet undeniable conflict of interest, was asked to examine Leigh Smith and give a professional medical opinion as to his competency.

Moore arrived at 9:30 in the morning and was met at the door by Dr. William Neale. A naturalist and surgeon from Leigh Smith's 1880 expedition to Franz Josef Land (Zemlya Frantsa-Iosifa), Neale had remained a faithful retainer from the time of that successful expedition and would until the end of Leigh Smith's life. Neale took Moore up to Leigh Smith's rooms and introduced him, a quaint and no doubt extremely awkward custom given the circumstances and the bitter history between them. Neale and another visitor then left the room, leaving Norman Moore alone with The Explorer. Moore found Leigh Smith courteous, even to the point of offering him his own chair, which Moore politely declined.

They proceeded to converse for three-quarters of an hour, primarily through the use of a speaking tube, which consisted of two cones connected by an air tube through which Moore's voice could be amplified to overcome Leigh Smith's deafness. Moore began by asking him if it was true that he had seen several doctors lately.

The Explorer replied: "One afternoon in Scotland they went up a valley & they had a lunch & some speaking and singing went on & that is the principal thing. It didn't amount to anything but someone gave me my health & I had too much to drink."[4]

Leigh Smith could not remember how long ago that had been. Dr. Neale would remember. Moore asked him how long he had lived at his present address.

Leigh Smith responded that "we'll ask the landlord; I cannot tell you."[5]

Moore asked who the two gentlemen were who were in the room when he arrived. Leigh Smith had not noticed two, only the doctor. He asked the doctor's name but Leigh Smith said that he did not notice but that he had seen him often enough. He began to relate a conversation with his brother-in-law, General John Ludlow, as if it had just happened that morning. Ludlow had been dead for more than twenty-five years.

Moore asked him how old he was.

"Over 70 & nearer 80. It might be over 80."[6]

Leigh Smith had difficulty remembering his address, but knew the name of the estate in Sussex that he had inherited from his famous sister Barbara: Scalands. But he could not recall when he had last been there. He could not remember who looked after the property while he was away but was certain that he had just settled on a man to look after the cattle. He remembered that he had two boys but could not recall their ages or which one was older.

Moore asked where his wife lived.

Leigh Smith replied "the other side of the water; the river that goes into the Thames."[7] In any case, he had not seen her for more than a year and had forgotten how long she had been away from him.

Moore asked him who his solicitor was. Leigh Smith could not recall with any certainty. He did not know precisely who was acting on his behalf but thought there might be several. The name 'Woolcombe' came to his mind but he could not say if this was the man who was acting on his behalf or not. Perhaps that was the name of his wife's solicitor. There had been a difference between him and his wife, but it was one he would rather not go into. But he was certain that when they had formally separated he had given her an ample allowance, ample. He could not remember what sort of allowance he had fixed upon his sons. He thought that he often gave them money, but could not recall the last time he had done that, or how much it had been.

Norman Moore asked if there had ever been any question about his fitness to manage his affairs. Leigh Smith said that he "should not bother about a little thing like that but dared say there had been any amount of squabbling."[8]

Asked if he had signed any letter or paper opposing the current proceedings against him, Leigh Smith answered that he had forgotten all about it. In his notes of the meeting, Moore transcribes The Explorer's response: "He said he should not think anything of it because if you paid attention to that sort of thing you might always be worried."[9] Moore gave the names of several doctors who had examined Leigh Smith but he could not attach himself to any of them.

How much money did he have?

Leigh Smith answered that he might be able to tell within £1,000 but would not. He did not know what his balance was at the bank nor could he remember the name of the bank. Then he remembered that he had his passbook in his pocket and pulled it out and said that he could not help laughing at anybody wanting to know about his affairs. He then looked at the first page of the passbook in order to learn the name of his bank.

Moore asked him again, since he now had his passbook in front of him, whether he knew how much money he had?

Leigh Smith would only say that it was rather difficult, and would not say what his income was. (It is unclear from Moore's notes whether the reason Leigh Smith would not say is that he could not properly read his own account book – whether from failing eyesight or mental deterioration – and therefore *could* not say.)

What seems clear is that the questioning went on in this manner for far too long, in a kind of repetitive hectoring that bordered on the faintly cruel. There could be no question that Norman Moore was performing his due diligence for the courts. But, given their tortured history, the affidavit now reads with more than a touch of unnecessary relentlessness. As if to prove the point, Moore even asked if Leigh Smith knew, on Christmas Eve, how far away they were from Christmas Day itself. Pitifully, Leigh Smith did not know. But he did know that it was the last month of the year.

At long last, the sad interview neared its end. Now, Moore reached for a topic completely unrelated to the family that Leigh Smith had largely forgotten about or the finances that he refused to or could not recall. And it was only at this point that Leigh Smith finally demonstrated that his mind was not completely vacant.

Moore asked about his career as an explorer.

As if searching for some vestige of his former self, Leigh Smith pointed to a large chart that lay on a table nearby. It was labeled 'Polar Regions.' He pointed out where he had been and now it was Moore's turn to seemingly reluctantly write that Leigh Smith could only find the locations "generally."[10] But it was clear that he knew that he had once been to faraway northern spaces.

Emboldened, Moore asked if Leigh Smith could give him the names of any of the explorers who had recently been discussed in the papers. He could not.

Leigh Smith had passed the point where he could remember such details. His condition, which left no room for anything but steady deterioration, only worsened until his death on the 3rd of January, 1913, little more than a year after the Norwegian Roald Amundsen reached the South Pole and drew a final curtain on four centuries of pole-seeking. In his gathering twilight, all the contradictory threads of his life were now hopelessly tangled and beyond any certain knowledge.

If his mind had allowed Leigh Smith to reach back with more than a sliver of clarity, he would have remembered that he had once been a man whose doughty leadership was so successful that the veteran Arctic whaling captain David Gray was moved to call him the very model of "quiet, cool, thoroughbred English pluck."[11] The Royal Geographic Society's Clements Markham referred to him as a polar explorer of the first rank.

Yet despite the active scientific research practiced on his polar expeditions, Leigh Smith published no personal account of his expeditions, leaving it to Clements Markham and others to write up the results of his explorations of Franz Josef Land for the proceedings of the Royal Geographical Society and the Zoological Society of London. John C. Wells, a Royal Navy captain asked by Leigh Smith to oversee the oceanographic stations of the 1872 expedition to Svalbard, described him in his published account of the expedition simply as "a friend,"[12] but otherwise did not identify him across 355 pages. Whenever the Royal Geographical

MR. LEIGH SMITH

Commander of the " Eira " Arctic Expedition

Fig. 2. Benjamin Leigh Smith at the time of the Eira expedition (courtesy Hancox Archive).

Society asked Leigh Smith to lecture on his expeditions or receive a medal for them, he always managed to find a reason why he couldn't attend.

Nevertheless, his leadership in the field was exemplary. As his purpose-built research vessel *Eira* sank off Franz Josef Land in August of 1881, Leigh Smith calmly directed his crew to salvage what they could. He then led his crew through an Arctic winter, all the while reserving enough champagne to allow his crew to raise a toast to Queen Victoria on her 63rd birthday on May 24th, 1882.

A month later, and ten months to the day after his ship went down, when the coastal ice finally offered an opening, he launched a voyage of escape south through hundreds of nautical miles of pack ice. Skillfully maneuvering small boats fitted with table cloth sails through ice and snow, amid soaking rains and treacherous seas, this remarkable Arctic journey was executed with no lesser grace than would be Ernest Shackleton's similarly stunning escape from Antarctica thirty-five years later.

It was after his dramatic escape from the Arctic that *The Times* wrote that the name of Benjamin Leigh Smith "would last as long as scientific men took an interest in Arctic discovery."[13] It was this reputation that became his last cogent memory. He had not forgotten that in his true self he had once been an explorer, even for a brief time The Explorer, one who had tried to plant his nation's flag at the top of the world.

No, he answered to Norman Moore's final question, he could not remember when he last went on an Arctic expedition.

"But if anyone asked him, *he would go again.*"

❦ 1 ❧

BENJAMIN LEIGH SMITH AND HIS TIMES, 1828–1871

When Benjamin Leigh Smith was born amid the rolling countryside of East Sussex on March 12, 1828, the British naval officer William Edward Parry was publishing the results of his attempt to reach the North Pole from the islands north of Svalbard the previous summer. Parry, one of the most active Arctic explorers of his generation, had served as junior officer for John Ross's search for the Northwest Passage in 1818, and then commanded three expeditions of his own in search of a solution to the mystery of the passage, before turning his attention to the North Pole.

The area of Svalbard from which Parry based his explorations, which for fifty years had been seen as a promising starting point for an expedition to the North Pole, would not see another Englishman for nearly another half-century. It would not be a cumbersome, flags-and-pennants-flying naval expedition of the type led by Parry, but instead would consist of a tiny civilian expedition on a small chartered sailing vessel and led by a polar neophyte, the now forty-three-year-old Benjamin Leigh Smith. Venturing reverently into the same area as Parry, Leigh Smith would eclipse the geographic work of his countrymen's full-fledged Royal Navy expedition.

One might wonder how a well-to-do, middle-aged country squire like Leigh Smith, who could have lived out his days collecting rents and making a run for Parliament, found himself in a position to challenge the polar geographic research of the largest navy in the world. The reasons can be found in the great transformational polar event of the intervening years between Leigh Smith's birth in 1828 and his first Arctic expedition in the summer of 1871. Ever confident in the discipline and organization of its navy to accomplish any task, Britain in the 1840s and 1850s experienced the massive cultural and institutional shock of the Royal Navy's Franklin polar expedition catastrophe.

John Franklin, a career naval officer, was no stranger to polar exploration, having commanded a vessel in search of the North Pole as early as 1818. In 1845, in what was planned as the crowning achievement of a long and distinguished career, Franklin was ordered to solve, once and for all, the long-standing geographic problem of the Northwest Passage. Placed in command of two naval vessels heavily-reinforced for work in the Arctic, HMS *Erebus* and *Terror*, Franklin left Greenhithe in mid-May and his expedition was last seen station-keeping in Baffin Bay, awaiting favorable conditions to enter Lancaster Sound.

What happened next took the better part of the next century and a half and the efforts of at least twenty separate expeditions to find out. Franklin led his fleet into the thicket of islands that comprise the Canadian Arctic, pausing for the winter at Beechey Island, where three sailors died and were buried. The following spring of 1846, the ships turned south into Peel Sound and Franklin Strait, where *Erebus* and *Terror* were eventually frozen into the ice about twelve nautical miles northwest of King William Island. Beset in the ice, they would never leave it. Franklin himself died in 1847 at the age of 61, and, after a further eighteen months of increasing hopelessness, his surviving commanders abandoned their ships and led their remaining crew members in a desperate attempt to walk out of the Arctic.

Of the 134 officers and men who began the expedition at Greenhithe, five were invalided home from Greenland and the rest vanished into the North American Arctic. Their story was eventually worked out largely through the superhuman efforts of four men: the Scottish long-distance walker John Rae who learned some of the details from the Inuit of Boothia Peninsula in 1854; the Royal Navy's Francis Leopold McClintock, whose 1857–59 expedition on board *Fox* discovered a brief written record on King William Island left by the survivors; the American explorer Charles Francis Hall, who recorded Inuit testimony about the fate of the sailors during his second expedition to the Arctic in 1864–69; and forensic anthropologist Owen Beattie and others in the 1980s, who found evidence to support a theory that Franklin's men had had their reason impaired by the effects of lead poisoning from improperly sealed food tins.

The many years and even decades of news produced by the many expeditions sent in search of possible Franklin expedition survivors dominated Benjamin Leigh Smith's formative years. During and just after his time at Jesus College at the University of Cambridge, no less than twelve separate expeditions involving hundreds of sailors were sent to scour the North American Arctic for any trace of Franklin, his men and his ships. Each of these searches was national news and almost every expedition made some contribution to filling in the complex geographic details and changing climatic conditions of the archipelago. And when the full extent of the catastrophe became apparent by the mid-1850s, it had the effect of dampening any further enthusiasm for polar exploration by the Royal Navy or any other national insitution for the better part of the next twenty years.

It is an open question how this protracted spectacle of government incompetence affected Leigh Smith's world view. His was a wealthy life almost nakedly devoid of the need for government at any level. At the same time, the public history of Leigh Smith's young adulthood was marked, not by a collective British pride in triumphant national geographic expeditions, but by a series of dramatic and largely private polar expeditions led by men from countries other than England, notably the United States, Sweden, Germany, and Austria-Hungary.

This atmosphere, during his college years, of private expeditions succeeding where public efforts had failed, was the exact opposite of the time Leigh Smith was born and in the decades preceding his birth. Then, from the Pacific explorations of James Cook to the exploits of Nelson at Trafalgar, there was very little, it seemed, that the Royal Navy could not achieve. One could even argue that it was this misplaced sense of technological and cultural superiority that made a tragedy like the Franklin expedition all but inevitable.

Yet such nationalistic feelings had been on the ascendant for at least half a century before Benjamin Leigh Smith was born. The 1827 explorations of Parry north of Svalbard mirrored a similar British naval expedition of half a century earlier. In 1773, Constantine John Phipps, a British naval commander and Member of Parliament who in 1766 had sailed to

Newfoundland with naturalist Joseph Banks, led the first British attempt to reach the North Pole since 1615. The expedition consisted of two specially-strengthened shore bombardment vessels, *Carcass*, commanded by Skeffington Lutwidge, and *Racehorse*, a former French privateer captured by the British in 1757 and commanded by Phipps. The expedition's total complement was 170 officers and men, with extra rations of spirits for each ship "to be issued at the discretion of the commanders, when extraordinary fatigue or severity of weather might make it expedient"[1] Phipps's mission was to reach the North Pole via the waters off the northwest coast of Svalbard. Prevailing geographic theory followed that he would encounter open water somewhere in that area and be able to follow that open water all the way to the pole. In the event of a wreck, there was even good hope of survival in the area, as there existed "three or four small settlements of Russians in Spitzbergen for the sake of the skins of quadrupeds."[2]

Phipps received a typical set of instructions directing him to make useful observations "of every kind,"[3] be they natural or navigational. That the Admiralty was supremely confident in the success of the mission can be seen in its admonition to Phipps, once he had reached the pole, to go no farther! He was ordered to have his expedition back at the Nore, a Royal Navy anchorage in the Thames estuary, before the onset of winter.

Phipps had a considerable amount of existing data on which to shape his course. For decades, the logbooks of whalers operating around Svalbard had recorded the changing nature of the polar ice in those northern waters. The edge of the mass of permanent ice would shift from summer to summer, some years crushing down upon the islands off the northern coast of Svalbard or the coast of the main archipelago island of Spitsbergen itself, in other years wending offshore and leaving an ice-free passage that trended northeast from the whaling stations of Amsterdam Island (Amsterdamøya) and Danes Island (Danskøya) all the way to the Seven Islands (Sjuøyane). Despite such occasional open waters, however, the pack ice above lat. 81° N always remained as an impassable barrier to the ice-covered waters around the North Pole.

Such seasonal variations in the permanent polar pack ice were used by a British dilettante named Daines Barrington in 1773 to argue that a ship need only force a bit further north before an ice-free corridor was located that would open a passage directly to the Pole. Barrington convinced the

Fig. 3. Racehorse and Carcass in the ice north of Svalbard, 1773 (from Phipps 1774).

Council of the Royal Society to ask the Earl of Sandwich to importune the King to order the Admiralty to mount a polar expedition north from Svalbard. With a fine bureaucratic disregard of a century and a half of whaling experience showing nothing but a continuous wall of ice north of Svalbard, the Admiralty agreed.

Phipps's expedition left England in late May, 1773, and by early July the ships had gained Magdalena Bay (Magdalenafjorden) in northwest Svalbard. En route, Phipps made a series of deep-ocean temperature observations using a "thermometer invented by Lord Charles Cavendish"[4] There, in the final safe stopping point before entering a tangle of historic islands that mark the northwest corner of the Svalbard archipelago and the beginning of the truly adventurous sailing, the ships were watered.

On July 5th, Phipps was called to the deck to see pack ice for the first time. As Phipps writes, he "perceived something white upon the bow, and heard a noise like the surf upon the shore; I hauled down the studding sails, and hailed the *Carcass* to let them know that I should stand for it to make what it was, having all hands upon deck ready to haul up at a moment's warning: I desired that they would keep close to us, the fog being so thick, and have every body ready to follow our motions instantaneously, determining to stand on under such sail as should enable us to keep the ships under command, and not risk parting company."[5]

Phipps's prudence was tested immediately, as the ships were forced to dodge in and out and around several large masses of drift ice. For several days they continued in this manner, waiting for the expected "opening [that] might be found to get through to a clear sea to the Northward."[6] The crews were soon tired of the continuous ship-handling in Arctic conditions, but found some comfort in "the spirits which had been allowed for extraordinary occasions."[7] Clearly, the titanic effort required to sail a tall ship through the maze of polar pack ice north of Svalbard classified as extraordinary when it came to the Royal Navy's daily ration of rum.

The two vessels reached the historic roadstead of Fair Haven in mid-July and anchored there in eleven fathoms. The area was given its amicable name centuries earlier by English mariners. They had found it the only anchorage in northwest Svalbard that – on account of several surrounding islands, like Vogelsang (Fuglesangen), Cloven Cliff (Klovningen) and the Norway islands (Norskøyane) – offered reasonable protection from the ice that drifted in from the east. While the ships were again watered, Phipps went ashore and saw to the northeast that the ice extended in an almost unbroken, uniform field. Unable to maneuver northwards, Phipps turned east along the coast until he encountered loose ice north of Woodfjorden, then turned north again.

On the 25th, Lutwidge from the *Carcass* went ashore on Moffen Island, a fascinating Arctic lagoon where, a century later, Leigh Smith would find the skeleton of a whale carved with centuries of ship's names. The island, about two miles in diameter, encircled a large pond of water in its middle. The nearly circular land surrounding the lagoon was about a quarter of a mile wide. Lutwidge found it covered with gravel and small stones, "without the least verdure or vegetation of any kind."[8] He also found a lone piece of driftwood on shore, and an inscription covering the grave of a Dutchman who had been buried alongside the lagoon two years earlier. It was easily the furthest north a human being had ever been interred to that moment. When Phipps learned of it, he thought it extraordinary that no one had ever mentioned the place before, since such an Arctic lagoon was highly unusual. He concluded that it might be because it had only recently been formed from the ocean currents that plied up the western coast of Svalbard.

On July 27, 1773, the expedition attained a new furthest north of lat. 80°48′ N. There the vessels were blocked by a line of ice extending nearly east to west, but Phipps had achieved a record that would stand for more than three decades, until the whalers William Scoresby, *père et fils*, gained it at lat. 81°30′ N on board the vessel *Resolution* in 1806.

Phipps continued to force his vessels east, occasionally entering narrow openings in the ice wall that extended a few nautical miles north. But each time, such promising leads invariably closed and forced Phipps to retreat. The ships continued eastward and on August 3rd reached the Sjuøyane, the seven northernmost islands in the Svalbard archipelago. They were then farther north and east than any exploring expedition before them. They were also beset by ice, which at some points seemed to rise higher than the mainmasts of the ships themselves. The pressure of the ice for a time led Phipps to contemplate abandoning the vessels. On the 5th, Phipps sent a midshipman named Walden to a high island about twelve nautical miles west of their position to gain a better view of the expedition's predicament. Walden returned the following day without any good news as to the state of the ice but his brief flying expedition was immortalized by Phipps, who named the rocky islet he had ascended Walden Island (Waldenøya).

With northward progress halted, Phipps nevertheless continued a program of scientific research, using such instruments as a thermometer designed for measuring water temperature and an apparatus invented for distilling fresh water from salt water. Phipps's log of the voyage contained much new data on Svalbard, including the first European description of the ivory gull and the polar bear ("much larger than the black bear …"[9]). Men in the small boats who fired on a walrus soon found the walrus attacking them in turn. There was also a magical foreshadowing incident between a large polar bear and a fourteen-year-old midshipman on board the *Carcass* named Horatio Nelson, who was almost killed when his rifle jammed during a failed attempt to secure the white bear's skin for his father. Paintings of the encounter would later be produced that extended the legend of the future hero. Two of the Sjuøyane would later be named for officers on the expedition, one for Nelson (Nelsonøya) and one for Phipps (Phippsøya).

For a week, Phipps combined his attempt to free the ships from the pack with a simultaneous effort to haul the ship's boats over the ice in case the mother ships became permanently trapped and the small boats became the only means of escape. By the 9th, however, the ships had overtaken and recalled the boats and the next day, with all sails set, the *Racehorse* and *Carcass* smashed through to the open sea. When one final attempt on August 22 failed to locate a workable opening in the ice to the north, Phipps quit the waters around Svalbard. On September 7, the expedition reached the Shetlands and from there fought through a succession of gales until regaining the Thames on September 24. Phipps hadn't reached the pole but he had indeed followed the Admiralty's prescribed timetable to the letter.

The Phipps expedition demonstrated that a direct open sea route to the North Pole from the waters between Svalbard and Greenland or from the waters directly north of Svalbard was unlikely to the point of impossibility. The many years of Arctic experience of the commercial whaler William Scoresby the Younger served, in the main, to further this impression. Eventually, Scoresby suggested – with the full support of an aging Joseph Banks – that his vast experience in the ice made him the perfect candidate to lead an expedition to solve the twin problems of the North Pole and the Northwest Passage once and for all. He was blocked in this ambition by one John Barrow, a professional bureaucrat who for forty years served as the Second Secretary to the Admiralty. Barrow warmly thanked Scoresby for his interest and then liberally borrowed most of Scoresby's ideas while making it plain that the Royal Navy was more than up to those two great Arctic tasks.

Scoresby and his father were from the same generations that had produced the father and grandfather of Benjamin Leigh Smith. Unlike the Scoresbys, however, the Smiths were not men of the sea.

Leigh Smith's grandfather, William Smith (1756–1835), was born into a family that traced its geographic roots to the Isle of Wight and its philosophical underpinnings to the religious conflicts that had torn

England apart for the better part of two hundred years. The Smiths were Dissenters, nonconformist members of the Protestant faith who had turned away from the predominant Anglican Church. William Smith has been variously described as a Unitarian[10] and a Congregationalist,[11] the latter affiliation conjoined at the time to the term Independent. It was a term as appropriate as any to describe both Smith himself and the generations of Smiths that would follow him.

The price the Smiths paid for their religious independence in eighteenth-century England was a steep one. Dissenters, along with Catholics and Jews, were barred from work in important government jobs and could not become officers in the army or attend Oxford unless they renounced their faith and took an oath accepting the Anglican creed. A Dissenter could attend certain of the colleges of Cambridge but would not be allowed to actually take a degree.

With the doors to employment in the government, the clergy, and the military largely closed to them, the Smith family, like many other Dissenters and nonconformists, turned instead to creating their own educational institutions and to making their livings in banking and in trade. Once established, William Smith would spend nearly half a century in Parliament in an attempt to reverse these historic discriminations, along with the great transnational sin of the age, human slavery.

William Smith's father, Samuel, was a grocer, a partner in a firm known as Smith, Travers & Kemble. The house imported tea from China and India and sugar from the West Indies, and through it Samuel Smith made a fortune. In 1754 he had married a woman named Martha Adams, the daughter of another nonconformist family of tradesmen. Over the next five years, Martha gave birth to William and to three daughters. Not one of the daughters survived beyond the age of four. The final daughter died at birth in 1759 and Martha, at the age of twenty-five, followed her in death a few weeks later. William, now the only surviving child, was only three when his mother passed: he would live until he was nearly eighty. Samuel Smith, who valued education above all, made certain that William received an excellent training prior to his expected participation in the family business.

A revealing portrait, painted in 1770 by Mason Chamberlain, shows William at the age of fourteen, standing before a table, looking through several books, as his father, "resplendent in periwig, knee breeches and frogged coat,"[12] has seemingly put his own reading aside to guide his son's interests. It is, as their descendent Charlotte Moore writes, "a classic illustration of the Age of Enlightenment."[13]

William completed a course of study at the Daventry Academy, a respected school for children of dissenting families, where he would have enjoyed the same liberal education that led Joseph Priestley to his Rational Dissent twenty years earlier. The belief in new fields of scientific inquiry, the belief that "minor differences in theology were much less important than a desire to discover truth,"[14] a belief in natural human rights, the rejection of mysticism and a government tied too closely to the dogmas of a dominant religion, each of these intellectual guideposts would mark William Smith's life and career.

In 1772, Samuel remarried and moved his reconstituted family south of the Thames to the enclave of Clapham Common. There they would soon be joined by a host of like-minded reformers. Within two decades, through groups like the Clapham Sect, the Common would become the staging area for the campaign to abolish slavery and, through such just causes, be seen as the harbinger of what would later become Victorian morality. Between his intellectual development at Daventry and the stimulation of his Clapham surroundings, William could be forgiven for a lack of attention to the grocery business, in which he became a partner at the age of twenty-one.

Not long after, in 1780, a legacy from an uncle made William financially independent. It allowed him to transfer his partnership in the firm and set off on an independent life of his own. The following year he married Frances Coape, another nonconformist whose family had made their money refining sugar imported from the West Indies. They began their life together by writing and traveling, making visits to manufacturing towns and art galleries throughout England. In 1784 they journeyed throughout Wales and two years later traveled through the Lake District, Scotland, and Ireland, riding in a phaeton drawn by two horses and guided by a postilion, moving from the estates of one acquaintance to the estates of another. They admired the scenery around Loch Ness and Urquart Castle and William climbed Ben Nevis. Throughout their lives they would rarely travel apart from one another. His biographers note that he was still writing affectionate poems to Frances fifty years into their marriage.[15] In between these trips they purchased a country estate in Little Parndon near Harlow.

In addition to their literary and geographic adventures, William and Frances were also busy producing children, thirteen of them. As if to illustrate the health and hereditary lottery of the age, their fourth child, a girl named Frances, died of smallpox at the age of four months in 1787; a second Frances, born the following year, would live to be ninety-two. In 1818, this second Frances married William Nightingale and it was their daughter Florence, born two years later, who herself would live to be ninety and world famous. The eldest son of William and Frances was named Benjamin Smith (1783–1860), and he would have been thirty-five and in the middle of an energetic life of finance and politics in the year of Florence Nightingale's birth.

Eighteen-eighteen was also the same year that John Barrow, with a portfolio full of William Scoresby's ideas for Arctic exploration, sent the first of the Royal Navy's many expeditions and ships in search of the Northwest Passage and the North Pole. Each was carefully stage-managed by the energetically misguided Barrow and occupied three decades of increasingly futile Arctic explorations by the Royal Navy and the British government. As historian Fergus Fleming writes: "When [Barrow] had a geographical opinion it was frequently the wrong one."[16]

To the commanders of the four vessels he dispatched in two separate expeditions in the spring of 1818, Barrow's instructions were as clear as they were impossible: attack the centuries-old problems of the Northwest Passage and the North Pole and resolve them by the end of the summer. The commanders of the North Pole effort, David Buchan and John Franklin, accomplished as much as could be expected. They led the ships *Dorothea* and *Trent* as far as an exploration of northwestern Svalbard, where, like Phipps and Nelson a half-century earlier, they found no obvious sea route to the North Pole.

To this brief thrust to the northwards was joined the vessels *Isabella* and *Alexander* under the commands of John Ross and William Parry, tasked with finding the long-sought Northwest Passage through the maze of islands of the North American Arctic. After some truly remarkable (and notably peaceful) encounters with Greenlandic Inuit, Ross turned the ships for England without fully exploring any of the inlets on the Canadian side of Baffin Bay that might have led to a solution of the Northwest Passage problem. By the end of 1818, the Admiralty was right back where it had started when the four ships left for the Arctic in April, and no closer to the North Pole than they were after the Phipps expedition nearly half a century earlier.

Parry returned to the North American Arctic the following year, 1819, in command of two vessels named the *Hecla* and the *Griper*. This expedition succeeded in penetrating halfway across the arctic archipelago to the Bering Strait and on his return Parry was promoted to commander and wrote the first of his accounts of Arctic exploration. A second Northwest Passage expedition under Parry from 1821 to 1823 in the *Hecla* and *Fury* fared less well, as did a third expedition with the same vessels in 1824. When *Fury* was wrecked in 1825 off Somerset Island, just north of King William Island, Parry doubled his crews on board *Hecla* and escaped back to England.

The following year, 1826, Parry and the Admiralty agreed to launch another attempt at the North Pole by means of a return to the same waters north of Svalbard explored by Phipps and Franklin. Again Parry commanded *Hecla* into the Arctic but this time with a new plan. He would not risk losing another ship in the ice. Instead, he would search along the northern coast of Svalbard for a suitable anchorage for *Hecla* and then lead two small boats northwards to the ice. There, he and his men would attempt to drag these boats northwards in the hope and expectation that an open sea around the pole would materialize and the boats could be sailed the remaining miles to their goal, which might even be the mountainous island many thought crowned the top of the world.

In crafting this plan, Parry was reaching back to an observation made by Skeffington Lutwidge during the Phipps expedition. Lutwidge had noted that, for a distance of thirty to forty nautical miles north of the Sjuøyane, there appeared to be "one continued plain of smooth unbroken ice, bounded only by the horizon."[17] Phipps's chart of the area showed flat, unbroken ice north of the islands. Parry then approvingly quotes Scoresby, where the whaler writes that he "once saw a field that was so free from either fissure or hummock, that I imagine, had it been free from snow, a coach might have been driven many leagues over it in a direct line, without obstruction or danger."[18]

Parry took these isolated and localized data of Lutwidge and Scoresby and from it devised a plan to slide two purpose-built small boats across the reputedly smooth and glassy ice field until they reached open water somewhere between the Sjuøyane and the Pole. The boats would be twenty feet long and have an extreme breadth of seven feet carried far forward as well as aft, with hulls made of ash and hickory covered with canvas. The canvas was coated with tar, which was then covered with a layer of fir, then a layer of felt and, finally, a layer of oak. The whole construction was closely fastened with iron nails and fitted with bamboo masts and duck sails. Running below and nearly the length of each side of the keel were steel runners meant to simulate a sledge, along with two large wheels on each side in the event progress could be had by rolling the boats northwards.

These unique boats, named *Enterprise* and *Endeavour*, were meant to be large enough to accommodate crews of two officers and twelve men along with all of their gear, yet small enough for these same fourteen men to hop onto the 'continuous plain of smooth unbroken ice,' don leather shoulder harnesses, and pull the boats behind them. This proved a faint hope, as the boats as constructed were massively heavy (Parry puts their empty weight at three quarters of a ton). Fully-loaded, each boat was near two tons, or nearly 300 pounds of dead weight for every man jack. Parry's instructions from Viscount Melville, First Lord of the Admiralty, were to find a suitable anchorage on the north coast of Svalbard, secure *Hecla* within it, and then move off northwards with his twenty-three companions in the small boats.

On Sunday, March 25, 1827, *Hecla* departed Greenwich. A few days later, after visits from Melville himself and with the crew given three month's pay in advance, *Hecla* was on her way northwards. She reached Hammerfest in northern Norway two weeks later, dressed the ship and fired a royal salute on the King's birthday on April 23rd, and took on board eight reindeer that Parry hoped to employ in pulling the boats.

The expedition encountered its first ice on May 5th at about lat. 73°30′ N, and four days later, at lat. 77° N, fell in with two whaling vessels, the *Alpheus* and the *Active* out of the Scottish port of Peterhead. Encountering several more whalers in the days ahead, Parry received the discomfiting news that each one considered the ice they had seen so far that season "to offer more obstacles to the attainment of [the North Pole] than it had done for many years past."[19]

On the 14th, the expedition was off Hakluyt's Headland (Hakluythovden), a thousand-foot high mountain that forms the northern point of Amsterdamøya and which for centuries had marked the turning point for all ships seeking to round the northwest corner of the Svalbard archipelago. Here Parry encountered his first real problems, finding, like Phipps and Buchan and Franklin before him, nothing but unbroken ice. Moreover, a strong southerly wind was coursing out of Smeerenburgfjorden, where he had hoped to anchor and land a planned relief cache of supplies at Hakluythovden. Despite every exertion by the crew, *Hecla* was blown north toward Fuglesangen almost on her beam ends. Seventy years later, in 1897 and almost to the day, a similar southerly wind would push Salomon Andrée over Fuglesangen in his balloon *Örnen* (*Eagle*), where a young crew member named Nils Strindberg would throw a letter to his fiancé onto the island.

Parry maneuvered the ship deep into the pack ice to get it away from the breaking seas and within a day the wind had died down and *Hecla* was carried past Fuglesangen and Klovningen and along the heavily-indented northern coast of Svalbard. Soon they had crossed the 80th parallel, hard on the keels of Phipps's farthest north. Parry couldn't resist reminding his readers that his ship had escaped the serious damage that David Buchan's *Dorothea* had suffered in exactly the same spot during his 1818 polar expedition.

Having reached the latitude where he planned to secure the ship and take to the boats, Parry instead set out to squeeze *Hecla* between the polar ice pack and the Svalbard shore in search of a suitable anchorage. In a region where every day lost was a major blow to his plans, this survey alone cost Parry a month, during much of which time *Hecla* was beset in the ice. Parry's impatience led him at last to launch the small boats into the pack, where he soon had to retrieve them or watch as jagged ice floes tore them apart. Search as he might, there was no smooth road. The ice edge was miles wide and up to twelve feet thick. Wrote Parry: "The nature of the ice was, beyond all comparison, the most unfavorable for our purpose that I ever remember to have seen."[20]

But Parry still held to the belief that, just beyond those jagged edges, his small boats would find ice floes and fields more suited to his purpose. Yet a second experiment in dragging one of the boats across the pack went so badly that Parry considered dropping one of the boats from the polar dash but keeping the same number of men to haul a single boat.

On the 13th of June, they got into enough clear water north of Low Island (Lågøya) to reach Waldenøya, where Parry eventually landed and sought to cache enough supplies to create a relief station. From Waldenøya, Parry could spy, ten nautical miles off, Little Table Island (Vesle Tavleøya), at that moment the northernmost known land on the planet. On the 14th, *Hecla* bested Phipps's farthest north and a few hours later drew above the 81st parallel. Here Parry was within a few nautical miles of Scoresby's record. Yet all he could see ahead of him were broken fields of ice extending in every direction, not the 'flat and unbroken' road Phipps had written of from near the same spot.

Ascending Waldenøya's heights on June 16th, Parry saw nothing but discouragement all around him and gave up searching for a safe anchorage among the Sjuøyane. He made one more attempt, sending Lieutenant James Clark Ross ashore at a small island north of Vesle Tavleøya. Ross landed some supplies but found no suitable holding ground for the ship. Besides standing on a new northernmost point of land in the world, Ross would later have the islet named for him by his commander. Today its accepted name is Rossøya.

Retreating southwards below the 80th parallel, Parry on the 18th finally found what he was looking for, an area within Sorgfjorden where the ship could be anchored and the small boats deployed without instantly encountering crushing ice floes. Parry writes:

> On the following morning I proceeded to examine the place, accompanied by Lieutenant Ross in a second boat, and, to our great joy, found it a considerable bay, with one affording excellent land-locked anchorage, and, what was equally fortunate, sufficiently clear of ice to allow the ship to enter. Having sounded the entrance, and determined on the anchorage, we returned to the ship to bring her in; and I cannot describe the satisfaction

which the information of our success communicated to every individual on board. The main object of our enterprise now appeared within our grasp, and every body seemed anxious to make up, by renewed exertions, for the time we had unavoidably lost. The ship was towed and warped in with the greatest alacrity, and at 1.40, A.M., on the 20th, we dropped anchor in Hecla Cove [Heclahamna], in thirteen fathoms, on a bottom of very tenacious blue clay, and made some hawsers fast to the land-ice which still filled all the upper part of the bay.[21]

Sorgfjorden is often cut off by ice drifting across its mouth from nearby Hinlopen Strait (Hinlopenstretet). Any ship caught in this trap would remain there all winter. Parry, however, was lucky. The drift ice in the summer of 1827 did not close off his choice of a harbor. Wasting no time, Parry devolved command of *Hecla* to Lieutenant Henry Foster and left the ship at five p.m. on the 21st. Depositing some more relief supply caches, first at Lågøya and then at Waldenøya (where he found his original cache already picked over by polar bears), the North Pole expedition proper began.

As it was still necessary not to delay our return beyond the end of August, the time originally intended, I took with me only seventy-one days' provisions; which, including the boats and every other article, made up a weight of 260 lbs. per man; and as it appeared highly improbable, from what we had seen of the very rugged nature of the ice we should first have to encounter, that either the rein-deer, the snow-shoes [sledges], or the wheels would prove of any service for some time to come, I gave up the idea of taking them.[22]

It took Parry only two days to lay in his caches and return to the edge of the world at Rossøya. There he and his men began to haul the boats northwards. They traveled at 'night,' a relatively meaningless term where the daylight lasts twenty-four hours, but at least the wind was not as strong during nighttime hours and the slightly diminished light it allowed them some relief from snow-blindness. They began the evening with prayers,

Fig. 4. Parry's boats stopped for the night, somewhere north of Svalbard, 1827 (from Parry 1828).

removed their sleeping furs and put on lighter traveling furs, and had some biscuits and cocoa. They set out in wet boots, traveling about ten hours at a stretch with an hour in the middle for rest. The boats would then be hauled onto the biggest pan of ice they could find, the sails thrown over them to form a canvas awning, and the men settled. Pipe smoke drifted up into the canvas, drying it somewhat. With a watch set against the appearance of polar bears or a break-up of the ice and a recitation of 'evening' prayers, they slept.

The going was "slow and laborious,"[23] and at some stretches it was taking them four hours just to advance half a mile. Even as they made a bit of progress to the north, oceans currents and winds would shift the ice further south, rendering their immense physical efforts all for naught. On one day, certain they had traveled over twelve nautical miles over the ice, their noon observation found that they had gone only five actual miles across the Earth. Recognizing a morale-killer when he saw it, Parry sensibly hid this data from the men. They, however, were not stupid, and often made bitter jokes about how long it was taking to get to the 83rd parallel.

By early July, the men's eyes were failing in the constant light. When it rained, the snow turned to slush and the men were forced to crawl on all fours in order to make any progress at all. Four days hard march after taking a sight that had placed them at lat. 82°40′23″ N, Parry found to his horror that they were three nautical miles *south* of that position. This was enough futility for even the most determined officer. The agony had lasted for thirty-five days, and on July 26th Parry called a halt to this "useless fatigue to the officers and men."[24] They had reached their furthest north of lat. 82°45′ N on July 23rd, some 172 nautical miles north of where their ship was anchored in Hecla Cove. To achieve these 172 nautical miles, Parry reckoned that they had actually hauled the boats over nearly 300 nautical miles of ice. If in fact there had been a smooth road north of Svalbard, their exertions would have put them at lat. 85° N – and only 300 nautical miles from the North Pole.

They regained Rossøya two weeks later, where they found that in their absence bears had eaten all of the one hundred pounds of bread they had laid in before departing northwards. Unable to land and haul the boats anywhere on Vesle Tavleøya, Parry headed for the cache on Waldenøya. Hauling the boats onto the lee of Waldenøya, Parry noted that his men were so tired that they still obeyed his orders but did not seem to understand them. He sent Ross around to the northeast corner of the island in search of the boat and supplies Foster had been instructed to place there. Then they sat down and waited for better weather.

Parry's brief penetration onto the polar pack ice north of the Sjuøyane would remain the sum total of the world's knowledge of the entire polar basin for much of the next half century. His book about the adventure along the north coast of Svalbard was published in the same year, 1828 – and almost to the same day – as the birth of Benjamin Leigh Smith, who would become the next Englishman to see in the geography of northern Svalbard and the Sjuøyane as the best route to the North Pole.

It was Leigh Smith's father, Benjamin Smith, who would style his grandmother's maiden name "Leigh" to the otherwise pedestrian "Smith" of William Smith in order to create a new and distinct family name well suited to a pre-Victorian upper class pretension. Benjamin Smith the elder became known as 'the Pater' and he was every bit of that. A raffish and Radical Member of Parliament whom *The Times* described as "a sufficiently flippant personage,"[25] the Pater, despite a prodigious reproductive life, never married. He was as radical in his personal life as he was in his public life and his politics. He fathered at least eight children out of wedlock with two and possibly three different women, including five with Leigh Smith's mother, commoner Anne Longden, and three with another woman named Jane Buss.[26]

He met Anne Longden, a twenty-five-year-old milliner from the East Midlands, in 1826. When she became pregnant, the Pater sequestered her in the remote East Sussex village of Whatlington, a tiny collection of structures that is now little more than a blink of the eye on the A21 from London to Hastings. There she was fashioned as 'Mrs. Leigh,' and it was there that she gave birth to the estimable, formidable Barbara on April 8, 1827. As Barbara Bodichon, the Pater's first child would through the force of her personality go on to become an artist and one of the great social reformers and feminists of the nineteenth century. Before she turned forty, she would do as much as anyone to extend university education to women, co-founding Girton College at Cambridge.

Benjamin Leigh Smith, the future explorer, followed very quickly on, in 1828. As the Pater's eldest son, Leigh Smith would have been the most heavily burdened with the highest expectations, a weary load he eventually tried to carry to the North Pole.

Besides Barbara and Benjamin, other children included the mercurial Isabella, 'Bella,' who would struggle throughout her life with an ultimately incapacitating mental illness; Anne, or 'Nannie,' who would live as openly homosexual as one could in nineteenth century England; and William, or 'Willy,' who to all apearances was as straight down the line as his siblings were radically flamboyant, and who was apparently content to remain throughout much of his life a simple gentleman-farmer on his inherited lands just outside of the town of Battle.

After Willy's birth, Anne Longden suffered a steady decline in her health. She died, still a young woman, in 1834, having never married the man she bore five children to. After her death, the children were looked after by aunts. Their firmly upper-class status was reinforced by Latin tutors and riding instructors and by such trappings as an eight-seat coach the Pater spent a fortune on in 1842. There is little reason to believe that he was particularly troubled by the millstones he had placed on each of his children by either their illegitimacy or the social isolation of his anti-establishment politics. In fact it is more than likely that he considered the two inextricably linked.

With men serving overseas in the military or emigrating in higher numbers than women and with consequently more women than men in England, meaning fewer potential partners, there existed an appalling bias against women in nineteenth-century English law that all but forced on women a kind of legalized prostitution. Men could divorce women accused of adultery, but not the reverse. Women could be cast out of a marriage and forbidden from seeing their own children. Everything a woman owned or earned became, upon marriage, her husband's. Leigh Smith's descendent, the novelist Charlotte Moore, believes that the Pater's approach was much more than an upper-class gentleman refusing to legitimize a union with a member of the working class. He simply refused to force a woman to, in effect, become his personal property. "Ben chose to make a stand against the conventions of marriage; he disapproved of the fact that, once married, a woman forfeited any right to property of her own and became little more than one of her husband's chattels."[27]

In the end, the Pater would do much more than that: he took his father William's political progressivism and, joining it to his own beliefs and proclivities, fashioned a kind of socio-sexual life experiment. He raised his first family – the one that included the brilliant Barbara and the restless Benjamin – as prosperous landed gentry. And then he extended his *Pater familias* to at least one if not two additional illegitimate families. With little regard for prevailing conjugal property law or public opinion, and in control of lots of inherited money and numerous mini-estates scattered across the green pasturelands of Sussex, Leigh Smith would have had numerous opportunities to both attract and impregnate local poor and working-class women who either could not or would not reject the advances of a prosperous middle-aged member of the gentry. That he took advantage of a ripe situation is not at issue, as there is little reason to doubt that men of similar means behaved in similar ways. That he sought such a life in order to make manifest his political beliefs regarding women and property is the more interesting story.

And this is where the Pater's tale becomes a bit murky. For if his family with Anne Longden was raised to be his 'first' or upper-class family, there is a suggestion that the second family, which he contrived as the "Bentley Smiths," and possibly even a third family, were conceived and organized on radically different economic lines: the second as deliberately middle class and the third as distinctly working class.[28] As a highly personal socio-economic experiment, the Pater could monitor the lives and careers of his variety of offspring – with each family unit cast in uniquely different economic strata – and gauge thereby the relative effects of inherited wealth to abject poverty in the development of the human being. If true – and given the prevailing laws and mores it is entirely possible that he arranged his life in this way not entirely or even mainly as a social experiment but rather because he was wealthy and could afford to do as he liked – it suggests a remarkably clinical compartmentalization of one's social, emotional, sexual, and economic lives.

Several of daughter Barbara's pencil sketches survive from this period and three of them in particular are stark depictions of lives lived by the poor and the gentry. In their Dickensian opposition they can perhaps be seen as glimpses into the social thinking of the Pater. The first sketch, from about 1840, presents the Pater as a well-dressed, balding man sitting in a finely-appointed drawing room complete with a marble bust of a female in the background. He is playing a game of chess with a young Willy Leigh Smith, who is standing and appears ready to make a move as his father contemplates the board. The Pater's face is soft, and reflects a seemingly pleased, indulgent father. It is an impression of an unhurried man leading an unhurried life.

The second sketch is likewise another depiction of upper-class wealth, education, and privilege. It shows Benjamin Leigh Smith, the future explorer, elaborately dressed in the cross-gartered stockings of Shakespeare's Malvolio from *Twelfth Night*, courting a scowling Olivia, played by his sister Bella, as an amused Maria played by Barbara kneels at Bella's feet.

The third sketch, made in 1847, when Barbara was twenty, could not be more severely different from the first two. It shows four children, all dressed in patches and rags, begging on the streets of Hastings. One boy holds a hoop to run with, while another child carries a burden packed into a flat box atop his head. A small girl is forlornly watching another boy as he begs for change from passersby by banging a tambourine to keep time for the puppets he is making dance via a string tied to his leg. It is a complete representation of small children trapped in hopeless poverty and facing the front of a lifetime of labor. And the scene takes place just a few miles from where Willy is playing chess with the well-fed Pater and where the future polar explorer is donning colorful costumes for his family's amateur theatricals. More to the point, given the Pater's unconventional sexuality, which Barbara learned of after his death when she learned of the existence of the Bentley Smiths, Barbara may have unknowingly sketched – not some tragically anonymous street urchins – but her own blood relations, deliberately placed in their stations by a father conducting a social experiment.

The third sketch also offers some insight into Barbara, the future social activist and now a justly and much-chronicled and celebrated historical figure. Throughout her life she sought constant improvement in the living and working conditions of women. Perhaps her first tangible attempt was made in November of 1854, when she founded a progressive educational institution, the School for Girls and Boys at Portman Hall. It promised "to bring a thoroughly good Education within reach of the working and middle classes."[29] It was intended that the teachers at Portman Hall would see to the "whole nature of their pupils, not omitting to give special instruction suited to fit them for the practical duties of life."[30]

Whether her brother, the future explorer Benjamin Leigh Smith, was as fundamentally disturbed as Barbara by the plight of the British working class is an open question. Few indications survive from his early life or his years at Jesus College at Cambridge to offer clues one way or the other. Leigh Smith entered Cambridge at twenty, in 1848, where he was reputed a good shot and yachtsman, qualifications that evidently placed one in good stead in the Fen country. He was one of less than three dozen undergraduates, at a time when Dissenters were still forbidden from taking their degrees and decades before Jesus College became a center for the education of hundreds of middle-class Englishmen each year.

When Leigh Smith reached twenty-one years of age the following year, the Pater bestowed on him investment income of £300 per year. Compared to the prevailing salary of a Royal Navy Marine of about £12 a year, Leigh Smith now possessed more than enough to relieve any

Figs. 5–6. Two sketches by Barbara (Leigh Smith) Bodichon. The first shows the Pater playing chess with Willie, ca. 1840; the second shows street urchins in Hastings, ca. 1850 (courtesy Hancox Archive).

financial worries about having to work for the rest of his life. Each of the Pater's daughters also received the same amount when they came of age, and Charlotte Moore writes that this was much more than a gift. It was to guarantee that these women would not be placed in the same situation as virtually every other woman of their age: that of being not only dependent on men and marriage, but in fact becoming the property of any man they might marry.

The beneficence to his children also shows that, whatever his political, social, and sexual proclivities, the Pater had managed his financial affairs well. Yet a letter from Barbara in December of 1852, when she was twenty-five and Leigh Smith twenty-four, hints at a blazing row between Leigh Smith and the Pater. The basis of the argument is unknown, but it was one that smoldered in Leigh Smith for some time. "I believe," Barbara writes, "that Papa will be astonished that you have taken his passionate words so seriously. His words never mean as much to him as you take them for."[31]

But clearly they did. What Leigh Smith interpreted as an explosion the Pater could have seen as a routine fatherly criticism of BLS's choice of career, of course. It is entirely possible that the father was irritated at the leisurely pace of his son's studies, even though the Pater could have considered himself as responsible for this tardiness as anyone, having fixed a fortune on the young man at the age of twenty-one.

In her letter, when Barbara reminds her brother that he has responsibilities to others besides his father, she reveals that Leigh Smith has moved away from home. Such a drastic family cleavage suggests the possibility of a more serious confrontation between father and son. If the argument was not a fight over money, then perhaps Leigh Smith had learned with the shocked horror of a young naïf of the Pater's other families? Worse, that he himself was part of a grand socio-sexual experiment. Perhaps there was a final reckoning over his illegitimacy and that of all his siblings – with half-siblings into the bargain? If in fact he found himself in loathing of the Pater's apparent womanizing and tight family control, it is possible if not probable that such feelings mutated to self-loathing when the same patterns emerged in Leigh Smith's own adult life, when he invested inordinate amounts of time coveting and controlling much younger women.

Whatever the reasons for the schism with his father, as the eldest son of a family of illegitimate dissenters Leigh Smith had been placed in an almost impossible position in Victorian society. He would come to have all the property anyone could hope for – which to the landed gentry meant rental income for life and an existence of extreme comfort and leisure. But as a dissenter from the Church of England he was nearly thirty before he could take his degree at Cambridge and this, combined with his illegitimacy, has to be considered when searching for an explanation as to why this otherwise dominant personality would later shy away from public acclaim for his polar accomplishments.

Dissenters were finally allowed to take their degrees from Jesus College in 1856, making Leigh Smith one of if not the first such student to receive his diploma. Even then, with his admittance to the Bar, he did not practice. It seems clear enough that he had his mind's eye on different frontiers, and he had more than enough money to afford to take his time exploring them. It is not difficult to see where he wanted to go. Instead of the law, the young man earned a master's certificate to demonstrate the competence to sail his own ships.[32]

One writer suggests that, in the 1850s, the unconventional children were further snubbed by their famous cousins the Nightingales.[33] Whatever the reason for this slight – the children's illegitimacy, Barbara's politics, or the fact that the Pater was originally urged to marry into the Nightingale family and had refused – it was all apparently forgotten or forgiven thirty years later when Leigh Smith named a prominent waterway in Franz Josef Land 'Nightingale Sound.'

When it came to the row with his father, Barbara – as revolutionary a personality as any in Victorian England – urged her brother to stand his ground, and her Churchillian exhortation borders on an abuse charge against the Pater. "Every one must bear & fight in the place he is put & every resistance makes one stronger & more able to resist."[34] Unfortunately, if Leigh Smith replied to Barbara this letter does not survive to give us more insight into her nebulous comment that she does "not quite understand your letter & therefore cannot say exactly what I think."[35] Yet the remark suggests a deep bond between the siblings and a sister's natural protectiveness of a younger brother.

Another possibility that cannot be discounted is that Leigh Smith had declared his intention to make a career in exploration and had been rebuffed by his father. £300 was a princely inheritance, but to build an Arctic research vessel one required a king's ransom of £10,000 or more. Such a rebuke would surely have stung, but given the timing it was certainly understandable. The Pater would not be inclined to buy a ship for his son while the Franklin disaster was at that moment in full carnage. The same year that Leigh Smith entered Cambridge, the Admiralty dispatched three separate expeditions to locate their lost ships. They then offered a massive reward of £20,000 for anyone who could find the lost crews and get them out of the Arctic. Had Leigh Smith, a young man keen on sailing and exploration, seen in the Franklin epic not a disaster but rather a heaven-sent chance to put both his money and his skill to work on a project that would make him famous as well?

The notion is not so far-fetched. Twenty years after the rift with his father, Leigh Smith would do something very similar, coming to the aid of Adolf Erik Nordenskiöld's expedition stranded at Mussel Bay (Mosselbukta) on the north coast of Svalbard and in the process winning for himself the Royal Order of the Polar Star from the King of Sweden.[36]

But the 1850s saw Leigh Smith not in the Arctic but tied to his studies at Cambridge. He was resigned to watching (and collecting notes on) the increasingly spectacular developments around him, each of which likely only intensified his impatience with the pace of his own life. Besides the encompassing saga of the search for Franklin, the technological transformations alone were accelerating at a bewildering rate as communications, sanitation, and transportation networks were systematically overhauled. The overwhelming stench of the wide Thames led to its banking with London's first modern sewer system in the 1850s. As railroads replaced canals as the major mode of heavy transportation, a new railway line from London to Hastings in 1851 cut the journey to the family properties in East Sussex from eight hours to a little over two. Leigh Smith could lunch at Jesus College and be on the family properties in East Sussex in time for dinner.

But more than this, the intellectual underpinnings of societies, economies, even the nature of humanity itself, all were revolutionized in the 1850s. Karl Marx published the *Manifesto of the Communist Party* just as

Leigh Smith entered Cambridge. The discovery of a human ancestor in Germany's Neander Valley in 1857, the year Leigh Smith finally took his degree at Jesus, combined with the publication of Darwin's *On the Origin of Species* two years later, with their Genesis-smashing implications that humans were descended from a common ancestor of non-human primates, were perhaps the culminating hammer blows to the moral foundations of Victorian society.

By 1854, Leigh Smith's sister Barbara was publishing her first major tract on the rights of women, even as the Crimean War led to the international fame of Florence Nightingale and other pioneers of modern nursing. Barbara's marriage to Eugene Bodichon, a French doctor living in Algeria, was as unconventional as her father's social and sexual arrangements had been. She lived half the year with Bodichon in Algeria and the other half without him in England, agitating for the rights of women. With no rights to property or access to decent jobs, Barbara saw the prevailing status of British women as one of prostitution in everything but name.

Against this tumultuous backdrop, Leigh Smith's formative decade witnessed the return of no less than fourteen different expeditions sent in an increasingly desperate search of any survivors of the Franklin expedition. Two of these, the first and second Grinnell expeditions, were financed by a wealthy American, Henry Grinnell, recently retired, flush with cash, and fascinated by Franklin's fate. Grinnell loaned two ships to the U.S. Navy and, manned with volunteers, they set out from New York harbor in late May, 1850. It was this first Grinnell expedition that later that summer located Franklin's winter quarters at the site of the graves of three of Franklin's sailors on Beechey Island. Further searches proved unsuccessful and, while attempting to return home, both vessels were caught in the ice and forced to overwinter. The ships eventually escaped, drifting back into the Davis Strait in the spring of 1851 where they broke free of the ice and returned to New York. The discoveries at Beechey were a sensation, but the expedition is best recalled as the first Arctic experience of its peripatetic medical officer, the wondrous Elisha Kent Kane of Philadelphia.

Kane was thirty when he first witnessed the Arctic. By the time he died less than seven years later, he was an international polar hero, freighted with honors for his work in the north. Slender on geographic discovery, Kane's work nevertheless created a new Arctic literature and left behind a deadly and confounding notion of an open polar sea. He became the subject of one of America's first celebrity biographies, written by his spiritualist-lover, and was buried in the kind of hillside bunker usually reserved for a pharaoh.[37] He would eventually have a crater named for him on the Moon.

Kane returned to his home in Philadelphia just long enough to drop off an eight-foot-long narwhal tusk for his hometown's Academy of Natural Sciences, and then just as quickly went north again. This time Kane placed himself in command and armed the expedition with both a new program to search for Franklin and a notion to make the first serious American attempt on the North Pole. Kane and his men charted the areas of Smith Sound, Kane Basin, and Kennedy Channel, pioneering what would later become Robert Peary's 'American route' to the North Pole. Even more than this, Kane's published accounts of the two Grinnell expeditions crackled with drama and suspense. This was something new in polar exploration – the Arctic as a kind of *Götterdämmerung* – and it set the model for nearly all future polar exploration literature. In between the cold and suffering, the Arctic offered an almost spiritual connection with the universe:

> On our road we were favored with a gorgeous spectacle, which hardly any excitement of peril could have made us overlook. The midnight sun came out over the northern crest of the great berg, our late "fast friend," kindling variously-colored fires on every part of its surface, and making the ice around us one great resplendency of gemwork, blazing carbuncles, and rubies and molten gold.[38]

Such writing was entirely absent in the expedition accounts of men like Phipps and Parry, and it was all but calculated to course hot blood through the veins of young would-be explorers like Benjamin Leigh Smith. No wonder he was fighting with his father. One imagines Leigh Smith sitting with a copy of Kane's mystical *Arctic Explorations*, peeking through it even as he was trying to plow through British case law in the spring of 1857.

Fig. 7. The Arctic of Elisha Kent Kane, full of drama, danger and heroism (from Kane 1856).

Another Arctic book appeared in 1857, as insouciant in its descriptions of high latitude sailing as Kane's tomes were dramatically desperate. This was *Letters from High Latitudes*, a breezy lark written by a carefree popinjay by the name of Frederick Hamilton-Temple-Blackwood, 1st Marquess of Dufferin and Ava or, a bit more simply, Lord Dufferin. In a smart little yacht named *Foam*, Dufferin planned a summer excursion to Iceland, Jan Mayen, and Svalbard. His combination of erudite silliness, playful flirtations with the locals, multi-lingual history lessons, and a genuine high

LORD DUFFERIN.

*Fig. 8. Frederick Hamilton-Temple-Blackwood, 1st Marquess of Dufferin and Ava, ca.
1869 (courtesy Toronto Public Library).*

Arctic sailing adventure, made the book a hit. He offered, for example, an insight into nineteenth-century remedies for seasickness, administered consecutively until one managed to lay down and stay down: "Brandy, prussic-acid, opium, champagne, ginger, mutton-chops, and tumblers of salt water...."[39]

He sailed first from Scotland to Iceland, giving most Britons their first glimpse of Reykjavík ("a collection of wooden sheds [surrounded by] a desolate plain of lava"); Icelandic language ("a singularly sweet caressing language"[40]); saga literature ("so much art and cleverness as almost to combine the dramatic power of Macaulay with Clarendon's delicate delineation of character, and the charming loquacity of Mr. Pepys"[41]); and even wandering into expansive topics such as the demise of the Norse colony in Greenland ("like the fabric of a dream"[42]); and the probable location of Vínland ("[not] farther [south] than Newfoundland, Nova Scotia, or, at most, the coast of Massachusetts"[43]). Toasted at a party in both Icelandic and Latin, Dufferin responds with his own remarks in Latin, deigning in his published account to "subjoin a translation of them for the benefit of the unlearned."[44] Other letters are left entirely in their original French.

Dufferin can be said to have invented the modern tourist weekend in Iceland: a rapid pony trip to the ancient legislative meeting spot of Þingvellir enjoyed with a coffee brewed from Geysir water, before a quick return to Reykjavík with an obligatory discussion of how the volcanoes of Iceland periodically contaminate "even the pure skies of England and Holland."[45] At a time when Leigh Smith was managing to get by on his £300 per annum inheritance, Dufferin records that the average stipend for an Icelandic clergyman was about £6 per year.

Back in Reykjavík, he renewed acquaintances with the Emperor of France, first as a guest of honor on board the emperor's yacht *Reine Hortense* and, later, at a ball where the local women were asked to come and show off their "ivory shoulders."[46] Dufferin was particularly interested in disproving a previous account of travels in Iceland that noted that Icelandic females were accustomed to flattening down their breasts. He engaged in this intensive anthropological field research by means of an evening of dancing with women in low-cut dresses. He thus satisfied himself that Icelandic women were every bit "as buxom in form as any rosy English girl I have ever seen."[47]

The French emperor offered to tow the *Foam* northwards and help Dufferin to make up for time lost by his studies of the women of Reykjavík, for his main object was an attempt to see Jan Mayen Land and especially the towering landmark of Mount Beerenberg. The tow lasted until *Foam* was less than 130 nautical miles from Jan Mayen, at which point the Frenchman decided that the island could not be located for the fog, and the vessels parted. Dufferin carried on under sail, but thick fog and pack ice prevented anything more than a long view of Beerenberg from about eight nautical miles off. Quite intrepidly he maneuvered his ship through broken ice around the island until he was close enough to the northern shore to launch a small boat and gain solid ground. He and his men then disembarked and dragged an old figurehead ashore and on up to a rock outcropping. There they ceremoniously mounted it alongside the white ensign of St. George and a tin biscuit-box holding a paper with the ship's name and the names of the men of the crew and the date of their landing.[48]

The harsh ice conditions meant that they had to depart immediately. Disappointed at not being able to spend more time exploring the primary objective of his summer cruise, Dufferin turned northeast towards Hammerfest in northern Norway, a run of 800 nautical miles that *Foam* covered in eight days.

Dufferin then made north for Svalbard, where *Foam* reached her greatest glories, closing on Amsterdamøya and dropping anchor in English Bay (Engelskbukta) on August 6th, 1856. For Dufferin, Svalbard, when he finally witnessed it, held none of the charms of Iceland. All he saw was a "numbness and dumbness [that] seemed to pervade the solitude. I suppose in scarcely any other part of the world is this appearance of deadness so strikingly exhibited"[49] It was probably too much to ask the magnificent geological stratigraphy of Svalbard to compete with the deep female cleavage of Iceland. Decidedly unimpressed, Dufferin only stayed about a week.

With his sprightly published account, pretentious but unstuffy, Dufferin achieved a minor celebrity, which later he parlayed into a series of increasingly responsible diplomatic postings. Almost certainly Leigh Smith would have read Dufferin's *Letters*. It was popular just at the time he was having doubts about a vocation in the law. Such a career would

Fig. 9. Lord Dufferin's Foam *gets her first look at Jan Mayen, 1856 (from Dufferin 1857).*

end before it even began, when his father's death left him in a position to contemplate the Arctic without the restraints of the formidable Pater looking over his shoulder.

The Pater died in 1860. He left his eldest son enough money and property in East Sussex and London so that, should he so choose, Leigh Smith could live the rest of his life in the comfortable management of his investments and the collection of rents from his tenant farmers. The land holdings alone were impressive and included a series of estates in the rolling green pasture lands of the English Weald. Amid deep copses and creekside stands of trees, Leigh Smith would have woken to the alternating honking of geese, quacking of ducks, and the subdued songs of the doves.

It was a formidable inheritance and there is no evidence that Leigh Smith ever despised either the land or the money, now seeing through its fourth generation since being assembled by his great-grandfather Samuel Smith out of tea and sugar imports a century earlier. But what he wanted now, as he entered his middle years, was to indulge his desire to see the Arctic. A whole genre of Arctic travel literature was under construction and all of it beckoned him north. Besides Dufferin's book, there is no doubt Leigh Smith would have read the other major popular account of an upper-class foray into the Arctic, when in 1861 James Lamont published his *Seasons with the Sea-horses: Sporting Adventures in the Northern Seas*. Where Lord Dufferin wrote of his brief contacts with Arctic shores with the foppishness one might expect of an English Lord off on a summer lark, James Lamont, F.G.S., took a much more serious, crabbed approach. That is clear enough in the dedication of his book, which is given over to the very model of the dour Scotsman, the geologist Charles Lyell. Lamont flatters his fellow countryman Lyell with the insight that his "delightful *Principles of Geology* has been my unvarying and instructive companion during ten years of adventurous wanderings, during which everything I have seen seems to me confirmatory of your Geological views."[50] Fulsome, certainly, but hardly misplaced. Lamont joined a long list of explorers, beginning with Darwin during the *Beagle* expedition in the 1830s, for whom *Principles of Geology* had informed everything they observed in the natural world.

Aside from his general interest in northern adventure, there are very definite reasons why Leigh Smith would keep a close eye on the Arctic travels of James Lamont. Unlike Dufferin, who was from a long-established upper-class family, Lamont and Leigh Smith were virtual carbon copies of children of successful nineteenth-century British middle-class entrepreneurs. They were also exact contemporaries, with Lamont born just six weeks after Leigh Smith in 1828 and departed this life six months after Leigh Smith in 1913.[51] And, just like Leigh Smith, at the age of twenty-one Lamont had inherited a fortune. The monies enabled Lamont to end a young career in the army, move to London, manage estates in Scotland and the West Indies, and, probably his most desired result, take his master's certificate and sail his own vessel in the Arctic.

Seasons with the Sea-horses is, first and foremost, the travelogue of a snob with upper-class pretensions, off on a boutique hunting experience in Svalbard. If one can read a man from his writings, you'd ship out any day of the week with Lord Dufferin, enjoying the wine and the women and tolerating his endless toasts in Latin and French. But in his foolish charm, Dufferin had completely missed the spirit of the times. It was Lamont, the serious student of Arctic history, geography, and biology with a grating nouveau-riche condescension and relentless focus on observing nature with his own eyes, who perfectly reflected the advancing materialism and fascination with science that was shaking the world of the 1850s to its stuffy, religious core.

To understand just how seriously Lamont took himself, he often quoted from Darwin's just-published *On the Origin of Species* and he sent a copy of *Seasons with the Sea-horses* to Darwin as soon as it appeared in print. Darwin in turn responded approvingly of Lamont's hypothesis for the evolution of the polar bear. Lamont speculated – correctly as it turns out – that polar bears had developed from northern brown bears, "who, finding their means of subsistence running short, and pressed by hunger, ventured on the ice and caught some seals ... so there is no impossibility in supposing that the brown bears, who by my theory were the progenitors of the present white bears, were accidently driven over to Greenland and Spitzbergen by storms or currents."[52] More astounding, Lamont thought this process through while sailing in Svalbard and *before* the 1859 publication of *Origin of Species*. In a measure of generousity that echoes the interplay between Darwin and Alfred Russel Wallace, Darwin even credits Lamont with arriving independently at the theory of natural selection.[53]

In August of 1858, Lamont sailed in his 142-ton yacht *Ginevra* to Norway. There, induced by tales of favorable and exotic hunting in the Arctic, he shaped a course for Svalbard. Given the lateness of the summer, *Ginevra* could only remain in the archipelago for a short time. But, cruising in the southern reaches of Svalbard in the area of the Thousand Islands (Tusenøyane), Lamont saw enough unusual wildlife and stunning geology to realize that he had to return.

That return came the following year, when Lamont began sailing toward Norway in early June of 1859. Putting into Lerwick on the 11th in the face of heavy seas and strong headwinds, the wealthy Lamont quickly noted the crushing starvation of the Shetlanders, but did not allow it to delay his departure for the north. He reached Hammerfest on the 23rd where he had a summer support charter waiting for him. This was the *Anna*

Louisa, "an extremely ugly, clumsy little tub of a sloop, of about 30 tons … [that] looked as if the intention of her builder had been that she should make as much leeway as possible, and upset at the first opportunity."[54]

Just as with Leigh Smith a decade later, Lamont found himself a strange man in command of a strange fleet. His Norwegian charter was a traditional one-masted cargo vessel called a *jagt* or *jakt,* in this case a walrus-hunter with an all-Norwegian crew made up of a skipper, two walrus harpooners, a cook, and eight other seamen. And like the Norwegian crew on board Leigh Smith's *Sampson* in 1871, the men of the *Anna Louisa* did not impress Lamont. It took some time to round them all up and dry them all out, but the *jakt* finally left port with a full complement on June 26th. The plan was for the support vessel to sail for southeastern Svalbard and rendezvous there with Lamont on board *Ginevra.*

Lamont sighted Sørkapp on July 2nd, and after sailing about in Storfjorden, made his rendezvous with the *Anna Louisa* on the 5th. On the 6th, unwilling to subject his pristine *Ginevra* to the carnage and smell of a summer of walrus hunting in the ice, Lamont, along with his guests, a Lord David Kennedy and his manservant, transferred to the "narrow and odoriferous bunks"[55] on board the *Anna Louisa.* Lamont gave the master of *Ginevra* instructions to meet up again in a month, and in the interim to collect as many fossils and hunt as many reindeer as he could, since the reindeer hides and meat would not bring the kind of overwhelming stench to *Ginevra* as would the blubber of the marine mammals Lamont wanted to shoot.

Once on board the *Anna Louisa,* Lamont proceeded to relentlessly kill seal, walrus, and polar bear wherever they could be found, along the way making a few geographic observations and curtly dismissing a plea for help from a badly frostbitten sailor of a shipwrecked *jakt.* Lamont slowed his expedition long enough to toss a few bottles of rum the sailor's way before continuing on with his hunting. He criticized Dufferin for believing that the Gulf Stream could bring pine to Svalbard, hypothesizing instead that it floats in from the rivers of Siberia. He also took to task those Arctic explorers who believed that the phenomenon of 'red snow' was a natural discoloration caused by a form of algae.

Lamont was correct about the pine, mistaken about the algae. He was also correct in his observation that the landmass of Svalbard was rising

Fig. 10. James Lamont, ca. 1860s (courtesy of the Royal Geographic Society (RGS–IBG)).

and in fact had been for some time. Whale bones and driftwood found up to two hundred feet above the level of the sea demonstrated that no storm could have thrown it there. Lamont put the rate of elevation at about thirteen feet per century, not far from modern geological estimates for various sectors of Svalbard of more than ten feet per century following the last Ice Age.

Right or wrong, Lamont was anything but shy in his opinions. He also seemed to take a grotesque thrill in the amount of carnage he and Lord Kennedy and his paid harpooners wrought on the wild animals of Storfjorden: "Lord David fired and struck the old bear on the back, completely paralysing her; we then scrambled through the icy mud up to where she lay, and despatched her. The cubs, quite black with mud, and shivering with cold, lay upon the body of their mother growling viciously...."[56]

Anna Louisa rendezvoused with *Ginevra* on the 4th, and to Lamont's fury his crew on board *Ginevra* had only managed to kill eight reindeer while cruising around the area of Bellsund. Worse, they had had the temerity to have "carefully eaten all the hind-quarters of the deer themselves, and had left nothing but ten lean fore-quarters for us!"[57] Fortunately, the sailing master had made a large collection of fossils and other geological specimens, which somewhat mollified Lamont's anger at not receiving the choice cuts of meat he felt were equal to his status. He ordered *Ginerva* northwards into Storfjorden after more reindeer, while *Anna Louisa* returned to the walrus hunt. One of the Norwegian sea-hunters related to him the tale of an incredible slaughter of over nine hundred walrus on one island alone in the summer of 1852. Lamont calculated that by the time of his voyage a thousand or more of the giant sea mammals were being killed in Svalbard each summer. He believed that the animals were attempting to retreat further and further north and away from their pursuers, taking refuge of sorts in the inaccessible islands along the more remote northern coast of Svalbard. Lamont freely admitted that the walrus were vastly overhunted, and thought they would be extinct within twenty to thirty years. But he did not let his feelings slow his trigger finger.

Lamont was curious to sail further north and east, toward the chimerical "Commander Gillies' Land, which lies sixty or seventy miles to the north-east of Spitzbergen,"[58] and thought there might be other lands in that direction, lands where walrus and polar bear existed in even greater

Fig. 11. James Lamont's men engaged in one of his favorite activities: killing Arctic marine animals (from Lamont 1861).

numbers. But no sailing vessels had ever been able to reach the northeast corner of Svalbard in order to test this proposition. Nor was Lamont any fan of the idea that there was an easy route to the north, otherwise known as the "open polar sea theory." "I am aware that the distinguished Dr. Kane held very strongly an opposite opinion; but the arguments in his book do not seem to me to be the slightest avail against the overwhelming amount of evidence in a contrary direction."[59] Lamont believed, along with Scoresby, that the highest latitude that a sailing vessel was likely to ever see was about lat. 81°30′ N.

As in so much else, Lamont was correct in this, as well as in his belief that the only way the pole could be reached was over the ice. If a ship could overwinter somewhere in along the northern coast of Svalbard, hunters could spend their time provisioning the expedition from the wildlife in the area, and then in the spring trained teams of dogs could possibly make the six-hundred-mile dash over the ice.[60] Parry had failed precisely for these reasons: he had failed to overwinter, had started his trek many months too late, had hauled his sledges and boats with men rather than dogs, and then adverse ocean currents had pushed the ice southwards faster than Parry's men could drag their heavily-burdened boats northwards.

Meeting up again with *Ginevra* on the 24th of August, Lamont left *Anna Louisa* behind in a small harbor while he sailed on his own yacht deeper into Storfjorden. Taking to the *Ginevra*'s small boats on the 26th, Lamont and a few of his crew sailed and then rowed to the head of Storfjorden. There, a fjord existed that some had long thought might actually be a strait that connected Storfjorden to the wide confluence of the three straits to the east known as the Southern Gateway (Sørporten) of Svalbard. The strait does in fact exist and is called Heleysundet. It separates mainland Spitsbergen from the island of Barentsøya. An adverse current stopped the small flying expedition, but Lamont's effort is now commemorated in Ginevrabotnen (Ginevra Bay), the body of water at the head of Storfjorden and just to the west of the sought-after strait.

By the end of August, Lamont had sent the *Anna Louisa* back to Hammerfest to cash in on his summer's hunting profits, which he would use to defray the costs of his northern explorations and hunting adventures, while he continued in *Ginevra* to round Sørkapp and make a late-season foray into Isfjorden on the west coast of Svalbard. It was during this interlude that Lamont had time to reflect on the nature of the seal and walrus and the polar bear he had spent much of the summer killing and how they illuminated the question of special creation versus natural selection. Writing as one would expect during perilous times for anyone contradicting the literal truth of Genesis, Lamont does not jump entirely off Darwin's cliff. But it is clear that he believes in a Darwinian universe, even as his writing settles for a form of theistic evolution:

> I acknowledge with humility my presumption in entering upon so profound a question in Natural History; but although I make no pretensions to the character of a scientific naturalist, still I have opportunities such as few have enjoyed, of observing and studying the habits and mode of life of strange animals in many strange countries; and the more I observe nature, and ponder on the subject, the more do I become convinced that Almighty

God always carries out his intentions with regard to the animal creation, *not* by "direct interpositions" of His will, nor by "special fiats of creation," but by the slow and gradual agency of natural causes.[61]

Ginevra anchored in a sheltered bay inside Isfjorden on September 2nd. There the crew replenished the water and firewood necessary for the return to the Hammerfest. More than three tons of meat was stowed on deck. They had killed just about everything there was to kill, with the exception of a narwhal and an Arctic fox, which Lamont very much regretted. Leaving Isfjorden on the 5th, *Ginevra* anchored in Hammerfest on the 11th. Lamont sold off everything he could sell and took home to Scotland two live polar bear cubs, six adult polar bear skins, and all the ivory his men had extracted from all of the walrus they had slaughtered. They were back in Leith Roads in early October. The final death toll: 46 walruses (plus 20 more killed but lost at sea); 88 seals (plus 40 more killed and lost); 8 polar bears; 61 reindeer; and one white or beluga whale. The rock and fossil specimens were all boxed and carted off to the Geological Society.

These first two sailing cruises to Svalbard had left Lamont fascinated but unsatisfied. The hunting had challenged him, as had the landscape and the ice, but he wanted to go further. Back at home, he entertained the fantasy that if he just possessed a ship with auxiliary steam power, he could make an attempt on the North Pole itself. In this, despite the truth he observed with his own eyes, he was enticed – by accounts of Norwegian walrus hunters and the speculations of open polar sea enthusiasts like August Petermann – with the thought that somewhere north and east of Svalbard there could after all be an ice-free channel that led to the pole. The fact that Britain had left the field of polar exploration after 1859 also pricked his sense of national pride. "So completely did these ideas gain possession of me that at the general election of 1868 I abandoned a seat in Parliament ... and set to work to build a vessel which should embody all Arctic requirements in a moderate compass."[62]

The result was the *Diana*, a three-masted schooner with thirty-horse-power compound steam engines. Her range of 10,000 nautical miles under steam power and ability to survive an Arctic winter was made possible by the tiny berthing and messing accommodations that made room for more coal and for the supplies that would be required if the ship were ever frozen in for a winter. In such an event, a 'man of leisure and means' would possess all the food and warmth necessary to survive an overwintering with a touch of class.

Launched into the Clyde in March of 1869 with seventeen iron holding tanks for the blubber he hoped to harvest, Lamont called her "a cross between a yacht and a modern Scotch whaler."[63] As with his voyages on board *Ginevra* and *Anna Louisa*, Lamont intended to shoot his way across the Arctic, and if possible engage in some whaling ("destroying these monsters of the deep"[64]), in an attempt to recoup at least some of the cost of the vessel and the expeditions he had in store for her. In *Diana*, he felt, he had built the best private vessel for Arctic exploration and pure Arctic conditions in all of maritime history.

In April of 1869, *Diana* steamed through the Caledonian Canal with a crew of fifteen, including an artist, William Livesay. At Tromsø on May 6th, six Norwegians skilled in hunting walrus and seal were taken on board. By the end of the cruise, Lamont would write that he had never shipped with "six lazier, dirtier, sulkier, more mutinous and cowardly rascals...."[65] Calling at Hammerfest, the execrable Lamont demanded that the local agent produce a small boat and some walrus gear Lamont had left with him over a decade earlier. One hopes that the agent produced his own bill of charges for ten years' worth of storage.

From Hammerfest, Lamont chose to sail eastwards to Novaya Zemlya, then northwards along that coast until stopped by ice, then work his way back westwards towards Svalbard while searching out any opportunity to get north through the pack. Lamont also wanted to try out a new method of killing walrus, by firing a large shell at them in order to make it easier to harpoon them while they were attempting to escape his guns. In the end, the shells blew up such large parts of the walrus that the carcass sank and could not be recovered. When he did manage to kill a walrus cow, he took the calf on board in an attempt to bring it back to England and sell it to a zoological park.

Diana sighted Novaya Zemlya on June 2nd, and there the crew commenced killing walrus in earnest, slaughters that Lamont employed with almost pornographic glee to describe the correct types of shells for penetrating thick walrus skulls at various angles. Lamont even saw an advantage for polar exploration in the gradual extermination of walrus populations. As long as the hunt continued, the walrus would be forced to retreat further and further north. Hunters would follow them north and in the process find a split in the ice somewhere between Novaya Zemlya and Svalbard that, in a season of open ice, would lead to the pole. Lamont understood, as much if not more than his contemporaries, the unlikeliness of such a pathway presenting itself. But, like his contemporaries, he could not resist being seduced by the possibility.

On June 19th, *Diana* was at 75°21′ N, 44°08′ E, and following a chart drawn up by Petermann two years earlier. If the chart was accurate, then an observer in *Diana*'s crow's nest, some seventy feet above the surface of the sea, should be able to see the peaks of Gillis Land, the southern extremity of which Petermann had placed at lat. 77°30′ N. Lamont could see nothing, and thought that the land might lie even farther north. Irritated, Lamont made a note to track down Petermann after the voyage and inquire by what authority he placed Gillis Land so far south.

The expedition reached Svalbard at the end of June, only to find Storfjorden and in fact the entire western coast of the archipelago blocked by a band of ice. Lamont directed his crew to sail for the northwest coast of Svalbard, where he hoped to round Hakluythovden and test how far *Diana* might be able to get north from that point.

Dropping anchor at Coal Haven (Kolhamna), near the present-day airstrip at Ny-Ålesund, with the snow-wrapped Tre Kroner mountains in the distance, Lamont enjoyed what he described as a 'typical' night in a bay in Svalbard. Everything was quiet beyond the rustle of activity on the decks of *Diana*. "Absolute stillness everywhere, save occasionally when the voice of a wild bird miles away over the glassy sea was borne to the ear, or the noisy falling of the edge of a glacier, like the sound of artillery discharges, was echoed from hill to hill. A clear, unclouded sky permitted the rays of the evening sun to crimson the snowy peaks, and to throw vast shadows across the glaciers."[66] He rowed around as much of Krossfjorden and Kongsfjorden as the ice would allow, shooting at birds and seals and taking notes and picking up the odd artifact – like a broken oar from a vessel called *Vigilant* – as he went.

Fig. 12. The Diana *at lat. 80° N (from Lamont 1876).*

Leaving the bay, they moved off northwards, rounding Hakluythovden and making for Moffen Island, where Lamont hoped to find more
walrus. Meeting up with a walrus hunter nearly beset at Moffen, *Diana*
towed the sloop to an anchorage in Fair Haven. There Lamont sent a
crewman twice each day to climb the heights of Utkiken (141 m/462´
high), a spot on Outer Norway Island (Ytre Norskøya) used 250 years earlier by the Dutch as a lookout point.[67] There they could scan for a favorable
way ahead.

Ice now lay in a sheet from Fair Haven to Moffen, so Lamont took to
a small boat to explore along the northern coast of Svalbard. After rowing
and hauling the boat through and over the ice for more than seventy nautical miles, Lamont and his companions returned exhausted and discour-
aged at the impenetrability of the pack ice. In the meantime, some of his
crew on board *Diana* had gone ashore to a graveyard of Dutch whalers and
returned with a collection of skulls of the Dutchmen themselves. After
more than a week of enforced idleness, during which Lamont concluded that no ship would soon reach the North Pole, he retreated south to

Isfjorden where, fortified with coffee, biscuits and brandy, he geologized, hunted reindeer, and mined ten tons of coal from a seam he named The *Diana* Coal Mine.

After ten days of larking about Isfjorden, Lamont made one more attempt to round Hakluythovden but again found the sea clogged by pack ice. Hiking to a promontory near Welcome Point (Velkomstpynten), Lamont could see that the object of his voyage, Hinlopenstretet, was also jammed with ice. A few more days spent lolling in Magdalenefjorden, rummaging for coal on shore and arguing over rum rations with the Norwegians, Lamont gave up on Gillis Land, Nordaustlandet, and the North Pole. "Never, I am convinced," he writes, "will a ship sail from Spitzbergen to the Pole."[68]

Rounding Sørkapp, *Diana* reached Edge Island (Edgeøya) and a bay on the southeast coast later named for the vessel. Soon after, Lamont gave up and returned to Tromsø, where he "discharged the sinful Norwegians,"[69] and then sailed for home, arriving at Dundee on October 6th. He would return to Novaya Zemlya the next summer, followed by a brief return to the northwest corner of Svalbard in 1871. But these voyages merely served to confirm him in his belief that even his steam-assisted *Diana* would never be able to visit the hidden northeastern coast of Svalbard, or find the mythical Gillis Land, or come anywhere near to the North Pole.

Reading the accounts of Lamont would have done nothing to dampen the desire for Arctic exploration of Benjamin Leigh Smith. If James Lamont could make such journeys with little more than a scientific bent, a master's license, the desire to hunt and an awful lot of money, well, Leigh Smith had all those qualifications, too. And for Leigh Smith there was now even more reason to try. While Lamont was making his first voyages to the waters around Svalbard, Leigh Smith had in the interim come into even more money, inheritance from a vague figure in family history referred to as 'Uncle Joe' Gratton.[70] Whatever influence Gratton exerted on Leigh Smith's development, it must have been profound to one extreme or the other, since he would later name a glacier in Franz Josef Land after him. Other relatives – direct or not – would also find their names placed upon one remote fastness or other in the new lands in the Arctic that would be soon be discovered by Leigh Smith, but Gratton Glacier strikes one as either grandly honorific or coldly ironic.

With the death of his father, as Benjamin Leigh Smith became the new *Pater familias* at the age of thirty-two, he was now the dominant figure in a family that included the estimable Barbara, the insane Bella, the gay Nannie, and the gentleman-farmer Willy. Nannie saw her brother as someone who had a kind of "personal *influence* that subtle thing that makes a person a power without even uttering a word."[71] Over the decade that followed the assumption of his new responsibilities, it would be Leigh Smith's younger brother Willy's daughter Amy, alone among the other nieces and nephews, who would become the prime object of Leigh Smith's affections, a situation that, given his new primacy in the family, was accepted as the norm. When she wounded him by accepting the engagement with Norman Moore, Leigh Smith turned his attentions to Mabel, the daughter of Bella and her retired and much-older husband, General John Ludlow.

Bella married the General in 1859 when she was twenty-nine and Ludlow was fifty-eight. John Ludlow had fought with distinction in the 1820s during the First Anglo-Burmese War, and then went on to join the Indian Police Force and help end the horrific practises of the killing of Indian girls by families who could not afford to marry them off and the immolation of a wife along with her husband's corpse.[72] It is to the deeply faithful and minutely detailed surviving diary of Ludlow that we owe most of the intimate glimpses into Leigh Smith's life between 1863 and Ludlow's death in 1882. These occasional commentaries are very likely the only such views we will ever have of the years when Leigh Smith grew from ambitious young man to internationally-recognized polar explorer. Most of these insights are in the form of family notes or gossip about the staff, as in the first entry that specifically mentions Leigh Smith. On April 12, 1863, the General writes that "Ben communicated a piece of intelligence connected with our coachman and former parlour maid which surprised me."[73] An entry from 1865 notes the death of Uncle Joe Gratton as well as his will that leaves everything to Leigh Smith's aunt, who promptly devolved it all to Leigh Smith, who was asked to manage it while paying her £1,000 a year. When Edmund, the three-year-old son of the General and Bella, sickened and eventually died in the winter of 1866–67, Ludlow's diary mentions that Leigh Smith was always around to help.

A year later, the General noted that Leigh Smith planned to stand for Parliament as member from the parliamentary constituency of Rye, but nothing came of his candidacy. Mostly, between 1863 and 1870, Leigh Smith shows up as something of an itinerant manager of funds and family. He escorted young relatives, like the nineteen-year-old Iona Bonham-Carter, to their first public balls. He played the occasional game of chess and otherwise helped intensively with an increasingly deranged Bella. He made plans to visit Egypt but does not seem to have made the journey. He gave one of his nieces a pony. He gossiped about how much money other, even more fabulously wealthy relations had settled on their offspring. He did visit Rome. Ten years after leaving Cambridge, and as he faced mid-life, Leigh Smith was clearly still casting about for a profession. The General, whose life possessed a not unpleasantly rigid routine, took note. "Ben talks of going abroad," Ludlow writes in his diary in mid-summer, 1869. "When will he settle down & have done with 'knocking about' which he so much delights in?"[74]

What the General did not know, but what he and the entire family would soon discover, was that Leigh Smith's days of "knocking about" had not even begun. In the summer of 1870, the General learned that Leigh Smith had hired *Gleam*, the 125-ton yacht of Sir David Baird, for a three months' charter at a staggering £500 per month. With it he hatched a plan to sail to Jersey, then Hastings, and then Scotland. To the family, such a charter must have been seen as a massive indulgence. For Leigh Smith, however, it was very much more. It is not known if he sailed as far north as Peterhead, the remote whaling port on the northeastern coast of Scotland, but, if so, and if he spoke with the whaling captains there, it was very likely this voyage that convinced him that he had the stuff of a great Arctic voyage in him.

Over the winter of 1870–71, this feeling must have only intensified. With the exceptions of the private voyages of Dufferin and Lamont, the British had all but given up on the north. Since the resolution of the major elements of the Franklin saga more than a decade earlier, the Royal Navy had sworn off the Arctic. It was not merely the Franklin disaster. War in the Crimea, the long transition from sail to steam, the laying of transatlantic and transpacific telegraph cables, each and all of these drew

British naval attention away from Arctic exploration. Dufferin and Lamont had opened a door to the private exploration of the Arctic to any
Englishman with a will and a wallet, and with the extra monies from
Uncle Joe Gratton, Leigh Smith now had more than enough money to
match his polar ambitions.

Even so, it was a far cry to believe that a wealthy neophyte just finished
with a summer holiday sailing charter might be the one to step in where
the entire Royal Navy now feared to go. Leigh Smith in the spring of 1871
was not yet the scientific explorer of the Arctic that he would become.
His conception of Arctic sailing at this stage was virtually identical as his
contemporaries Dufferin and Lamont: the Arctic was where one could
engage large amounts of money in hunting exotic species and navigating
in high latitudes. The hunt furthermore held the promise of defraying the
enormous costs of such a voyage.

Still, the seeds of a much greater ambition were clearly there and, in
late April, 1871, the General writes as much, albeit with unselfconscious
humor: "Ben has bought a big & stout yacht without having seen her. She
has been cased in the North Sea & was built for going among the ice.
Ben says he is 'going to the North Pole' – but it seems that he cannot get
anyone to accompany him.… His object is sport & he has been to Blissets
in Holborn to buy rifles.…"[75]

This yacht was the *Sampson*, an 85-ton topsail schooner purchased
from a John Pallisser of Comragh, Ireland. Built by Messrs. John White
of Cowes, Isle of Wight, in 1852, *Sampson* had already made two Arctic
voyages while owned by Pallisser. That was apparently enough of a rec-
ommendation for Leigh Smith to decide that this was the vessel he could
use to sail far beyond the usual courses he encountered as a member of the
New Thames Yacht Club. With no countrymen brave enough or foolhardy
enough to go with him, Leigh Smith turned his gaze to Norway, the
gateway to the North. His plan was to take *Sampson* into the same waters
explored before him by Phipps, Nelson, and Parry and, if possible, go even
farther than these titanic names in the history of British polar exploration.

At the age of forty-three, Leigh Smith believed he could finally realize
his calling. Within six months – with his first experience in the Arctic a
ringing success – Leigh Smith would become preoccupied with the scientific exploration of the north. Between 1871 and 1882, his five expeditions

into the Arctic would discover dozens of new islands, engage in the survey of uncharted coastlines, pioneer deepwater oceanographic research, carry live polar bears to the zoos of London, collect fossils and other geological specimens on remote shores and dredge marine invertebrates from the ocean floor to add to the burgeoning natural history collections in Britain. These increasingly daring expeditions would climax in a spectacular story of shipwreck and survival at a place no one even knew existed in 1871. And his fame would largely eclipse the twin curses of his youth in the eyes of polite Victorian society: his family's dissent and his own illegitimacy.

❧2❧

EXPEDITION ONE: SVALBARD, 1871

On Tuesday, May 16, 1871, while *Sampson* lay moored at Grimsby Docks on the Humber River awaiting favorable winds, Leigh Smith began a journal he would keep regularly for the next five months.[1] His companions for the expedition were an all-Norwegian crew from Tromsø. Only the mate and the captain, a "well-known" Norwegian sealing skipper and explorer by the name of Erik Andreas Ulve (1833–1896), spoke any English.[2] There is no indication that Leigh Smith spoke or understood more than a few words of Norwegian. In Tromsø, Leigh Smith mentions that five additional crewmembers came on board to make a crew of fourteen, suggesting that *Sampson* left England with a total complement of nine including Leigh Smith himself.

For the next five months, the Norwegians on board *Sampson* made seemingly little impression upon the Englishman, unlike the consistently negative impression they made on Lamont. His journal reveals a man preoccupied with winds and tides, rocks and islets, and ocean temperatures and depths, with only brief views of his own personality showing through a thick veneer of scientific curiosity. Most of the intimate glimpses were revealed in and around Tromsø, where Leigh Smith more than once remarked on the beauty and athleticism of the women of northern Norway. Yet, unlike Lord Dufferin, who could avidly linger for several pages on the attributes of Icelandic women, as soon as Leigh Smith opened one of these personal doors he just as quickly closed it, and returned to his observations of the winds and skies, flora and fauna, geology and oceanography.

Early on Friday morning, May 19th, *Sampson* crowded on all available canvas and sailed out of the Humber, shaping a course north by northeast for the west coast of Norway. In moderate to fine breezes, *Sampson* coursed along between three and six knots, covering 239 nautical miles from noon on the 19th to noon the 21st, before running into shifting winds and fog and having its daily run cut to fifty-one nautical miles. Meandering along, Leigh Smith found his first chance to engage in some field research. With the dip of a survey bucket overboard, he collected samples of "great quantities of green stuff on the surface of the water [that] extended for several miles." Nearby, Leigh Smith sighted a whale. His journal descriptions left something to be desired, and the "great quantities of green stuff" proved to be fish spawn, but he was finally off on his own and eager to make meaningful contributions to science. In the light winds, the all-Tromsø crew, anxious to be home after an extended absence, took to matching "their luck in getting favorable breezes whilst on deck."[3]

During the afternoon of May 24th, after a cumulative run of 432 nautical miles from England, the crew sighted land to starboard they believed to be in the vicinity of Bergen. Leigh Smith began to notice the increased daylight in the more northerly latitudes and by midnight on the 24th he writes of "scarcely any darkness during the night-time." He began a running comparison of the coast of Norway with that of Scotland, contrasting the latter with the "plentiful snow on [these Norwegian] mountain tops." *Sampson* moved slowly northeastwards, passing several Norwegian cod-fishing boats. The weather was very warm and the seas smooth and the low clouds were so thick that they appeared to cut off the masts of the fishing boats. The *Sampson* crew dropped lines in fifty fathoms and fished up a meal of cod.[4]

By Saturday the 27th, still gliding along on smooth waters, both Leigh Smith and the crew became increasingly agitated about reaching Tromsø. Since he needed to engage more crew in that northern port to take with him to Svalbard, Leigh Smith was concerned lest he be too late and "the best men [already] all gone to Spitsbergen." He seemed as well to absorb a lesson of caution when, with several of the crew, he lowered a dinghy and gave chase to a large shark that was "showing a fin about three feet above the water." As they put a rifle bullet into it, the fish threw up its tail into the air "and fortunately for us did not touch the boat or our Arctic voyage would have ended in a very brief manner, as there were no boats that could be sent from the ship without some considerable delay getting them off the deck."[5]

The next day the weather turned and *Sampson* began to reel off first eight and then nine and a half knots. With increasing winds and a heavy sea rising, the crew was forced to take in or reef much of the sail. The captain shaped a course eastward of the Lofoten Islands and into the Vestfjord with its shelter from both northwest and northeast winds. Leigh Smith began to regret all the calm sailing they had enjoyed, as "so much indulgent weather is not qualified to prepare one for an Arctic cruise." By the evening of the 28th, with rain "blowing strong and thick [it] was not quite so comfortable on board as it had been during the former part of the voyage."[6]

Early on the 29th, as *Sampson* passed the islands of Røst and entered Vestfjorden with its high surrounding mountains and variable winds and the schooner's progress slowed again to a crawl, Leigh Smith decided that "a good steam launch would be a valuable addition to a sailing yacht."[7] Two years later, he would go this technological inspiration one better, when he chartered James Lamont's screw steamer and Arctic veteran *Diana* and, with *Sampson* as a reserve tender, voyaged to Svalbard in relief of the Swedish polar expedition under Adolf Nordenskiöld.

As he entered this gateway to the north with its increasing disorientation from the elongated summer days, Leigh Smith also began a kind of Norwegian reverie, noting several coastal boats "of the old ancient style of Norsk vessels. They do not alter the rig of them or the hulls according to the modern style. They have one large square lugsail which does them good service with fair winds, but with head winds they have to lie neutral." Alongshore he observed a long trend of rock and mountain and a few scattered huts, with little vegetation save the ubiquitous birch trees. The one modern vessel that overtook *Sampson* was the *Sophie*, an auxiliary screw-steamer bound for white or beluga whale hunting in Svalbard. Leigh Smith would later hear from another vessel that *Sophie* had caught seventy belugas around Svalbard in less than a month, which offered him further evidence that he might finance his expeditions through sea hunting. Gliding in calm winds through a narrow, fast-running tidal gut near a village he identifies as Sandtoiv, Leigh Smith has a "musical box" brought on deck, "being a very fine evening to give the crew a treat." It's one of many such gestures he would employ on his subsequent expeditions in order to bring small pieces of England to the Arctic.[8]

On June 1st, sixty nautical miles out from Tromsø, Leigh Smith recorded an outside temperature of 35° F and a cabin temperature of 42° and remarks that they had made it thus far without having to light a fire in the cabin. Picking through fickle winds and rocks and shoals, *Sampson* finally anchored in Tromsø on the afternoon of June 3rd. Numerous vessels were already in port, awaiting favorable winds for the reach to Svalbard.

Once *Sampson* was hauled alongside and moored to the Norwegian brig *Tromsoe*, Leigh Smith went ashore to collect his mail and engage in a bit of ethnographic research. "The houses are all built of wood, being varnished in the rooms gives them a light and cheerful appearance. The people dress well and look to be enjoying good health and I think the fashions are studied as much here as in any of our towns by both sexes. The women are very good-looking and for a small place they muster very strong.… People do not seem to care about going to bed here. I think they are acting on the old maxim, 'Make hay while the sun shines,' and as they have a long dreary winter, they intend to make up for the lost time."[9]

The next day, a Sunday, Leigh Smith observed men and women rowing to church across the fjord. After dinner, he walked to a shipyard to see a small Arctic cutter named *Isbjørn* (*Polar Bear*), which was being fitted out to carry an Austro-Hungarian polar expedition led by the team of Karl Weyprecht and Julius von Payer "with a view of getting to Gillie's Land." Weyprecht was the leader of the maritime piece of the expedition, while Payer would be the explorer on the ground.[10]

The object of 'Gillie's Land' was a long-time Arctic chimera, the location and naming of which had become something of an obsession for German and Austrian expeditions of the 1860s and 1870s inspired by the geographer August Petermann.[11] Petermann's own desire was to see some major feature like Gillie's Land named for King Wilhelm and the greater promotion of German polar exploration.[12] But it was Weyprecht and Payer's pursuit of the Gillie's Land mystery that led them further north and east the following summer and resulted in the discovery of Franz Josef Land.

Known variously as Gillie's Land, Gillis-Land, Giles Land, or The Commander Giles Land, the land was reportedly first sighted east of Nordaustlandet in 1707 by Cornelis Giles, a Dutch whaling captain for whom the spot was initially named. Petermann, studying old charts and using those that actually mentioned it, placed it east of the eastern point of Nordaustlandet by fifty nautical miles. The veteran Norwegian sealing captain Johan Kjeldsen (1840–1909) sighted it in 1876, five years after Leigh Smith's first expedition, but it was no great land. It was most likely the ice-covered island with its glacial appearance that was eventually given the name White Island (Kvitøya).[13] It would come to figure prominently in the balloon expedition of Salomon A. Andrée as the forlorn place where he and his crew finally perished. The island was often confused – as indeed it was during Leigh Smith's first expedition – with Kong Karls Land, a group of islands in southeastern Svalbard first seen by the English whaler Thomas Edge in 1617.[14]

The pursuit of Gillis Land is what brought Weyprecht and Payer to Tromsø in the summer of 1871. On June 8th, Weyprecht came on board *Sampson* to introduce himself to Leigh Smith, and during their conversation Leigh Smith discerned that Weyprecht did not possess much confidence in the *Isbjørn*. Weyprecht explained his plan to trend along the south coast of Svalbard to "Walter Thymen's Strait [Thymen Strædet; eventually named Freemansundet, a 35-km-long by 6-km-wide strait separating Barentsøya from Edgeøya], [and] if impeded by ice to take the boats across the ice to reach Gillie's Land."[15]

On the 11th, Weyprecht returned to *Sampson*, this time bringing Julius Payer with him. Together they dined on board with Leigh Smith, probably on some of the fresh cod caught by the crew the previous evening. These June 1871 meetings in Tromsø were of some moment, given Weyprecht and Payer's discovery of Franz Josef Land the following summer and Leigh Smith's own later explorations and shipwreck in that newfound archipelago.

Listening to the Austrian plans, Leigh Smith quietly began to formulate his own personal method of Arctic exploration. Already, his experiences along the coast of Norway had begun to teach him the values of patience, flexibility, and opportunism when it came to wind, tide, and weather. Soon he would add experience in the ice to his list of qualifications. In a note that was almost certainly added after his return from Svalbard, Leigh Smith proclaimed that, "in [his] own humble opinion, it is utterly impossible to form any definite plans before leaving as the winds prevailing from any quarter have a great influence on the ice in general."[16]

This thought was the beginning of Leigh Smith's eventual voyaging strategy: go where conditions allowed you to go, and record such data as conditions allowed you to gather. As W.J.A. Grant wrote of the 1880 Franz Josef Land expedition, even Leigh Smith did not know exactly where they were going that year, since he had long decided "to be guided entirely by circumstances, and if the ice prevented him from getting far north, or finding anything fresh to do in one direction, he could then try somewhere else."[17]

In Tromsø, Sampson was loaded with three walrus boats to go with the ship's dinghy, along with "harpoons, lances, walrus lines and other gear requisite for the [walrus] boats during the voyage."[18] On June 15th, Sampson rode the tide out of Tromsø and began to work its way north through light and inconsistent winds to the island of Sørøya, from where the expedition would take its departure for Svalbard. When they anchored on June 21st near an island Leigh Smith identified as Sanda, he went ashore to meet the foreman of the local fisheries, the appropriately named Mr. Roe, as well as his daughter, "a buxom, healthy-looking lass of twenty summers, rejoicing in the name of Petra Christine Marie Roe, who seemed to take great pleasure in waiting on us and would have fain prevailed us to have taken coffee enough to have lasted us for our Arctic cruise."[19] The vision of Ms. Roe seemed to bring with it fresh breezes from the northwest, and the following day Sampson cleared from the northern coast of Norway bound for Svalbard.

After two days of steady winds that pushed Sampson a consistent six knots northwards, Leigh Smith on June 25th sighted his first iceberg at a position of 74°06′ N, 24°26′ E, approximately seventy-five nautical miles southeast of Bear Island (Bjørnøya). It was Leigh Smith's first view of Arctic ice and as such a harbinger of adventures to come. He "considered it a novelty and now begin to realise that we are in the Arctic seas." Two hours later, Sampson encountered an impassable barrier of ice barring the way to the north, and so the men shaped a course eastward in search of a way through. For the rest of the day, Sampson threaded through icebergs and pack-ice, before becoming trapped "in an artificial lake amongst the ice and [with] no outlet."[20]

Thus began nearly two weeks of plodding back and forth amid ice-covered seas between lat. 73° and 75° N in the vicinity of Bjørnøya.

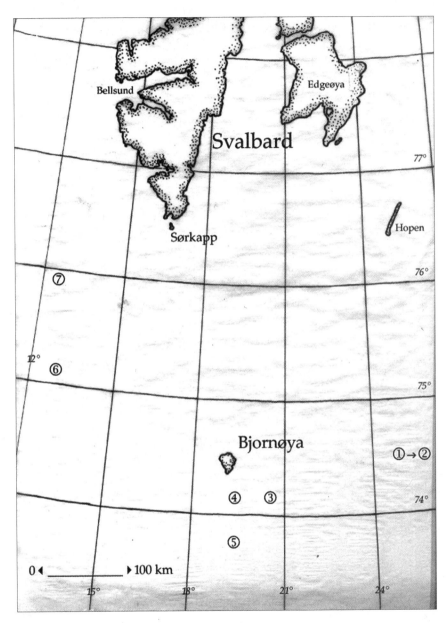

Fig. 13. Chart of Leigh Smith's first ocean stations, recorded around Bear Island (Bjørnøya), June 26–July 6, 1871. These locations testify to Sampson's difficulty in finding a route through the ice north and east of Bjørnøya, finally settling on an advance north along the west coast of Svalbard. Chart derived from Petermann, 1872, 'Originalkarte.'

Leigh Smith soon acclimatized to his chosen environment. "It seemed rather strange at first to be thumping so much against the ice but we seem to be quite reconciled to it and look upon it as a matter of course."[21] Like Weyprecht, Leigh Smith also started off in a search for the elusive Gile's Land, but soon thought better of it and accordingly set course to the west of Bjørnøya. By July 6th, as *Sampson* continued to wallow along at a paltry knot and a half, Leigh Smith grew tired of the slow pace of the voyage, remarking that it was "three weeks since we sailed from Tromsø, a very long passage for such a short distance."[22]

Yet he was not one to waste any time. He used the meandering cruise to begin a series of ocean stations, recordings of both surface and deep ocean temperatures along with samples of ocean bottom sediments. These systematic efforts at scientific data collection was the major element that would set apart all of his Arctic voyages from those of earlier British Arctic tourists like Dufferin and Lamont. Between June 26th and July 7th, during the slow voyage from Tromsø to Svalbard, Leigh Smith carried out seven such ocean stations. In *The Depths of the Ocean*, the pioneering Scottish oceanographer John Murray credited these early deep ocean data from northern seas with helping define "warmer layers of water beneath the colder surface waters of the Arctic Ocean."[23]

On June 26th, Leigh Smith for the first time used what he referred to as a "Cassell's deep-sea thermometer" to record ocean temperatures at various depths.[24] With this instrument, Leigh Smith began to record a series of ocean temperatures at various depths, and to use this data to speculate on the nature of the intricate and dimly understood oceanography around Svalbard. At his first station, he found his first counterintuitive evidence that the deeper he surveyed the warmer the ocean temperature became: 32.5° F at the surface, 34° at thirty fathoms, and 35.5° at a hundred fathoms. This initial data, along with similar results obtained during this same summer by Weyprecht on board *Isbjørn*, were the first of many such recordings that would support the idea that a layer of comparatively warmer Arctic seawater might exist between the surface and the bottom. In time, this current would become known as the West Spitsbergen Current. In just a few weeks, Leigh Smith had already come a long way from his first observations of "great quantities of green stuff" in the ocean.

The scope of his research widened as the expedition wore on. The following day, Leigh Smith was able to dredge up bottom sediments from 200 fathoms. For the next week, as *Sampson* wallowed around Bjørnøya, Leigh Smith continued to record ocean temperatures from the surface down to 230 fathoms.

In the first week of July, *Sampson* finally made some progress north, and at 4 a.m. on the morning of July 7th, large numbers of birds were seen flying toward what the crew assumed must be land. Svalbard was sighted twelve hours later, and by 8 p.m., Bellsund was forty nautical miles away to the east. After finding Green Harbor (Grønfjorden) clogged with ice, Leigh Smith continued north past Prins Karls Forland and made for Danskøya. He was now entering the historic waters that had beckoned him for so many years.

By July 12th, riding a light northeast breeze in moderate 40° F temperatures, *Sampson* was twenty nautical miles offshore of Albert I Land, northwest of Kapp Mitra. Leigh Smith writes of a "sea as smooth as glass, scarcely a ripple to be seen. No ice to be seen in any direction and any ordinary vessel could cruise here in perfect safety."[25] The following day, as *Sampson* tacked to the east, the conditions changed rapidly: temperatures dropped, icebergs appeared to the north, and Amsterdamøya lay just ten nautical miles northeast.

With seemingly remote prospects for rounding Hakluythovden on the north point of Amsterdamøya, *Sampson* maneuvered toward Sørgattet, the strait that separates Danskøya from the mainland. Reluctant to risk *Sampson* in the shallow strait, a small boat was put over to collect water and eider duck eggs on Moseøya, a small islet off the southern point of Danskøya. There Leigh Smith picked up a blank cartridge "of English manufacture for [a] breech-loading fowling piece," leading him to conclude that James Lamont on board his steamer *Diana* had recently passed that way.[26] Leigh Smith and his mates shot twenty eider ducks and collected a hundred eggs.

Finding no fresh water, *Sampson* maneuvered around the west coast of Danskøya and came to anchor in three fathoms of water in Kobbefjorden, just east of a small islet named Postholmen that was situated in the middle of the small bay. The crew found a good place for filling water, along with shelter from all but westerly and southwesterly winds. Leigh Smith took

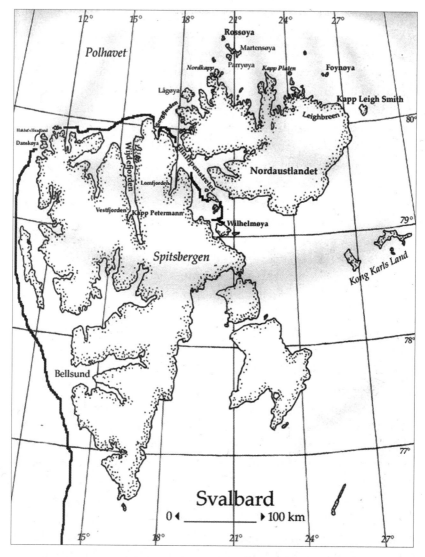

Fig. 14. Track of Sampson along Svalbard's west coast to Danskøya, round Hakluyt's Headland, and to Sorgfjorden (July 7-31, 1871). Sampson then penetrated Hinlopenstretet as far as Wilhelmøya (August 1-31, 1871). Tumlingodden, from where Leigh Smith and others thought they could sight 'Gile's Land' (from this point they were actually seeing Kong Karls Land), is the eastern point of Wilhelmøya. Petermann thought Gile's [Gillis] Land was actually further north and east. He was correct in believing that what Leigh Smith had seen was Kong Karls Land. Chart derived from Petermann, 1872, 'Originalkarte.'

his hunting dogs ashore on Danskøya and walked inland. He ascended a snow-filled ravine to the top of the ridge that would later be named for the American journalist-explorer Walter Wellman (Wellmankollen) and from there had a panoramic view of Smeerenburgfjorden. Northeast winds, he noted, had cleared the fjord of its ice.

As Leigh Smith returned to *Sampson*, another yacht anchored in Kobbefjorden, groaning with a catch of fifty seals and two whales all taken in Smeerenburgfjorden. The other vessel reported that ice still clogged Hakluythovden, and that James Lamont in his steamer had escaped southwards. On Saturday, July 15th, still another hunting yacht anchored in the bay and the crews of all three vessels joined on board *Sampson* where one of the men with a concertina provided some entertainment.

The following day, Leigh Smith recorded a balmy noontime temperature of 62° F. With bright sun and an easterly breeze, he decided on a miniature half-day expedition. Taking four men in one of the small boats, they pulled for Sørgattet, intent on a rowing circumnavigation of Danskøya. No seals were seen, and what ice there was had grounded in the shoal water of Smeerenburgfjorden. Rowing in the shoals against a strong tide, the five men reached the site of the abandoned whaling station of Smeerenburg on the southeast corner of Amsterdamøya. There Leigh Smith found great quantities of driftwood amongst the low and marshy flats.

The men then pulled through Danskegattet, the narrow strait separating Amsterdamøya from Danskøya. Leigh Smith noted the numerous rocks and shoals, and warned any vessel with a draft exceeding nine feet from attempting the passage. The boat rounded the northwest corner of Danskøya at Kapp DeGeer and returned to *Sampson* at 11 p.m. loaded "with 200 eggs which we had collected on our journey on the islands."[27]

The winds shifted around to the southwest on Monday, July 17th, and with them an expectation that the ice might have been pushed away from Hakluythovden. Accordingly, *Sampson* left Kobbefjorden at 2 p.m. and sailed northwards, rounding the headland three and a half hours later and shaping a course for Vogelsang Island (Fuglesangen). In dense fog, Leigh Smith 'heard' Fuglesangen before he saw it. "It is a great resort for the auks [little auks or dovekies], guillemots and other birds which build their nests in the cliffs; they make a great noise which you can hear in still weather one or two miles out and in foggy weather is a good warning when approaching land."[28]

Just before midnight, *Sampson* anchored in Fair Haven in just two fathoms. Leigh Smith went ashore, most likely to the promontory at Ytre Norskøya, to look northward, and distressingly saw ice as far as the eye could see. There was no passage north or east. Ice pressed down on *Sampson* itself, and the crew was forced to put a line on shore and warp the ship close in toward land to avoid it. When the warp snapped later that night, *Sampson* was shifted around a point to a more secure anchorage.

The next morning, Leigh Smith went ashore again to check the state of the ice northwards, but found the same result. He also found several graves, "the coffins were of very rude construction and skeletons still in them. They are supposed to be the remains of sea-men buried here in the former whaling seasons at Spitsbergen. At that time these islands were used as a rendezvous and to try out the blubber, having had boilers erected on shore."[29]

By Friday, July 21st, after seeing another yacht use its small boats to tow itself eastward on the tide, *Sampson* put its own boats ahead to try the same thing. Rowing for four hours until the east-running tide played out, *Sampson* meandered to the mouth of Red Bay (Raudfjorden) before anchoring to some ice. Another day of towing with the tide put *Sampson* off Velkomstpynten, the northern edge of Reinsdyrflya and the entrance to Woodfjorden. "Here we find the benefit of a small ship as our moderate draft of water enables us to get close inshore and a few grounded icebergs keep the pressure of the smaller ice-floes clear of the ship."[30]

Leigh Smith took a dinghy and rowed the two miles to shore at Red Beach (Raudstranda), finding the beach sand "corresponding to the name ... given it by Parry's expedition." He commenced "a very rough journey" overland to a hill on the western shore of Liefdefjorden, in search of open water to the east. He returned to the ship six hours later cold, wet, and unsuccessful.[31]

Later that same day, Leigh Smith went ashore again, this time with better results. "In walking inland for about a half hour we came to a garden of Eden and no person would credit that flowers would grow in such a country and in such a short space of time. The ground was literally covered with a yellow flower similar to our primrose and several other kinds of which we gathered specimens. Here we found a beach inland as far as three or four miles which looked as if it had at one time been a sea-shore."[32]

Returning to *Sampson*, Leigh Smith found a number of other vessels, all waiting for the ice to clear and open a path eastwards. For five days, the ships waited for clear water, making repeated trips ashore for provender. As Leigh Smith remarked, "it will not require many visits to kill all on the ground." Finally, on July 27th, the ice and the "very disagreeably cold" fog above it began to clear. *Sampson* sailed slowly toward Verlegenhuken and the entrance to Hinlopenstretet. There, Leigh Smith was able to make his first deep-sea temperature recordings in two and a half weeks. At midnight, he also recorded his highest latitude yet on the voyage: 80°13′ N.[33]

Seeing a mass of ice to the east and north, Leigh Smith decided at midnight on July 27th to penetrate southwards into Hinlopenstretet as far as possible. Even though at that moment the strait seemed relatively free of ice, Leigh Smith was by now convinced that ice conditions around Svalbard were never static for very long. *Sampson* would now spend the whole of August exploring Hinlopenstretet, a long passage that runs northwest to southeast and splits Svalbard in half.

Before proceeding into Hinlopenstretet, Leigh Smith explored Sorgfjorden, especially the area around Heclahamna. This was the first of his many nods to the history and, one might even say, the archaeology of British exploration of the Arctic. Parry's *Hecla* had anchored in this harbor on the east side of Sorgfjorden in 1827, while the expedition's boats were pulled over the ice toward the pole. Leigh Smith seemed anxious both to pay homage to Parry wherever he could, and to gently critique the national polar hero where he thought it appropriate. He disagreed with Parry's idea of separating his small boats from the expedition's mother ship. "In our case with a small vessel we are never far from our boats when they are absent and the crews reap great benefit from the rest and warmth they get on returning to ship which is far preferable to remaining in boats for a week in these regions."[34]

On Saturday, July 29th, Leigh Smith set out to climb a mountain on the south side of Sorgfjorden ("supposed to be two thousand feet in height") and where he expected to find a cairn left there by Parry.[35] "After a long and very rough journey, we clambered to the summit of it where we were amply repaid for our labor. We had a good view of the coast from North Cape to Hakluyt's Head including all the adjacent islands, and inland as far as eye could trace it seemed to be one immense glacier." Leigh

Smith eventually found and dutifully rebuilt Parry's cairn, and gazing around him from this height the awesome panorama commanded a "very stillness [that] seemed to be quite oppressive to us." He was beginning to gain an appreciation for the feeling of relative scale one acquires amid the immensity of the Arctic landscape. After nine hours away, the forty-three-year-old returned to *Sampson* "very tired."[36]

The next day, Leigh Smith recorded an almost uncomfortably warm noontime temperature of 72° F, prompting him to remark that if not for the surrounding ice on land and sea, "no person could imagine they were in the Arctic regions."[37] He went ashore to hoist the New Thames Yacht Club ensign at Crozier Point, on a flagstaff that had been erected there by Parry's crew. Triumphantly, he found several pieces of hemp rope, "about three-inch, Government private mark – a yellow thread in the strand – which could have been left here by no other vessel than the *Hecla*."[38] In the space of a few moments, he had made two direct connections with the great Parry.

On the 31st of July, *Sampson* weighed anchor and proceeded out of Sorgfjorden and into Hinlopenstretet. Leigh Smith remarked that the other *jakts*, still lying at anchor, showed no inclination to follow. And indeed the weather in the strait was very different from that prevailing within the sheltered bay. With strong winds blowing from the southeast and with fog, grounded icebergs, and large floes making navigation hazardous, *Sampson* worked southward toward Lomfjorden. The warmth had vanished – the temperature was forty degrees lower than it had been just a day earlier in Sorgfjorden. The transition was sudden and sharp, and a reminder of how quickly one's environment changed in the north. "Everything on deck is one mass of ice, the dense fog freezing as it settles on the ropes and sails and likewise on ourselves."[39]

In the thick fog, they narrowly avoided a collision with the eight-mile-long Isrundingen, the sheer glacial edge of the Valhallfonna that flows into the west side of the strait. For Leigh Smith, the massive looming ice front was a "very close shave and made everyone on board open their eyes with astonishment."[40] As they cleared Isrundingen, *Sampson* came to anchor in five fathoms in a tiny bay on the north side of Lomfjorden. Here Leigh Smith recorded a rather extraordinary sight: one hundred or more beluga whales that all appeared to be floating erect in the bay, their white heads two feet above the surface. Unable to approach more closely with harpoons, Leigh Smith speculated that perhaps a large stream flowing into the bay provided a source of food. He then rowed around Kapp Fanshawe to the bird cliffs at Alkefjellet, where he scattered thousands of guillemots by echoing his voice off the cliffs.

Sampson left Guillemot Bay (Lomfjorden) on August 4th, making a series of short tacks to avoid the icebergs. Leigh Smith sighted the Black Mountain (Svartberget) on the east side of the strait, the 'black mountain' that – like so many locales in Hinlopenstretet – would be used for longitude determinations in 1898 by the Swedish–Russian Arc-of-Meridian Expedition.[41] That night, *Sampson* came to anchor under several grounded icebergs on the south side of Wahlbergøya. Two *jakts* on walrus hunts were already there. Leigh Smith recorded that the southern extremity of the island extended farther south than on existing charts, and provided *Sampson* with good shelter.

The snug anchorage appeared just in time. A gale soon sprang up and blew for two days. One of the other *jakts* narrowly missed destruction when the berg to which it was moored suddenly toppled over. When the storm finally moderated on the evening of August 6th, Leigh Smith went ashore with his dogs and, walking inland, found an extended beach where he found a collector's paradise: plentiful shells and fossils, along with skeletons of both a polar bear and a walrus, and the ubiquitous Siberian driftwood that descends on every stony beach of Svalbard.

Looking eastward toward Torellneset on Nordaustlandet, Leigh Smith saw his way south blocked by ice. He longed for a clear sky "to see whether we can get a glimpse of Giles Land of which there is so much talk." His comment leads one to believe that he was beginning to have his doubts about Giles Land, and not just because of his own experiences. "We have met with men this voyage in some of the vessels who positively affirm that they have seen it, and some state that they have been there, but from personal experience they are greatly addicted to lying."[42]

It is possible, through Captain Ulve, that Leigh Smith had encountered some of the Norwegian sealing captains who had so recently located what became known as Kong Karls Land. In 1853, a Norwegian ice pilot named Erik Eriksen, sighted Kong Karls Land from Edgeøya and mistook it for Giles Land.[43]

Still, the lure of new and elusive lands in this fogbound seascape was compelling. Whenever the weather cleared, Leigh Smith would to go ashore to ascend the nearest mountain and scan the southern horizon for Giles Land. As early as August 9th, while at anchor off Wahlbergøya, Leigh Smith had gone ashore, ascended a mountain, and through a break in the clouds and fog "we fancied we could see land in the far distance."[44] This may have been Svenskøya in Kong Karls Land, laying more than 61.2 nautical miles to the southeast.

On August 12th, *Sampson* made a start in dense fog for Thumb Point (Tumlingodden), the eastern point of Wilhelmøya. The area was visited and given a preliminary survey in 1868 by the German *Grönland* expedition under Karl Koldewey.[45] When Leigh Smith cruised in the area, the name Wilhelmøya had not been settled, since it was not clear whether the area was a point of land sticking out from the mainland, or an island upon itself. As Leigh Smith writes: "This land called Thumb Point is supposed to be an island but no one has surveyed it accurately."[46] Mooring to an iceberg in the vicinity of Kapp Freeden later that day, Leigh Smith began a series of local surveys in order to solve the problem.

On the morning of the 14th, he took one of the small boats and rowed to a bay on the northwest corner of Wilhelmøya. There he disembarked with a small team and began a walking circumnavigation of the island. Crossing a hill to the west side of the land, Leigh Smith shaped a course to the southward, hiking over soft, muddy ground for several miles. In the process he solved the problem. He crossed a hill to the southeast side of what he now knew to be an island, and walked into a flat area of swampy yellow clay.

More than twelve hours after leaving *Sampson*, the team was still trying to reach better ground along shore. The appearance of the sun for the first time in a fortnight cheered the men. At two a.m. on the 15th, after rounding the northeast corner of the island, they spied *Sampson* weighing anchor to the north and rushed to meet the ship before it disappeared. The ship sailed anyway, and the men took to their boat and did not regain the ship until it anchored off Tumlingodden at six a.m.

They had been away from the ship without food on a strenuous hike for twenty hours, but had answered the Thumb Point/Thumb Island question. The island and several features around it were later named by

Petermann after supporters of Koldewey's German polar expedition of 1868.[47]

On Saturday, August 19th, Leigh Smith made another trip ashore to the summit of the mountain at Tumlingodden to look for Giles Land "and saw supposed land in that direction."[48] Indeed, *Place Names* notes that the mountain was "ascended by the Norw. sealing captain, E.A. Ulve, on Aug. 19, 1871 from where he sighted 'Gillis-Land.'"[49] It is clear enough that what they both were looking at was in fact Kong Karls Land.

New land or not, by the next day the novelty of the sighting 'Giles Land' had infected the entire crew. As they waited out the ice in hopes for a passage either east or north, even the ship's harpooner hiked to the top of the mountain and claimed to see the long-sought chimera in the distance.

Now, in late August, Leigh Smith saw no chance of progress south or east through the ice. The temperatures were falling daily. The first snow dusted the area on August 23rd. A vessel from Tromsø met up with *Sampson* on the 24th and reported that all passage beyond the North Cape (Nordkapp) of Nordaustlandet was blocked by a mass of ice. For Leigh Smith, still stuck on the southern end of Hinlopenstretet, and despite his modest successes to this point, the summer was rapidly becoming a lost one.

On the 28th, Leigh Smith rowed to the Bastion Islands (Bastianøyane) to hunt for polar bears and have one last look to the south and east. Ice was everywhere. There was no navigable water in either direction. He and his party lit a fire and took coffee in the lee of a rock. It was time to extricate *Sampson* from the strait. It was now cold enough that ice was beginning to form on still water. The sun dipped below the horizon for the first time on the 30th. At noon on the 31st, with all boats ahead rowing and towing, *Sampson* slipped from its iceberg mooring and floated on the ebb tide northwards. By midnight they had passed Wahlbergøya, halfway up the strait and, four hours later, passed Kapp Fanshawe.

At 10 a.m. on Friday, September 1st, *Sampson* rounded Shoal Point (Langgrunnodden) and, much to his delighted surprise, Leigh Smith found "the coast is quite clear as far as we can see eastward."[50] Two hours later, at Low Island (Lågøya), they found an abandoned Norwegian *jakt*, masts and spars cut away and all cargo removed, yet still riding at anchor inside of a reef. Having barely escaped Hinlopenstretet, a superstitious man might have turned around at this point. Instead, Leigh Smith

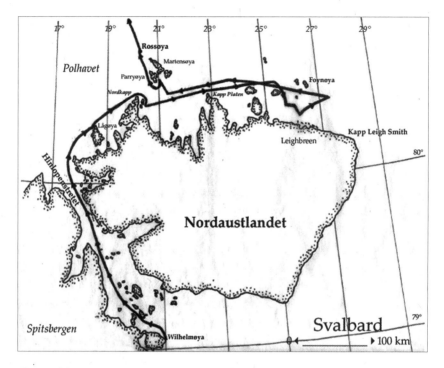

Fig. 15. The break-out from Hinlopenstretet (August 31, 1871) and the flying expedition eastwards past Kapp Platen (September 4, 1871), to Foynøya (September 5, 1871), to Kapp Leigh Smith (September 6, 1871). Sampson then retreated along the north coast of Nordaustlandet to the Seven Islands (Sjuøyane). There, north of Rossøya, Leigh Smith made his farthest north of lat. 81°25′ N at 11 a.m. on September 11, 1871. Sampson then made for Wijdefjorden where Leigh Smith charted Vestfjorden (September 12–16, 1871). Chart derived from Petermann, 1872, 'Smyth' & Ulve's.'

continued east. It was a bold decision, especially given the lateness of the season, and Leigh Smith would be rewarded for it. Over the next ten days he made the majority of his significant Svalbard discoveries.

Sampson passed Nordkapp just before noon on September 2nd and came to anchor off South Castren's Island (Søre Castrénøyane) in eight fathoms. On shore for two hours, Leigh Smith found more driftwood than he had seen at any other point in Svalbard, not an inconsiderable observation given the amount of Siberian wood that drifts onto those remote shorelines. Two *jakts* that had been sea-hunting north of Russia in Novaya

SHIPWRECK AT CAPE FLORA

Fig. 16. Norwegian walrus-hunting jakts off the northern coast of Svalbard, 1880 (courtesy Hancox Archive).

Zemlya showed up at the same anchorage. Leigh Smith politely sent over a bottle of brandy and some preserved meat and vegetables to each, and was rewarded with return gift of a Novaya Zemlya fox skin and some ptarmigan shot in Wijdefjorden.

A strong southwest gale forced *Sampson* from its temporary berth on the afternoon of the 3rd so she rounded North Castren's Island (Nordre Castrénøyane) and found clear water to the east. By 8 a.m. on the 4th, they had crossed Nordenskiöldbukta and in thick fog stood three nautical miles north of Kapp Platen, still with clear water to the east. From here, Captain Ulve shaped a course northeast, and around 5 p.m. that afternoon, they sighted the small island of Drabanten. This tiny bar was later joined to Karl XII-øya by wave action, losing its identity in the process. Petermann's chart of *Sampson*'s track does not show the vessel approaching the island(s), but Leigh Smith is clear in his journal that a boat from *Sampson* was sent through broken ice in search of seals or walrus on the island, but found neither.

Sampson stood its ground for several hours, the fog being too thick to maneuver in. When the fog cleared a bit the following morning, September 5th, *Sampson* cruised toward what emerged as two small islands and then a third island about three nautical miles to the southwest of the first two. These were the first confirmed sightings of Brochøya, Foynøya, and Schübelerøya, small islands that would figure so large in the *Italia* saga of 1928. Along with most of the other features Leigh Smith would soon after note in this sector of Svalbard, these islands were later named for accomplished nineteenth-century Norwegians. After the cruise, Captain Ulve handed the new geographic data to Professor Henrik Mohn of the University of Oslo. Mohn then consulted with August Petermann upon an eventual thirty-three new place names in northeast Svalbard, and Petermann published them in two articles and two charts in his *Mittheilungen*.[51] Schübelerøya was named for a botanist at the University of Oslo while Brochøya honored a mathematician. Foynøya was named for the famous Tønsberg whaler Svend Foyn, whose explosive harpoon revolutionized the hunting and processing of whales in the nineteenth century.[52]

From the newly discovered islands, *Sampson* tacked still further eastwards and, at noon on September 6th, came to the limits of Svalbard. "We can see land bearing from our present position SSE," Leigh Smith writes, "stretching to a very low point to the sea and inland it appears to be one continuous glacier."[53] Because of the fog, they had not been able to take their position for several days, but they figured *Sampson* to be thirty nautical miles east of Repøyane. The "very low point" they had seen Mohn and Petermann would later name Kapp Leigh Smith, the eastern limit of Svalbard, and the "continuous glacier" became Leighbreen.

From the masthead, there was still no ice to be seen to the east. Neither could they see any vessels, all other ships having made their retreat as it was now very late in the season. Leigh Smith was sorely tempted to attempt a rounding of this new northeast point of Svalbard, but he knew that if ice came in from the north, or they encountered an ice wall to the south, they would have no escape route. If they were trapped, they did not have enough supplies on board to support an overwintering.

At 4 p.m. on Wednesday, September 6th, they turned the ship around and tacked to the westward. Two hours later, *Sampson* passed a quarter mile north of what Leigh Smith called "Sampson Island," bearing twenty nautical miles east from Repøyane.[54] It was one of twenty-two new islands within Svalbard sighted and named during this one research cruise. On his very first attempt, Leigh Smith had done more than all the previous English explorers of this sector of Svalbard combined.

By the following morning, *Sampson* had cleared Repøyane and shaped a course for the Sjuøyane. Before abandoning the north for the year, Leigh Smith wanted to see the islands named after so many British naval explorers. He also had a notion to make one quick reconnaissance toward the pole itself.

Under a bright moon, *Sampson* approached the ice-shrouded Sjuøyane around midnight on September 7th and by the following afternoon was only two nautical miles off the southern edge of Martensøya. Drifting in Straumporten, the strait between Phippsøya and Parryøya, Leigh Smith sighted the same derelict *jakt* he had noted off Lågøya a week earlier. He thought she had most likely broken her anchors and floated north on the recent southerly winds. *Sampson* anchored in seven fathoms next to a large grounded iceberg on the east side of Parryøya, and Leigh Smith went ashore to pay a visit.

On the morning of 9th, Leigh Smith stepped ashore onto a sandy beach, where he located the usual large quantities of driftwood along with the backbone of a whale and reindeer tracks in the sand. Atop "a very peculiar rock which we will call Pinnacle Rock," the shore party hoisted the New Thames ensign to celebrate the highest latitude they had yet attained.[55] From this height, Leigh Smith saw nothing but open water as far as he could see both north and west. As he had at Danskøya, he then rowed around Parryøya, and reaching a bay on the south side of Phippsøya, boarded the derelict *jakt*. She had not broken her anchor; someone had boarded her, cut away her anchors and cable, and set her adrift.

Ice from the east began to hem *Sampson* in, so the boats were employed to tow the ship through a reef off Parryøya that screened them from the force of the ice. Clearing the southeastern corner of the island and passing between Parryøya and Nelsonøya, *Sampson* headed north along the western edge of Sjuøyane, making for Table Island (Tavleøya). To the northeast, they saw the derelict yet again. As Leigh Smith noted, she was "driving away with the tide and no doubt she may accomplish what no human being has done, reach the North Pole."[56] There is more than a hint of a suggestion here that he longed to be on board and go along for the voyage.

At 7 p.m. on September 10th, *Sampson* arrived off Rossøya and Vesle Tavleøya, the northernmost islands in Svalbard, and a boat was lowered so Leigh Smith could go ashore. Again the New Thames ensign was hoisted, a salute fired, and Leigh Smith collected a few specimens of the northernmost rock in the world. He then rowed through the narrow strait separating the two small islands and circumnavigated Rossøya before returning to *Sampson*.

The only ice to be seen was a few grounded bergs. So, after retrieving the boat, *Sampson* hove to in a strong westerly gale. At 6 a.m. on September 11th, *Sampson* made sail and proceeded northward. For five hours she sailed north by west at five knots. Leigh Smith recorded that not an iceberg or ice of any description was to be seen.

Near 11 a.m., they finally approached the edge of the pack ice. This was no spot for a vessel to linger in. The seas were heavy, so the expedition turned around and began its retreat. When the sun appeared momentarily, they fixed their highest latitude at 81°25′00″ N, just short of Nordenskiöld's record of 81°42′ N of Svalbard in *Sofia* in 1868. This was the farthest north Leigh Smith would attain on any of his five expeditions. As they sailed southwest past Waldenøya, rather than celebrate his farthest north, Leigh Smith marveled that they had gone the entire Arctic cruise without the need of a fire in the cabin.

Retreating southwestwards, *Sampson* bore up and made for Wijdefjorden, the crew intent on replenishing their meat and water supplies before returning home. In the event, the excursion turned into a chance for the crew to hunt before they returned to Tromsø and for Leigh Smith to engage in more surveying.

Sampson entered the large deep fjord and located a previously uncharted island off Kapp Petermann on the evening of September 12th. The ship came to anchor on the south side of the small island in eight fathoms. Boats were sent into both Vestfjorden and Austfjorden in search of reindeer. Leigh Smith began to chart Vestfjorden and write up a set of sailing directions for any vessel that might explore this remote corner of Svalbard in future summers. Working from a small boat, he sounded from the island to Kapp Petermann, finding no bottom at twenty-five fathoms until he was half a mile from the kapp when he dredged up "stiff red clay" from seven fathoms.

New ice was already forming at the head of Vestfjorden, and it became difficult to row through it and continue the survey. But Leigh Smith carried on as far as he could reach into the mid-channel of Vestfjorden, finding no bottom at twenty-five fathoms as far as his miniature icebreaker could reach. By September 14th, the crew was returning from their hunting forays, and in calm, snowy weather, set to work skinning nearly thirty reindeer. Five-foot-long sharks, possibly Greenland sharks, appeared when the reindeer carcasses were set overboard for a cleaning, and the sharks themselves were caught and dissected for their livers. Thrown back overboard, Leigh Smith observed them swimming astern of the ship, not seeming "any worse for being subject to such an operation."[57]

At 1 p.m. on the September 16th, *Sampson* weighed anchor and headed down the bay, arriving at the entrance at midnight. They made for Moffen Island but sailed round it without seeing any walrus. After a stay at Velkomstpynten on the mainland, *Sampson* rounded Hakluythovden at 2 a.m. on September 20th, and in a strong north breeze set all sail for Tromsø. The return to the Norwegian mainland was very rapid, *Sampson* reeling off as many as nine knots running under square sails with the wind directly aft.

Recording a "very singular change" upward in the surface water temperature off Sørkapp, Leigh Smith began his analysis of the hundreds of ocean temperature measurements he had recorded during the cruise. "From the Prince Charles Foreland as we came further south we found the temperature of the water to be gradually decreasing owing no doubt to a current known to be constantly setting southwestward along the S coast of Spitsbergen, round the S. Cape and thence northward along the west coast. From the large quantities of ice between the NE land and Giles Land there must evidently be a stream of cold water coming southwestward with the current which checks all influence the Gulf Stream has on other parts of the coast."[58]

Leigh Smith was beginning to find a way to reconcile the relatively warm surface temperatures he recorded north and west of Svalbard with the colder temperatures he had recorded south and east of the islands both on the journey from Tromsø and then when *Sampson* was stuck at the southern end of Hinlopenstretet. "We have found when at the Henlopen

Straits south entrance that the temp of water never exceeded 31° at surface, whilst at the Seven Islands the temp of water at surface was never *less than* 31° at surface [italics added]."[59]

Leigh Smith was correct that a cold, westward-setting blocking current that passed south of Svalbard would account for the ability of ships to pass up its west coast for long periods of the year, while ships like his own and Weyprecht's *Isbjørn* were stopped if they tried to force a passage through to the elusive Giles Land east of Svalbard. Leigh Smith realized, however, that he had only one summer's worth of data to rely upon. He was determined to return the following year to begin the creation of a series of observations over time that would contribute to a solution of the problem.

Early on the morning of September 27th, *Sampson* anchored again in Tromsø. The crew was disappointed on several counts. The entire haul from the cruise was thirty-three seals, eight bears, and forty-five reindeer. Only now were they told they would all receive an equal share in the voyage, which led to regret that they had not engaged more energetically in their hunting. In Tromsø, it had been the best summer for herring fisheries in twenty years. Had the crew stayed home and fished in their own waters, instead of following a wealthy English wanderer around Svalbard, they would have enjoyed a much more profitable season.

When Captain Ulve left *Sampson* in Tromsø, it was left to Leigh Smith to get the ship back to England with an all-Norwegian crew already resentful over their summer losses. Adding to their misgivings was Leigh Smith's purchase of a polar bear cub from a ship recently arrived from Novaya Zemlya, which he named 'Sampson' and intended for delivery to the Zoological Gardens in Regents Park.

Leigh Smith himself was in a better mood. He flirted with a pretty young Tromsø woman, and received new visits from Weyprecht, whose *Isbjørn* had returned to the mainland but had to be towed in by steamer from Hammerfest. Julius Payer, denied any real chance for overland exploration during the expedition, had chosen to walk from Hammerfest. "Their voyage," Leigh Smith writes, "has not answered their expectations in any respect. They have not got one polar bear or seal the whole voyage on account of the great quantities of ice on the east coast of Spitsbergen. They have failed in their attempt to reach Giles Land."[60] It was a stark contrast to Leigh Smith's own efforts.

Soon, however, Leigh Smith encountered disappointments of his own. The young woman was already engaged and, upon sailing from Tromsø on October 11th, Sampson the polar bear repeatedly attempted to escape. During one such episode, while the crew looked on with bemusement, Leigh Smith dove after the cub to grab its hind legs before it jumped over the taffrail. *Sampson* the ship fared little better, its desultory Tromsø crew unwilling to fight headwinds all the way to England. Unable to put much force behind his English commands to a Norwegian crew, Leigh Smith turned back. *Sampson* returned to Tromsø, dropped anchor, and ended her 1871 Arctic cruise on October 31st.

Such minor setbacks could not diminish the magnitude of his accomplishments. Leigh Smith had gained a summer of experiences with varying ice conditions north of Svalbard, had solved several geographic problems, located dozens of previously unknown islands, and initiated a series of ocean stations in the Arctic. His experiences with a small sailing vessel in such waters only intensified both his desire to return and to do so with a properly equipped screw steamer. His first expedition to Svalbard was critical in defining the complex northeastern coastline and eastern limits of Nordaustlandet, and pioneered Arctic oceanographic research. It established a pattern that Leigh Smith would follow on all four of his subsequent expeditions: draw up a general plan of geographic and oceanographic reconnaissance, then vary that plan according to the ever-shifting ice conditions between Greenland, Svalbard, and, eventually, the as-yet undiscovered Franz Josef Land.

Leigh Smith might be shocked to learn that the ice-laden East Spitsbergen Current that in the summer of 1871 blocked the passage of both his *Sampson* and Weyprecht's *Isbjørn*, is even today under intensive study.[61] This current carries Arctic waters from the polar basin south between Franz Josef Land and Svalbard, then west along the southern coasts of Svalbard, where it rises up against the Spitsbergen Bank that runs from Edgeøya southwest to Bjørnøya. There, it sets up a confusing series of oceanographic phenomena as it clashes with the warmer waters of the West Spitsbergen Current as the latter flows north out of the North Atlantic. Nearly one hundred and fifty years later, these waters are still an extremely challenging arena in which to attempt navigation and scientific research.

~3~

EXPEDITION TWO:
JAN MAYEN AND SVALBARD, 1872

General Ludlow recorded Leigh Smith's homecoming comments, dramatically relating that the expedition had been surrounded by ice and casually adding that they had gotten out "all right."[1] Leigh Smith must have gone into greater detail during another visit about a month later, as the General recorded that the expedition had killed numerous polar bear, reindeer and seals. Still one more month on, in late November, a letter arrived from Barbara saying that "she was busy making drawings of the *North Pole* from Ben's sketches."[2]

The good feelings were marred somewhat by a snipe in the pages of the literary magazine *Athenæum* just before Christmas. The General writes in his diary that the journal indicated that Leigh Smith had reached lat. 81°13′ N "the highest lat. as yet observed on board ship." The anonymous *Athenæum* writer continued: "We would however like to see this confirmed as whalermen and merchant captains generally are not altogether very particular about the accuracy of those observations."[3]

It was a bitter first taste of the life of a public figure, and forever afterwards Leigh Smith was determined to avoid it altogether. As for his extended family, he presented them with haunches of reindeer meat for their New Year's celebrations, and reindeer and polar bear and seal skins to warm them throughout the Sussex winter. The General appreciated the gifts, but in a fair caution hoped that what he called Leigh Smith's "hobby" would not carry him "too far, i.e. into risks that may be fatal."[4]

By the spring of 1872, Benjamin Leigh Smith was forty-four years old and had an exemplary private expedition to the Arctic behind him. He was determined to lead a second exploring expedition to the Arctic in the summer of 1872, in part to continue to restore British credibility in Arctic exploration. As his 1873 expedition companion H. C. Chermside writes, with Leigh Smith's 1871 expedition to Svalbard, "the old [British] zeal ... for Arctic discovery has been maintained by the private enterprise of English yachtsmen."[5] This echoed contemporary feeling, as expressed in a newspaper article anticipating Leigh Smith's return from the Arctic in September 1872, wherein the writer remarks "that if no public expedition of great pretensions is being carried on here, at least the enterprise of one Englishman is on the alert."[6]

More importantly, he sought to further the impressive oceanographic and geographic research of his first expedition in the summer of 1871. Much of this work, such as the bathymetric survey of Vestfjorden or the addition of thirty-three new place names to the maps of Nordaustland-et or the defining of the eastern limits of Svalbard, was largely straight-forward and non-controversial.

His startling and counterintuitive recordings of deep-sea temperatures from 1871, however, had led Leigh Smith into something of a scientific controversy. These data suggested a variance of as much as 9° F between surface water temperatures and warmer currents 400 fathoms below the surface, "a fact so extraordinary," according to his 1872 scientific compan-ion, a Royal Navy captain by the name of John C. Wells, "as to lead scien-tific men to assume that this, our assertion, is so contrary to the laws laid down by modern savans [sic], that they do not declare that the statement we made was impossible to be received."[7] It was primarily for this reason – a search for new data to support the radical 1871 observations – that Leigh Smith determined to sail Sampson once again into the Arctic.

Leigh Smith had encountered other, more applied, problems during the 1871 cruise. Only two of his all-Norwegian crew spoke any English and Leigh Smith's journal evinces no desire on his part to learn Norwe-gian, even as he clearly admired Norwegian women. Wells put the crew selection down to a "mistaken theory," an apparent belief that Norwe-gian whalers and sealers alone possessed the requisite knowledge to get a sailing vessel safely into and out of the Arctic. This, Wells writes, was a mistake, especially when Sampson encountered ice-free water north of Svalbard in 1871 and had a chance to reach the Open Polar Ocean he and many others believed lay just beyond the edge of the polar pack ice. But "the superstitious fears of these curious people overcame every attempt to prosecute a voyage so well begun, and our friend [Leigh Smith] was most reluctantly compelled to relinquish an opportunity of sailing into the sea whose very existence is denied by some...."[8]

In this, however, Wells was in error, and not only because Leigh Smith would have discovered no great polynia had he been able to sail farther north. On the day of his farthest north, it was already September 11th, and Leigh Smith himself recorded in his journal that the seas at the edge of the polar pack ice were building dangerously. Fortunately for all on board, *Sampson* did not sail any further north where she would have been trapped and forced into an overwintering for which neither the ship nor anyone on board was prepared. Leigh Smith had already avoided a similar fate earlier in the expedition, when *Sampson* rounded Nordaustlandet near Kapp Leigh Smith, and he wisely decided against attempting a circumnavigation of the entire archipelago fearing the ship would be frozen in for the winter.

As for the possibility of an open water polynia near the pole, it seems incredible that Wells still clung to this notion as late as the 1870s. The British antiquary Daines Barrington had suggested in the 1770s that a polar sea free of ice existed just beyond the ice barrier north of Spitsbergen, and numerous nineteenth-century naval expeditions paid a heavy price testing its possibilities. Elisha Kent Kane had given the idea perhaps its biggest boost in the 1850s. Yet, as Clive Holland has written, "in matters concerning the North Pole, and especially the 'Open Polar Sea' beyond it, the ability of otherwise rational men to delude themselves was remarkable."[9]

The other problems with the Norwegians that had presented themselves when *Sampson* returned to Tromsø made Leigh Smith determined to avoid similar cultural confrontations in 1872. He thought this could be achieved by signing on sailors from Hull, supplemented by sea-hunters from the Shetland Islands. According to Wells, he himself was given only two days to answer Leigh Smith's invitation to join him in the Arctic to collect the summer's plan of oceanographic data in the form of soundings, dredging, ocean temperature readings, and measurements of currents, which suggests that he may not have been the first choice for the assignment. Yet he took to it with enthusiasm, and echoed Chermside's

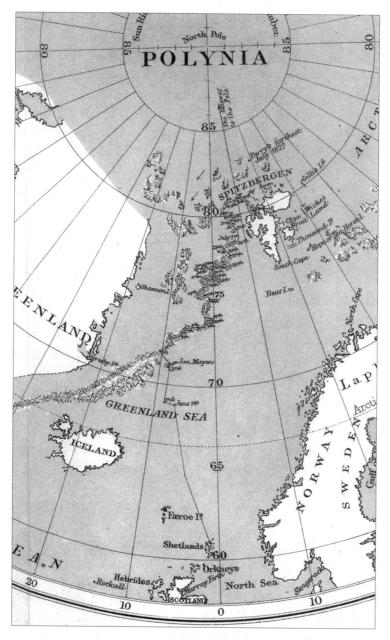

Fig. 17. *Chart of Leigh Smith's progress from England to Jan Mayen along the edge of the polar ice to Svalbard (from Wells 1873).*

lament about the state of official British polar exploration. "For many years past the English Government has relaxed its efforts, and the lead is being taken by other nations, such as the Germans, Swedes, Norwegians, Russians, and Americans."[10]

Leigh Smith's plan for 1872 was to first explore Jan Mayen, the island Lord Dufferin had only briefly touched on, and then sail back to Svalbard. But the luck that had followed him in 1871 was nowhere to be found in 1872. While he managed to conduct a memorable reconnaissance of Moffen Island and his crew caught far more seals than in 1871, unfavorable ice conditions first altered his course and then damaged *Sampson* so badly it was beached for repairs at Wijdeforden and almost wrecked.

The summer of 1872 would be partially redeemed by a brief meeting with the great Swedish explorer Adolf Erik Nordenskiöld, during which a bond was formed between the two men with fortuitous benefits for Nordenskiöld's Swedish Polar Expedition the following year as it struggled to escape the north coast of Svalbard. But in the end Leigh Smith was forced to make for England in September, without sailing nearly as far to the north or east as during his first Arctic expedition. These developments would eventually lead him to reconsider his use of a sailing ship as his primary exploration vessel in the Arctic.

For Wells, his main scientific task was clearly the deep-sea oceanographic research Leigh Smith required to support his surprising data from 1871. The strategy was to replicate the 1871 cruise a closely as possible, with *Sampson* attempting to sail further north toward the pole before retreating south and east around Kapp Leigh Smith and then the whole of Svalbard. But as he had learned during his first cruise, Leigh Smith knew that no Arctic expedition could adhere to any strict timetable. This approach, one that seemingly made a virtue of necessity, nevertheless eluded most of the expeditions that voyaged into the Arctic in the nineteenth century, including the one Leigh Smith would meet north of Svalbard in 1872.

The expedition left Hull on May 13th and ran directly into north winds that forced *Sampson* to shelter at Edinburgh for a day. The heavy seas delayed the expedition's arrival at Lerwick in the Shetland Islands until May 26th, where "somewhat old" charts forced the vessel to scrape her way through the narrow, rocky north entrance.[11] While the ship was re-supplied and more crew members added, Leigh Smith and Wells hiked seven miles in a driving rain to locate the ruins of the then-275-year-old castle of Patrick Stewart at Scalloway.

Lerwick seemed a busy place to Wells. As *Sampson* readied her departure, two hundred locals were in the process of emigrating to North America. The carpenter and four additional sailors from the Shetlands brought the total expedition to seventeen, and Wells noted the "formidable array of whaling and sealing weapons" they would use to fill the forty-ton water tanks on board with seal and whale blubber for the return trip.[12]

On May 28th, *Sampson* again put to sea and, accompanied by occasional numbers of fin and bottle-nose whales, made for Jan Mayen. Leigh Smith seemed determined to avoid the main cause of the 'revolt' of his Norwegians in 1871, namely the failure to secure any real profit from the voyage. Wells noted that the crew busied itself with overhauling the whale boats, sturdy vessels constructed of pine and sheathed in zinc to protect them from contact with the ice floes *Sampson* would be working around. He watched them stow four whale lines of 960 yards apiece in each boat, followed by lances and harpoons with fixed handles (for whaling) and detaching handles (for seals and walrus). At the bows were swivel guns for throwing a ten-pound harpoon twenty yards.

On June 3rd, *Sampson* anchored off Maria Muschbukta on the northwest coast of Jan Mayen.[13] Leigh Smith and one sailor went ashore to explore the area around the bay, the first British explorer to set foot on the island since William Scoresby, Jr., in August of 1817. Wells and another sailor ascended the ridge a mile north of the bay, gathering botanical specimens along the way.

Wells sought to reach the eastern slopes of the island, but the rough going over snow-covered volcanic scoria and cinders made that impossible. He returned to the beach via the Nordlaguna, which was still ice-covered, and joined Leigh Smith in throwing stones at bird colonies nesting in a "pyramidal rock [that] shot up into the air about 1,200 feet above us," a reference to the appropriately described Fugleberget near Nordlaguna.[14] The temperature of both air and water hovered around 32° F.

On the beach was a treasure-trove of flotsam and jetsam: glass floats from Norwegian herring fishermen; Siberian driftwood; masts of merchant ships; remnants of whale-boats "everywhere lie shattered on these sands."[15] Like Scoresby, Wells noted the *teredo*-infested wood and concluded that it had drifted across the Arctic from some northern coastline where warmer climate and water temperatures allowed for the existence of the wood-boring mollusks.[16] These early indications of the Trans-Polar Drift Wells identified simply as "some ocean current."[17] The sailors gathered some of this wood in order to make coffee early the next morning and then, not wishing to be caught on this exposed shore by a storm, were off quickly, the coffee and other supplies brought ashore testifying to Leigh Smith's preparations for such a possibility.

When they awoke five hours later, June 4th the bay was still calm, so Wells and Leigh Smith were again rowed ashore by two sailors.[18] Leaving the sailors to watch the small boat, Leigh Smith and Wells ascended the ridge once again until they could see the ocean to the south, as well as "two craters marked upon the chart."[19]

Seeing Beerenberg (Mount Beerenburg) free of clouds, they ascended a part of the way to the top of the world's northernmost active volcano. From this vantage they "were rewarded by the discovery of a hitherto unnoticed crater, whose position we carefully noted."[20]

After ten hours, they returned to the small boat and then to the ship, where they reluctantly decided that the lack of a suitable anchorage at Jan Mayen precluded a closer survey of the island. *Sampson* was soon beating her way north and west and within a few hours had reached the edge of the polar ice. Trending north-northeast along the edge of the pack, the hunting began in earnest. As Wells occupied a series of ocean stations, the Shetlanders killed and processed two whales and 250 seals, a vast increase over *Sampson*'s 1871 haul around Svalbard. It was enough, apparently, to satisfy the crew, who would receive half-a-crown for every ton of oil they returned to Hull.[21]

For a week after the exploration of Jan Mayen, *Sampson* edged in and out of the polar pack while the Shetlanders slaughtered everything within reach of their harpoons. Then, Wells writes, it was time "to return again to the somewhat dry demands of scientific inquiry."[22] Sailing northeast from Jan Mayen to Northwest Spitsbergen, Wells occupied fourteen ocean stations, twice the number from 1871. Most of these soundings were taken between 100 and 200 fathoms and, like those of 1871, showed a slight but definite increase in the temperature of the ocean from the surface to depth. In addition to the single station, single observation stations, Wells on June 18th adopted a technique of recording temperatures at several depths at one station. This produced a result, over four of six such stations, of a steady increase in ocean temperatures from the surface to the maximum depth, including the final station on July 12th that showed the extraordinary (and almost certainly false) temperature reading of 64° F at 600 fathoms off Amsterdamøya. But the anomaly only served to emphasize the pattern: deep-ocean temperatures around Svalbard were warmer that the temperatures at the surface. Warmer waters were flowing into the area and affecting everything in their course, from the weather to the ice.

The first station, made 170 nautical miles from the polar pack, was no doubt a test of the surveying gear, as no further stations were made for two weeks. When the sampling commenced in earnest, *Sampson* was cruising at the edge of the pack ice. As *Sampson* maneuvered into the ice, searching for a lead to the north, Wells had varying levels of success in his data collection. His notes from June 15th, that he only "had time to sound in 50 fathoms,"[23] offer a glimpse into the logistical challenge of deploying a single sampling wire from a sailing vessel surrounded by large floe ice.

On June 18th, Wells recorded the largest temperature difference yet, when the thermometer recorded 33° F at the surface compared to 48° F at 200 fathoms. On the 20th, he began to record his temperatures from beneath the lower surface of the ice (six fathoms down) and again the results were the same: colder surface waters supplanted by increasingly warmer waters at depth. On July 7th, Wells dredged up an unusual species of starfish which he used to suggest that the warm waters were not of volcanic origin, a natural supposition given *Sampson*'s cruising area near the volcanoes of Iceland and Jan Mayen.

By July 10th, with the crew "required elsewhere," Wells was forced to end the soundings.[24] He and Leigh Smith made one final sounding, the anomalous data of July 12th. As for this almost absurdly high reading, Wells himself writes that it was "remarkable."[25] But they did everything they could to discount instrumentation error. He writes that Leigh Smith himself "carefully registered" this station, checking the thermometer both before and after it was deployed overboard.[26] Leigh Smith, apparently aware that this particular reading would raise eyebrows, had the

1872.	Station.	Lat.	Long.	Depths in fathoms	Temperature.			
					Air.	Surface.	Min.	Max.
June								
1.	1.	68 52 N.	6 40 W.	600	42°	37½°	30°	37½°
13.	2.	75 6 N.	2 30 W.	100	36	31	28	35
15.	3.	75 7 N.	3 48 W.	100	36	32	28	35
				50	..	31	29½	32½
17.	4.	76 13 N.	2 22 W.	100	34	31	29½	34
18.	5.	76 3 N.	0 10 E.	150	35	33	30½	40
				200	..	33	30½	48
19.	6.	76 21 N.	1 5 E.	150	35	32	30½	32
				250	..	32	30½	39½
20.	7.	76 35 N.	0 3 W.	6	34	33	30	33
				25	..	33	30	35
				150	..	33	30	39½
22.	8.	76 41 N.	2 10 W.	150	35	32	29½	39½
27.	9.	77 18 N.	5 0 E.	25	37	34½	32	34½
				250	..	34½	32	39
July								
1.	10.	78 20 N.	7 2 E.	6	36	36	33	36
				600	..	36	33½	36½
6.	11.	79 54 N.	6 34 E.	6	35	34½	33	34½
			,,	12	..	34½	33	35
				25	..	34½	33	37
				50	..	34½	33	37
				200	..	34½	33	40
7.	12.	80 4 N.	5 12 E.	Bottom 600	37	34½	31½	39
10.	13.	80 23 N.	9 0 E.	12	35	31	28	31
				50	..	31	28	31½
12.	14.	80 32 N.	9 50 E.	Bottom 600	36	31	28½	64

Fig. 18. Chart of ocean stations conducted by Sampson in 1872 (from Wells 1873).

thermometer checked after the cruise by its designer, L. P. Casella, who found it working properly.

Earlier in the year, Leigh Smith had given a similar set of deep-ocean sounding instruments to the Scottish whaler David Gray (1827–1896), captain of the Peterhead steam whaler *Eclipse*. It is a mark both of Leigh Smith's generosity and his scientific objectivity that he was willing to subsidize the collection of an independent series of ocean stations in the Arctic. Between April 13th and July 3rd 1872, *Eclipse* made nine stops to record oceanographic data using Leigh Smith's donated equipment. Wells added these to the fourteen made by *Sampson* for a total of twenty-three ocean stations recorded by the two vessels in 1872. Most of the *Eclipse* soundings were made between 200 and 400 fathoms, on a northeasterly line running from Greenland to Norway.

Grey's recordings on *Eclipse*, made when the vessel was as much as 90 nautical miles inside the ice pack, showed the same trend as those recorded by Wells from *Sampson*. Deep-sea temperatures were higher than those at the surface. It was increasingly evident that a complex warm ocean current was at work in the high Arctic. Wells himself could not identify the source of this current, though he was mistakenly convinced that it was not a northern extremity of the Gulf Stream. In fact, it is exactly that, and now known as the North Atlantic Current or, at even more northerly latitudes, the North Atlantic Drift.

As the title of his book, *The Gateway to the Polynia*, suggests, Wells thought it more than likely that there was a "stream of warm water coming from the north" that originated at or near the North Pole.[27] Combined with Leigh Smith's 1871 observations of open water east of Nordaustlandet and north of Rossøya in Svalbard, as well as his ocean stations south of Svalbard – with their suggestion of potential inversion layers of warmer polar waters – Wells clearly supported Petermann's notion that the polar pack might surround an open sea at the pole.

If he was incorrect regarding the source of Leigh Smith's warm deep-sea current, Wells was correct in assuming that further research would have several advantages. Not the least of these was a greater understanding of how ocean currents influenced the weather of northern Europe and more generally throughout the northern hemisphere. The specific research technique he suggested, that of an expedition of circumpolar navigation

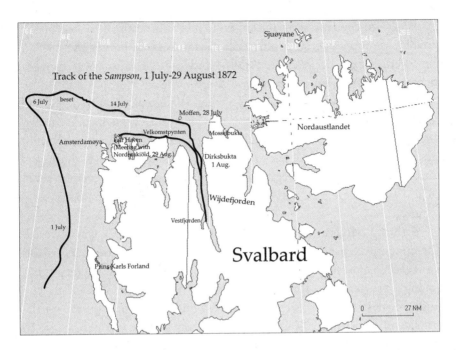

Sjuøyane

6 July   beset   14 July

Moffen, 28 July

Velkomstpynten   Mosselbukta   Nordaustlandet

Amsterdamøya   Fair Haven
(Meeting with
Nordenskiöld, 29 Aug.)   Dirksbukta
1 Aug.

Wijdefjorden

Vestfjorden

1 July

Prins Karls Forland   Svalbard

0   27 NM

Fig. 19. Track of the Sampson, *July 1–Aug. 29, 1872.*

that would collect not only depth soundings but also dredge up marine organisms from the bottom of the Arctic Sea, was soon to be taken up by Leigh Smith in Franz Josef Land and by Fridtjof Nansen in the polar basin itself.

For almost a month, from June 23rd to July 17th, *Sampson* probed the edge of the ice field. The ship was beset twice, the first time for three days beginning on June 23rd at lat. 76°42′ N. Approaching Prins Karls Forland on July 1st, a heavy collision with submerged ice carried away the ship's false keel. On the 6th they were beset again at lat. 80°18′ N and for five days carried north with the ice to lat. 80°30′ N. The harpooners often went ahead of the ship and shifted the ice aside manually, a technique Wells admired but thought best handled by a proper steam vessel. When the wind shifted around to the west and a lane of open water appeared, the expedition could finally break out to the north and east.

If the ice conditions permitted it, Leigh Smith hoped to stop at the circular, lagoon-centered Moffen Island. From there he would seek out the Swedish expedition under Adolf Nordenskiöld, which was thought to be constructing an advance base somewhere in the Sjuøyane for an expedition to the pole the following spring. Wells was convinced that had *Sampson* possessed steam-power the previous year, when it sailed to lat. 81°25′00″ N, she could have punched through to the open sea he thought lay just beyond the ring of pack ice. But the lack of steam and "the superstitious fears of the Norwegian captain and crew" had prevented what 1872's "English crew ... without the least fear of failure" would certainly achieve.[28]

Sighting Moffen on the 28th, one of the small boats was lowered. The crew rowed ashore only with great difficulty, as the low-lying island was twice lost to their line of sight, causing detours of eight nautical miles amongst the scattered ice floes. The charts were not helpful either. The single break in the lagoon that was shown on Wells's chart on the northern side of the circular island they found instead on its western edge. In the meantime the fog lifted and *Sampson* called back the shore party so the sea-hunt could continue.

After a few days of chasing walrus, Wells and Leigh Smith returned to Moffen, this time to its eastern edge, where Wells claims that they collected specimens of Terek sandpipers (*Xena cinerea*), and then stepped across and around a tremendous slaughterhouse of walrus remains from previous hunting expeditions.[29]

Wells writes that they then spied an enormous skull of a whale, partially embedded in the shingle and far away from the water's edge. As they approached they saw that it was in fact an entire skeleton, with the other bones gradually disappearing into the shingle and flotsam and jetsam that wind, current, and ice had accumulated along the lagoon's berm. The fact that the skeleton was intact would suggest that this was the skeleton of animal that might have beached and died on the island naturally and had then been raised along with the surrounding shingle as a result of glacio-isostatic uplift, rather than an animal killed and hacked to pieces by whalers.[30]

A sketch of the whale in Wells's account gives fantastic dimensions to the skeleton and steep, volcanic crater-like slopes to the island itself.

Fig. 20. The Moffen Island whale skeleton (from Wells 1873).

As they closely examined it, Wells and Leigh Smith saw that the skull was covered with inscriptions "recording the many visits to the spot by Norwegian and other whalers."[31] These notations would almost certainly have included the names of these vessels and the years of their visits to the island.

Such an artifact constituted a unique glimpse into the archaeology of sea-mammal hunting around Svalbard in general and into the natural and human history of the unique and now-protected micro-environment of Moffen itself. It recalls Melville's description of a large whale skeleton used as a temple on the fictional island of Tranque (Melville also knew his Scoresby, and referenced his measurements of Greenland whales and even the "Leviathanic Museum … in Hull, England [now the Hull Maritime Museum]," the English port from which *Sampson* sailed.)[32]

Unfortunately, Wells, who earlier used four pages to describe a fly in his cabin, expends less than a paragraph on this extraordinary palimpsest. Or, as Melville exhorted all who might encounter such an all-encompassing creature, "to magnify him in an archæological, fossiliferous, and antediluvian point of view."[33] Wells did not record the names or arrival dates of a single vessel carved into the whalebone. Perhaps because of its size and the challenge of excavating the stony shingle of Moffen Island, Leigh Smith did not see any simple way to recover it as he did with so many other fossil specimens on his five Arctic expeditions. No such artifact has been recorded in the extensive scrimshaw collections of the maritime museum in Hull.[34] Even though such bones (especially the jaws, which were used as archways throughout the British Isles) had been a staple return of the Hull fisheries, by 1872 the industry had been in decline for some time.[35] Leigh Smith did bring a complete whale jaw back to East Sussex, where it eventually became the entryway to the tennis courts at his family home at Scalands and where it still stands today.

Leaving Moffen to continue their pursuit of walrus, *Sampson* was again pinned down by ice and her keel further damaged. After several failed attempts at sea to remove the broken timber, the vessel began to take on water. When *Sampson* pulled alongside a vessel that Wells identified as the whaler *Norsel Jack* out of Tromsø, its skipper advised Leigh Smith to run to Gray Hook (Gråhuken) and beach the ship for repairs in Wijdeforden. It was a place Leigh Smith knew well from the previous summer. It was where *Sampson* had paused in the fjord so the crew could find fresh meat and water and Leigh Smith could survey the area before the return journey to Norway.

Reaching Wijdefjorden on August 1st, 1872, with *Sampson*'s pumps working overtime, the ship stopped briefly in Dirksbukta,[36] a small bay now long closed off by sanding up and called Dirk's Point (Dirksodden), before anchoring off an uncharted island that Wells gave the unfortunate name of Gilles Island. One would have thought that Leigh Smith would have warned him away from any such confusion or connection with the long-sought Commander Giles Land.

While the crew rowed ashore in search of a suitable area to beach the ship, Wells and Leigh Smith explored the surrounding area. Wells was alternately enthralled by "this charming coast-scene" and depressed by the "vast mountain sides … destitute of green places [and the] melancholy and solitary plains."[37] As with other expeditions on the verge of collapse, the bleak surroundings combined with their inability to keep their ship afloat led the men to begin "to inquire with ourselves into the enigma of human existence."[38] Freed from the comforts as well as the constraints of civilization, Wells writes that their "health was at its best: we breathed more freely; we enjoyed everything."[39]

On the third day in Wijdefjorden, *Sampson* was brought close ashore on a high tide and then beached. But even then the source of the leak could not be located. Sealskin coated with tar and oakum was nailed over the likeliest spot, and the ship shoved back into the icy fjord.

By August 7th, with the ship stuck in the northward-drifting ice, Wells and Leigh Smith rowed ashore at another unmarked spot to inspect a small wooden hut they measured at twelve feet by eight.[40] Wells described it as having a fireplace of clay and rough stones, with two rough stone benches for furniture. Outside the door stood a cross marked with an inscription in Russian and the name and date of the last inhabitant. Recounting that whaling and sealing crews had often made use of such structures to survive after a shipwreck, Wells writes that he and Leigh Smith "were careful not to injure [the huts they visited in Wijdefjorden], never knowing how soon they may be required for the reception of some fellow-seaman."[41] It is a rare example of an expedition deliberately *not* pilfering a site in the Arctic.

In the eighteen days *Sampson* drifted amongst the ice of Wijdefjorden, Leigh Smith and Wells were rowed ashore several times and managed to shoot thirty-six reindeer. On August 11th, they hiked to a body of water near Dirksbukta that Wells called Salmon Lake, a fairly large body of water today called the Salmon Lake (Lakssjøen). Looking forward to an afternoon of fly-fishing, they were much disappointed to find the lake frozen over, a sharp reminder of the advancing season.

On August 13th, despite the leaky ship and the approaching fall, Leigh Smith held a council and took a decision to make one more try for the north. That afternoon they killed a single beluga whale, and then stood by and watched two Norwegian sloops trap and kill seventy-eight more by using nets fastened between their vessels and the shore. A few days later, Wells and a Shetlander named Magnus made an eight-hour climb to the top of a peak that gave out a view spanning Wijdefjorden and Isfjorden. If this account is accurate, the ice must have carried *Sampson* deep into Wijdefjorden, where it perhaps took refuge in Vestfjorden, the only place from which such a hike and view would have been possible.

Freed at last from Wijdefjorden on August 18th, *Sampson* made a final and brief attempt to force her way to the north. Before long, ice streaming from the northeast forced the ship to take refuge behind Velkomstpynten, where the anchor was broken. *Sampson* was soon joined by three more fishing sloops and two steam vessels, all seeking shelter from the worsening conditions. Further attempts to hold the ship in position resulted in one of the small boats capsizing.

On August 24th, *Sampson* reached across Raudfjorden and then, on the 29th, Fair Haven, where the ship stopped in Fowl Bay (Fuglefjorden). There, Leigh Smith found Adolf Erik Nordenskiöld and the twenty-two other members of his Swedish polar expedition already at anchor on board the steamer *Polhem*. Wells described the expedition leader as "a very pleasant man advanced in life" though Nordenskiöld, at thirty-nine, was five years younger than Leigh Smith.[42] Both were from prominent, educated, and wealthy families and enjoyed thereby a significant amount of shared social status.

Leigh Smith received Nordenskiöld and others from *Polhem* on board *Sampson* "with great kindness, and next day himself visited the vessels of the expedition."[43] Nordenskiöld was waiting for a re-supply of coal from two support ships, the *Gladan* and the *Onkel Adam*, that had yet to make their appearance, and Wells noted that Nordenskiöld's planned starting point in the Sjuøyane was still a long way off and it was late in the season.

Nordenskiöld had already been warned a week earlier by the captain of a Norwegian steam-powered fishing vessel about the ice conditions north and east of Fair Haven.[44] Leigh Smith and Wells added to this warning from their recent experiences in Wijdefjorden.[45] Nordenskiöld ignored the advice and ordered his convoy to sail northeastward anyway. Wells thought that even if the Swede was successful in reaching his planned jumping off point on Parryøya, he still faced an immense amount of work to ready his base camp before winter proper set in.

Wells observed several prefabricated structures and boats that nevertheless would require considerable effort to reassemble even if the expedition could find suitable ice-free ground for them in the Sjuøyane.

> We noticed the materials for three of these huts – a dwelling consisting of four sleeping-rooms, fourteen feet by thirteen; a long room for the men, twenty-two by fourteen; a central room nineteen by twenty-two; and a kitchen twenty-two by sixteen.... [The boats] were light and exceedingly strong, double in structure: one portion was made of the fine wood of the willow, the second layer of ash.... The journey was to be commenced on the first of April, 1873, and the provisions were sufficient to last until the first of July, by which time they hope to have accomplished this long meditated journey to the northern Pole of the earth.[46]

Wells seemed satisfied by Nordenskiöld's plan to use reindeer driven by Laplanders to pull the boats north since the expedition could kill and eat the deer as they showed signs of exhaustion, and then take to boats to make the final distance across the open sea he was still convinced they would find around the North Pole. As he reviewed Nordenskiöld's plans, with their clear echo of Parry's 1827 polar expedition, Wells reiterated his belief that a steamship was the only effective way to reach the pole. And if such a vessel were caught in the ice, Wells argued, it would merely "drift south, at the rate of about six miles each day" until it returned to the 'gateway to the polynia' north of Svalbard.[47]

The two explorers parted from one another on August 30th, but not before Leigh Smith promised Nordenskiöld that he would return to Svalbard early the following summer and call in on the Swede for news of his polar expedition. Soon thereafter, Nordenskiöld sailed east and discovered that he was not able to penetrate further than Mossel Bay (Mosselbukta), where *Sampson* had recently called. There, all three ships of the

Fig. 21. Sampson *parting from Nordenskiöld's expedition (from Wells 1873).*

Swedish expedition were caught by surprise and frozen in for the winter. Instead of a crew of less than two dozen supported by a single vessel, Nordenskiöld was suddenly faced with feeding sixty-seven people from three ships over the long course of a Svalbard winter, along with the crews of several Norwegian hunting *jakts* knocking on his door. The following June, his plight largely ignored by his own government and with all but one of his reindeer escaped, Nordenskiöld would find himself very glad of Leigh Smith's promise.

As for Leigh Smith, his somewhat disappointing summer concluded with visits to Kings Bay (Kongsfjorden) to collect specimens of marble, Green Harbor (Grønfjorden) to collect fossils, and Prins Karls Forland for some dredging work. Then the expedition sailed for England. *Sampson* returned to Hull on September 26th.

Leigh Smith returned from Svalbard in the fall of 1872 without having sailed nearly as far to the north and east as during his first expedition. However, the brief meeting with Adolf Erik Nordenskiöld had nonetheless formed a strong bond between the two men, a bond that would lead

Leigh Smith to seek out the Swedish expedition as soon as he returned to the north coast of Svalbard in June of 1873. In addition, Leigh Smith in 1872 had continued his series of deep-ocean temperature recordings, which, along with the ongoing work of Weyprecht and Payer, continued to lay the foundations of high latitude oceanography.

Over the course of the summer, his continual discussions with John Wells on the merits of using a steam vessel for polar exploration would have a profound influence on his thinking as he began to formulate plans for a new expedition to Svalbard in 1873 and especially for his eventual construction of his own research vessel, the *Eira*.

4

EXPEDITION THREE: SVALBARD, 1873

The General noted Leigh Smith's return to Hull and dutifully records that "Ben got a small whale, 2 Bears, 103 seals, 32 reindeer. He discovered an Intinct [*sic*] Volcano and fell in with the Swedish expedition."[1] Leigh Smith himself paid a visit to Ludlow a few weeks later, badly hung over from a celebration the previous evening at the Oxford and Cambridge Club "where he entertained Mr Lamont the Arctic voyager who wrote *A Season with the Seahorses*."[2]

It was perhaps at this meeting that Leigh Smith broached the subject of chartering Lamont's steamship *Diana* for a third voyage to the Arctic, or perhaps Lamont made the offer himself. In either case, Leigh Smith spent the winter of 1872–73 readying for another expedition. A note in the General's diary in April of 1873 records that Leigh Smith "is going to Hastings to be present at some barometrical experiment."[3] While it did not rank high on the General's list of interests, it was clearly important to Leigh Smith.

For 1873, Leigh Smith planned to conclude the private oceanographic and geographical explorations in the seas around Svalbard that he had begun in 1871 and continued in 1872. The logistics of the 1873 expedition, however, were far more complicated than those of the first two voyages.

Rather than using a single ship as he had done with the sailing vessel *Sampson* the previous summers, Leigh Smith chartered the *Diana* and employed *Sampson* as a reserve supply tender. With the added supplies he could carry on board *Sampson*, Leigh Smith planned once and for all to round the northeast limit of Svalbard at Kapp Leigh Smith and conduct a survey of Kong Karls Land.

Among those invited to join to expedition was a twenty-three-year-old Royal Engineer, Lieutenant Herbert Charles Chermside, who would visit the Arctic for the first and last time in a long life of military service. It was to Chermside that Leigh Smith entrusted the keeping of the expedition's logbooks. These three unpublished journals, along with a log kept by *Sampson's* captain, William Walker, detail an expedition that, while it failed in its primary objective to round Nordaustlandet, did succeed in relieving Nordenskiöld's expedition beset near Mosselbukta and maintained an array of contacts with whalers and sealers – for example the Peterhead whaler David Gray and the Norwegian skipper Frederick Christian Mack – regarding local conditions around Svalbard.

The patriotic motivation to pick up where the government had abandoned the field was still strong in 1873. As Chermside wrote after the expedition, it had been "nearly fifty years since attempts at reaching the highest latitudes [was] abandoned by British public enterprise and all such exploration [was being] carried on by foreign nations," especially Germany and Sweden.[4]

For Chermside (1850–1929), the 1873 expedition marked his first major field experience, one in which he would act as surveyor, hunter, photographer, and chronicler. An Etonian, he had received the Pollock Prize as the top graduate of the Royal Military Academy at Woolwich in 1870.[5] This earned distinction set him far apart from the typical line officer of his day, most of whom paid for their commissions through the purchase system until it was abolished the year after Chermside's graduation.[6]

Chermside's surveying and photographic skills would have naturally drawn Leigh Smith to him. But it is in his journal entries, written in a large, flowing hand, that he reveals himself as a humorous, adaptable companion, a good shot, and a man curious about the world around him; in other words, the perfect individual to record the adventure with wit and insight. These same traits apparently served him well throughout his life. Thirty years later, as a colonial governor in Australia, he would be described as someone with a "readiness to share sacrifice, [an] approachable personality, wide range of interests, clear and forthright public speeches and [a] willingness to learn by travel...."[7]

By the summer of 1873, the results of Leigh Smith's first voyage to Svalbard in 1871 had appeared in two articles and two charts in *Petermann's*

Mittheilungen.[8] The much more meager results of the 1872 expedition appeared in rather disjointed fashion in a popular account written by Wells.[9] For his third voyage, Leigh Smith seems to have chosen Chermside not only for his abilities mentioned above but also so that he could combine the results of all three of Leigh Smith's expeditions into a comprehensive article that Chermside would later deliver before a meeting of the British Association for the Advancement of Science in August of 1874.[10] These, of course, were meetings that Leigh Smith himself avoided almost on pain of torture.

This British Association paper is divided into two sections, the first twenty-five pages consisting of a recap of the three expeditions and the final forty pages given over to a general discussion of the oceanographic conditions around Svalbard and its presumed value as a route to the North Pole. For the day-to-day details of the 1873 expedition, one must refer to Chermside's rather massive, three-volume log kept on board *Diana* from May 10 to September 26, 1873, and now stored at the Scott Polar Research Institute at Cambridge University.[11] Additional details come from the logbook of *Sampson*, kept by its captain, William Walker, during its voyage that summer from Hull to Svalbard and back and also now stored at the Scott Polar Research Institute, as well as copies of half a dozen letters sent home by expedition member Richard Potter (1855–1947).[12]

Leigh Smith's first two Arctic experiences – in particular the difficult ice conditions of 1872 – led him to reconsider the use of a single sailing vessel in the Arctic. Searching for a more durable vessel for his 1873 expedition, he decided to charter James Lamont's steamer *Diana*, which had been especially constructed in 1869 for Arctic cruising and hunting. Lamont's subsequent expedition to Svalbard had even left the ship's name behind in the place of Diana Bay (Dianabukta), an open bay on the southwest coast of Edgeøya where the vessel briefly anchored that summer.[13] The screw steam yacht was powered by 30 hp compound steam engines and its hull strengthened below the waterline with double layers of Australian bark and the bow clad with iron plates.[14]

With *Diana*, Leigh Smith thought that he would for the first time possess an ice-strengthened vessel with the power necessary to attempt to round Svalbard and survey Kong Karls Land. He was also committed to finding the whereabouts of Nordenskiöld. The addition of *Sampson* as a reserve tender allowed Leigh Smith to carry a larger load of supplies, many of which would come to Nordenskiöld's aid early in the Arctic summer of 1873.

On May 10th, 1873, Chermside came on board *Diana* at Dundee, where he was given, as he writes, "a spacious chamber 5´6˝ × 3´6˝ which the steward was pleased to call my 'state room.'"[15] *Diana* had a crew of seventeen, including a harpooner. Chermside was joined by a fellow Etonian, seventeen-year-old Richard Potter (1855–1947), and the naturalist and Reverend Alfred Edwin Eaton (1845–1929) as guests of Leigh Smith.

Another thirteen sailed on board *Sampson*, which had already departed Hull on April 30 and arrived at Lerwick on May 7th. On May 10th, the reserve vessel began laboring her way through heavy seas to Svalbard.

The two vessels, outfitted with a year's worth of provisions, planned to sail for Svalbard and rendezvous on July 1st at Kobbefjorden on the west coast of Danskøya. Replenished from the stores on *Sampson*, *Diana* would then sail east along the north coast of Svalbard as far as Gilles Land, "should such exist."[16] If the mythical Gilles Land did in fact appear, they would course along its western coast, using the land as a barrier to any pack ice flowing from the east, and sail as far north as possible. The extra provisions were also crucial to Leigh Smith's other stated objective: to bring relief to Nordenskiöld's expedition that was now assumed to be in trouble.

Chermside was grateful to Leigh Smith for giving him the chance to take part "in an expedition in these regions, the exploration of which has always had a strange fascination in my mind."[17] He was perhaps less grateful as *Diana* left the Firth of Tay and began to roll in the open sea and the soldier found himself absent from dinner for the first time in his life. Potter shared a cabin with Eaton and recorded "a good, long, rolling swell on which finished Eaton off at once as on getting up he was very ill & had to go to bed again instead of performing divine service (much to my sorrow).… Towards the evening Chermside got seedy and the steward was so bad that he could not make our beds. This morning the wind was blowing much stronger against us so that we were only going 2 knots. Ben Smith was ill & has not been able to eat anything all day, so that I, much to my surprise am the only one who has not been sick."[18]

Rather than fight a north wind, *Diana* put in to Lerwick in the Shetlands, where Chermside found himself "astonished at the absence of beggars," which is perhaps more a comment on 1873 London than the prevailing economy of the Shetlands.[19] Delayed in the islands for a week, Chermside met an old man who recalled to him the arrival of Parry's polar expedition in Lerwick in 1827. It was the very absence of the British government from the polar field since Parry that had provided much of the impetus for Leigh Smith's private efforts.

The expedition departed the Shetland Islands under steam on the 18th, and Chermside was re-introduced to the sea. When the winds turned favorable, the ship's steam was run down and the sails hauled up. Just as this was completed, the winds died and the ship wallowed, making Chermside sick once again until steam could be got up again and the ship propelled northwards. Not until the 20th did they get a strong SSW wind that sped *Diana* along towards Svalbard.

Diana met the ice at 72° N, 1°6′ W on the 23rd, and just as it had with Leigh Smith two years earlier the new experience gave Chermside a chance to exercise his pen. "The ice floats about in white snow-covered detached blocks never much above 5′ from the surface & of every shape & form, the pieces being eaten into most fantastic shapes by the action of the water, the sides are a beautiful green & if only a bright sun were upon it, the effect would be lovely. Bump there we go as I write bang against a block, as far as the eye can see the sea is covered with these floating blocks … bump, bump…. We are now in the long wished-for Polar regions…."[20]

They met their first Arctic ships three days later. The first was the Swedish vessel *Vega*, which had been in the north hunting seals and was "evidently surprised at our flying the 'blue ensign' & at once asks if we are an 'expedition.'"[21] A few hours later, they met a Peterhead whaler called *Active*, which relayed the news that fast ice lay just to the north.

Five days later, a much longer information exchange took place when *Diana* came alongside another Peterhead whaler, David Gray's steam-powered *Eclipse*. An avocational scientist, Gray was first and foremost a deep-ocean hunter. He shared with Leigh Smith the news that *Eclipse* was returning from its spring hunt with 250 tons of oil from a catch of two whales and 48,000 seals. So much oil was processed that they had been forced to throw some of the steamer's coal overboard to make room for more blubber.

Leigh Smith was carrying papers, letters and news for Gray, who had not been ashore since March. In the mist, *Eclipse* was rafted alongside *Diana* for a day as the officers and guests shared lunch on board *Diana* and then "a capital dinner ... with a long conversation & numerous yarns."[22] Gray explained how he could use the remains of the blubber extraction process to drive the ship if his coal stocks became low. Using this method, he told his dinner guests that *Eclipse* had once "steamed over 100 miles on the tail of a whale...."[23]

When Chermside mentioned that he was surprised at the absence of blubber smells on board *Eclipse*, Gray explained that it was cold enough that none of the seal or whale products putrefied at these latitudes. Gray then gave a tour of his cabinet of natural history curiosities, which included parasites collected from whales, narwhals, and the stomachs of bearded seals.

By June 6th, impatient with the slow progress north, Leigh Smith ordered *Diana* east towards Prins Karls Forland in Svalbard. When the mountains and glaciers came into view the following day, Chermside had his first views of Svalbard and busied himself mixing chemicals for his photographic gear.

After *Diana* anchored near the glacier at the head of Kongsfjorden, Chermside and Potter rowed to a near-shore lake whose surface was covered with birds. "I think I have never enjoyed an evening more," he writes as he took in the sight of the pyramid-like summits of the Tre Kroner. "There was a glorious Arctic sun still high in the heavens, that even at midnight shone in all its pride above the Northern Hills, casting on their covering of the purest snow a sheen of golden light, so dazzling as to seem unearthly."[24]

The next day, Potter and Chermside ascended a nearby mountain to find a cairn already there. When they dismantled it, they discovered notes in French and Swedish proclaiming that the Swedes had reached the spot in 1861. In the meantime, the much slower *Sampson* on May 22nd had fallen in with the ice around lat. 70° N, and the crew began working north along the edge of the ice, sealing as they went. They sighted Prins Karls Forland on June 20th and the next day, as Captain Walker writes in his

Fig. 22. Nordenskiöld's three ships lying beset in Mosselbukta (from Kjellman 1875).

log, "came to anchor in Magdalena Bay in 13 fathoms above the small island at the head of the bay; caught 3 seahorses."[25]

Departing Kongsfjorden on June 9th, *Diana* rounded Hakluythovden in the evening of June 10th. After some exploring in this area and leaving word for *Sampson* in Kobbefjorden, they met up with a Norwegian fishing *jakt* early in the morning of June 13th. The captain, whom Chermside called "Charlie the Norseman," told Leigh Smith that Nordenskiöld and the rest of the Swedes were lying beset and starving in Mosselbukta.

"This is news indeed," writes Chermside, and Leigh Smith wasted no time in ordering full speed to the rescue.[26] Charlie the Norseman was given a bottle of rum and Leigh Smith's compliments and then rowed smartly back to his *jakt*.

Diana reached Mosselbukta, which Chermside described as a mere "unprotected indulation [sic] in the coast on the E side of Wiide Bay [Wijdefjorden]" in four hours.[27] There, the three Swedish vessels – the 200-ton, 108′ iron steamship *Polhem* along with the steamer *Onkel Adam* and the brig *Gladan* – were frozen into the northeast corner of the bay, in ice that Chermside estimated at three to seven feet thick. More than three nautical miles of ice separated the ships from open ocean.

All the flags on *Diana* were run up. The ladder was put over forward but the "hardy Swedish sailors" ignored it, swinging themselves on board to be greeted with tinned meat and schnapps. "We smoke & chat & drink each other's health & talk & have quite a spirited party."[28]

Leigh Smith and Nordenskiöld shared similar ages, social status, education, and wealth. If there was a difference between them it was that Nordenskiöld was willing to leave his ship and try to reach the pole over the ice, whereas Leigh Smith was the classic gentleman-adventurer who would go ashore for a long hike in search of his fill of game birds but seems never to have seriously contemplated a polar sledge expedition.

Nordenskiöld had planned to sail to Sjuøyane and construct a base camp on Parryøya with several prefabricated structures. From that point, Nordenskiöld hoped to lead an expedition to the pole in April, 1873, using boats and sledges pulled by reindeer which in turn would be driven along by four Lapps.

Soon after the two explorers had parted from one another on August 30th of the previous year, Nordenskiöld had sailed north and quickly discovered that he was not able to penetrate further than Mosselbukta. Worse, the two supply ships that should have dropped their cargoes and returned to Sweden were caught and frozen into Mosselbukta along with the *Polhem*. The huts and observatories meant for Parryøya were instead erected at Mosselbukta, and Nordenskiöld was forced to divide his limited rations amongst sixty-seven people from three ships. By April of 1873, the winter hardships notwithstanding, Nordenskiöld began his attempt on the North Pole with three teams, several sledges, boats, and a single surviving reindeer. The conditions were extremely difficult, with broken seas and fog. One crew member who left in search of driftwood was never seen again.

The expedition managed to reach Sjuøyane, where the view to the north brought home to the men the utter hopelessness of attempting to cross the vast fields of broken ice. However, rather than return directly to Mosselbukta, Nordenskiöld retreated via Nordaustlandet in order to

Fig. 23. Nordenskiöld's winter quarters at Mosselbukta (from Kjellman 1875).

explore that area, so when Leigh Smith arrived off Mosselbukta he was still away on this exploring expedition.

By evening on the 13th, Leigh Smith had his crew members moving hundreds of pounds of provisions by sledge from the British to the Swedish ships. It was, Chermside writes, "a great triumph for the judgment of B.L. as regards ice, current, winds, etc., as in his letter to *The Times* in the winter, & ever since, in spite of many contrary statements, he had predicted that they would be lying there. This he takes in his usual quiet way."[29] Potter wrote a hasty letter to his father, noting that the Swedes had survived a fairly mild winter on half rations, "so will be glad of the provisions which Mr. Smith is giving them."[30]

Leigh Smith's letter to *The Times*, written from the Oxford and Cambridge Club the previous November, spelled out his concerns over Nordenskiöld's fate. He thought, correctly, that the Swedish expedition had put in to some safe harbor, unloaded their cargo but, before the two supply ships had been able to get away, they had been locked in the ice. He felt that the Swedes would survive the winter on the strength of their supplies and their ability to live off the land. Then, in a rare moment of both public expression and private introspection, Leigh Smith writes of the last time he saw the Swedish fleet at Fuglefjorden, "rosy with the ray of the evening and the morning sun."[31] As *Sampson* cleared the fjord on its way southwards, Leigh Smith writes that he felt "something like the shame of desertion" and promised he would search for Nordenskiöld when he went north again in the spring.[32] These are clearly the words of someone who saw Nordenskiöld as a friend and colleague rather than a polar competitor.

The survival of most of Nordenskiöld's crew (another died of scurvy) was in sharp contrast to the deaths by starvation and exposure of nineteen Norwegian whalers trapped in Svalbard by the severe ice conditions at the same moment in time. By mid-September, 1872, no less than six walrus-hunting vessels had been frozen in near Velkomstpynten. Seventeen sea hunters managed to escape in small boats to a hut at Isfjorden but, once there, all died over the winter. Two other sea hunters refused to leave their uninsured ship and were later found dead in a small boat, their ship having been crushed.[33] It was a horrific death toll for one season on Svalbard.

Yet, despite their successful overwintering, by early June of 1873, Nordenskiöld's expedition was in a bad way. The expedition's chief scientist, the physicist August Wijkander, noted that the first vessel to reach the Swedes arrived on June 7th, followed the next day by two fishing vessels from Tromsø. They delivered letters and newspapers and a little butter and flour. It was apparently this meager relief on the part of Nordenskiöld's agent in Tromsø that convinced the Swedish government that a large relief ship from Sweden was not required.

They could not have been more incorrect. Wijkander appealed without success to the fishing *jakts* to return to the mainland for relief supplies, but the Norwegian skippers were reluctant to abandon their seasonal work before it had even begun. "By this time all but one of the people aboard *Onkel Adam* had come down with scurvy, and half of the crew of *Gladan*, too. Even if all of the ice had magically disappeared from Mossel Bay … there just were not enough [healthy] men available to sail them home."[34]

Just as the Swedes began to sink into renewed despair at their worsening situation, *Diana* along with *Sampson* appeared just beyond the ice that clogged Mosselbukta. Wijkander writes of the almost miraculous appearance of "an English gentleman, Mr. Leigh Smith [who] offered the expedition with great generosity ... lime juice, tobacco, rum, fresh potatoes, and preserves for more than two weeks for all men, which we received with great gratitude."[35]

Lieutenant P. M. von Krusenstjerna, commander of *Gladan*, observed that the fresh provisions allowed the men suffering from scurvy to recover in little more than a week and so "are able to join in the severe work of sawing a passage through the ice in order to deliver us out of our ice-prison."[36] A member of the *Polhem* crew went further, writing on June 19th that all of "the sick have rapidly improved and that already in six days. Such a generous and at the same time beneficent gift deserves indeed to be made known."[37] The expedition's medical officer, Axel W. Engvall, writes in a report to the Swedish Board of Health that they would "not have got off with less than one or more deaths" if Leigh Smith had not arrived when he did.[38]

As Nordenskiöld's Lapps, "in their curious hats & long blue frocks ... and bright leggings, smoking their pipes," looked on, Chermside acted as quartermaster as provisions were off-loaded from *Diana* for the Swedish survivors. "Half a ton of beef, 40 tins of cabbage, 20 tins of salmon, 1 case of sherry, 1 case of brandy, 10 tins of carrots, 2 cases of lime juice, 59 lbs of tobacco, 5 bags of potatoes & 10 gallons of concentrated rum."[39] Along with Eaton, Leigh Smith took lunch with the Swedes, going over their scientific results for the winter. Chermside, for his part, had by this point perfected his sly style of revealing the quirks of his compatriot's characters: "Eaton was much pleased with their collection of sea-weeds."[40] Earlier in the year, and apparently at her request, Eaton had written to Leigh Smith's sister Barbara Bodichon with the news that he had compiled lists of all of Svalbard's flora as well as "of the Seals and Whales, Birds and Shells" so that in between his collecting forays he would be able to see at a glance where he had gaps in his efforts and strive to fill them in.[41]

Chermside visited the Swedes' small village of science huts and saw the three ships locked in four feet of ice about a quarter mile from shore. The *Onkel Adam* was in the center, with *Polhem* to port and *Gladan* to starboard. He thought that they couldn't have picked a worse place to be stranded, as between the ships and the open sea was a screen of grounded ice and several large hummocks. From his few weeks of experience with ice conditions around Svalbard, he thought it unlikely the rotting floe would keep the three vessels trapped for much more than another month.

Potter wrote to his father that he and Chermside spent much time ashore shooting, bagging Eider ducks, looms and a few ptarmigan. When not so occupied on land, Potter and Chermside invested hours in taking and processing photographs. "We had some difficulty with the photographs at first as the cold was too great, but now we have taken to warming the bottles and seem to be getting on all right as we got a good one of the *Diana* to-day. Chermside knows more about it than I do, so he does the most difficult part of it and I help him."[42]

Diana remained at the edge of the floe near Mosselbukta until the morning of June 15th, when steam was gotten up and the ship moved off toward Sjuøyane. Leigh Smith hoped to catch up with Nordenskiöld there, for if the Swede had managed to reach the pole he was scheduled to return to Parryøya on June 23rd and would almost certainly welcome if not require some assistance. When ice blocked *Diana*'s approach to Parryøya, ice anchors were deployed to moor the ship to a floe halfway between Parryøya and Waldenøya. Leigh Smith, along with Chermside and Captain Alex Fairweather, *Diana*'s skipper, rowed the three nautical miles to Waldenøya and climbed to its highest point to gain a view to the north.

From this perch, they could see that all of the islands off the northern coast of Svalbard were linked by ice. Ice blocked the ways to the north and east as well. The three regained the ship and then began a long exploration along the ice edge, gliding through still, clear water and making occasional soundings as they went. "A deep sea sounding [on Sunday, June 22nd] of 800 fathoms gave no bottom & we got plenty of exercise hauling in the line."[43] They again returned to Sjuøyane, as "the owner is very anxious to get to Parry's Island to see if there is news or trace of the Swedes."[44]

Once again they anchored to a floe and this time Leigh Smith, the captain, and two crew members trudged across the ice toward Nelsonøya in search of Nordenskiöld. Chermside and Eaton rowed back to Waldenøya to collect some lichen. There Chermside found an old coffin filled

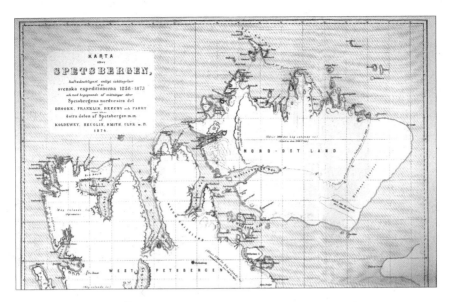

Fig. 24. Nordenskiöld's 1875 chart of Svalbard, showing his route from Sjuøyane southwestwards to Nordaustlandet and back to Mosselbukta (from Kjellman 1875). The map also shows the continued fascination with the "Giles Land," thought to exist somewhere to the east of Svalbard.

with stones and a bone or two. They had brought miniature caskets of their own, as Chermside thought of them, for Eaton's botanical collecting. They ascended to the highest point of the island, collecting lichens, flowers and grasses along the way, and then writing the names of their prizes in Latin "with care and precision, on the lids of the nice little wooden coffins prepared for any rarity vain enough to bloom & pining for sepulcher in a museum, by the indefatigable Eaton."[45] They reached *Diana* just as Leigh Smith returned to announce that he'd found no sign of Nordenskiöld on Nelsonøya.

On the 29th they made a journey to Tavleøya and, climbing to its height, stood for a long time gazing north. Chermside seemed to realize that he would very likely never again set foot on land so far north, so he looked intently "over the ice towards the mystic pole, that defies approach." When it was time to return to the ship, "it is almost with a feeling of awe that one turns away from the outmost (or inmost) threshold of the dread unapproachable tract of frozen ocean...." As they reached the shore, lit their pipes, and waited for the launch, the euphoric, heroic feeling began to recede until they were once again, as Chermside writes, merely "ordinary."[46]

Having arrived at Magdalenafjord on June 20th, Captain Walker of *Sampson* had sent one of his small boats north to Danskøya and the planned rendezvous point at Kobbefjorden. It returned the following day with the news that they had reached Kobbefjorden and brought back "letters from the *Diana* and found a [separate] letter, on a small island near Kobbe Bay [Kobbefjorden], from the Danish expedition dated 11th Oct. 1872."[47]

On July 1st, *Sampson* got underway toward the Sjuøyane and they soon ran into *Diana*, which was maneuvering south. The steamship took *Sampson* in tow and brought her into Sorgfjorden the same evening. As coal, stores, and fresh water were transferred to *Diana* over the next three days, Chermside climbed to the top of what he called Parry's Hill (Heclahuken), where two years earlier Leigh Smith had found a flag staff left by Parry in 1827. The staff was now gone, and Chermside relates a rather extraordinary tale of its disappearance from the 486 m/1,596´-high summit. He writes of a group of Norwegians trapped at Sorgfjorden, presumably during the catastrophic freeze-up the previous fall, who "nipped it as a mast to a piece of drift ice + proceeded on their way."[48]

On July 6th, Leigh Smith was on board *Sampson* to talk with Captain Walker and review his charts prior to making his main push north and east. Once the transfer of supplies between *Sampson* and *Diana* was completed, a few of the men went ashore to "collect whalebones, ancient + very bleached."[49]

Chermside in the meantime hiked to Mosselbukta, presumably alongside the low-lying streams and swampy ground that run up from Sorgfjorden and then down to Mossellaguna. There he found Nordenskiöld's huts barred, the windows boarded and smoke no longer rising from the chimneys. The Swedes had made their escape at last.

Nordenskiöld himself had journeyed south over the ice from Phippsøya to Kapp Platen. Stopped by open water east of Kapp Platen, Nordenskiöld sought to cross Nordaustlandet to its southeasternmost point at Kapp Mohn. Discovering a uniquely impenetrable landscape of 'ice canals,' Nordenskiöld and Palander studied the area before giving up any hope of traveling further south.

The impassable glacial landscape forced Nordenskiöld west, toward Wahlenbergfjorden, which he and his men reached in mid-June just as Leigh Smith was relieving the Swedish base camp at Mosselbukta. Nordenskiöld and his party finally returned to Mosselbukta on June 23rd, less than a week after Leigh Smith had departed. No other expedition of Nordenskiöld's, writes George Kish, was "as beset by trials and bad luck as the expedition of 1872–1873."[50] Only the timely arrival of Leigh Smith had prevented the Swedish expedition from tipping into a complete Arctic catastrophe, a fact later recognized with the Royal Order of the Polar Star for Leigh Smith.

Chermside learned all of this when he returned to Sorgfjorden and saw *Polhem* anchored alongside *Diana*. Prior to a brief exploration northwards before his return to Sweden, Nordenskiöld had come to thank Leigh Smith. The other two Swedish vessels had already made their way south on June 30th, quickly departing the scene as soon as the ice had moved out of Mosselbukta. Potter wrote a hurried note home to his father, the M.P. Thomas Bayley Potter, saying that the *Polhem* had come in the night before and was leaving that day. "I must finish this letter," he concluded, "as we are just going on board the *Polhem* to say goodby." The contrast between the ordeal the Swedes had just endured and Leigh Smith's cruise was apparent, as Eaton finished with a cheery postscript saying that he had "never enjoyed anything as much as this trip, and don't feel the cold a bit. It is warmer here than it has ever been, the temperature being 49 deg. We have plenty of sport with the birds, eider ducks, etc., and find them all capital eating...."[51]

The meeting between Leigh Smith and Nordenskiöld must have been brief indeed, or perhaps private, for Chermside makes no mention of it in his otherwise expansive journal. Both men were serious in their respective intent to explore the north, and the brief summer was already advanced. It was perhaps at this meeting that Nordenskiöld mentioned the possibility that the north cape of Svalbard was in fact an island and suggested naming it for the man who saved him, while the ever-humble Leigh Smith deferred the honor to his young aide-de-camp Chermside.

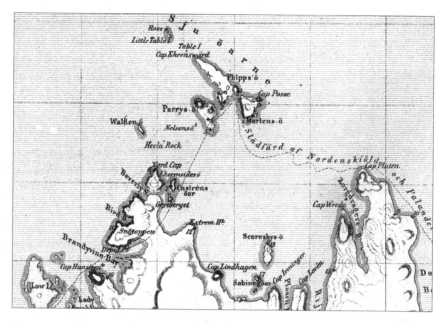

Fig. 25. Detail from Nordenskiöld's 1875 chart of Svalbard, showing the area of northern Svalbard bounded by Rossøya, Lågøya, and Kapp Platen (from Kjellman 1875). It was in this area where Leigh Smith spent much of his 1873 expedition in search of Nordenskiöld, and where he decided that Beverly Bay was in fact a sound or channel separating Nordaustlandet from the island to the north.

On July 7th, *Diana* moved out of Sorgfjorden and down Hinlopenstretet to a group of islets called Fosterøyane that Nordenskiöld had explored in 1861.[52] There Leigh Smith's expedition was itself beset by ice that stretched all the way across the strait from Kapp Fanshawe to Selanderneset. Retreating into Lomfjorden, Chermside found a "vertical pillar of flat stones covered with inscriptions in Norwegian."[53] Fishing *jakts* with ill or injured crew would call on *Diana* for a chance to be treated by Eaton, who passed for the only doctor north of Tromsø and served as a kind of replacement for Envall, who had performed much the same duty during the Swedish expedition's stay in Svalbard.

On July 14th they were hailed by Norwegian skipper Frederick (Fritz) Christian Mack (1837–1876), of whom *Place-Names* writes, "several important geographical discoveries in the Arctic are due."[54] "Like all

Fig. 26. Further detail from Nordenskiöld's 1875 chart of Svalbard, showing that the island north of Nordaustlandet had already by 1875 been named 'Chermsides ö' for the then-twenty-three-year-old Herbert Chermside (from Kjellman 1875).

these Norwegian skippers that I have met," Chermside writes, "he is a well-informed superior class of man...."[55] Mack had also been sent by Nordenskiöld's agent in Tromsø with supplies for the beset expedition but had arrived after the relief from Leigh Smith. (Three years later, Mack would write a plaintive letter to Leigh Smith complaining that he had been swindled by two putative foreign polar expeditions, had been without work for a year and a half, and was at the end of his tether.[56] He died only a few months later.)

The next day, *Diana* escaped Hinlopenstretet and anchored back in Mosselbukta only a short distance from the Swedish camp. "How different on a calm sunny summer evening like this it looks from the dreary icebound haven of 4 or 5 weeks ago."[57] With the way north blocked by ice pressing on the north coast, *Diana* maneuvered down Wijdefjorden, where Chermside and Potter went ashore for a bit of surveying while Leigh Smith initiated dredging and collecting operations. *Sampson* in the meantime had caught up with *Diana*, and for several days the two vessels – along with a collection of Norwegian fishing smacks – anchored in Lomfjorden to await favorable conditions.

Leaving its escort on the 14th, *Diana* passed beyond Kapp Petermann and anchored near a small island in Austfjorden that Leigh Smith named after *Diana*. On this newly-christened 'Diana Island,' they went on a reindeer hunt, returning with no fewer than sixty-eight reindeer, two or three seals, and seven white-fronted geese, which Chermside describes as a "new species to Spitsbergen."[58] Chermside notes that the hunting was a very trying experience, as the "excitable sailors are not trained gillies, will not keep line, do not know when to stand, when to show, when to squat, or act in concert at a distance...."[59]

The expedition remained anchored near Diana Island for several days, surveying the island and a nearby shoal, while the crew performed chores of painting the vessel, flensing and salting skins, and preparing heads for mounting. They continued dredging operations and on the 26th began a running survey as *Diana* retreated back toward the mouth of the fjord in another attempt to get north.

On July 27th, the expedition sighted ice-covered Lågøya and did their best to avoid the treacherous seas around it, which Chermside noted were foul with "black wicked rocks & reef."[60] The following day they took up dredging in 120 fathoms with a whale line and a heavy iron dredge weighing one cwt (112 lbs).

Chermside described several other aspects to this dredging operation. First, they fashioned a "swab" from a "long broom of oakum used to clean the decks," which was used to gather up starfish and seaweed, echinoderms, and stones from the bottom. To this was added a small tin to form a scoop to capture stones or gravel, along with a small hoop net and a sounding lead to gauge the character of the bottom. Deep-sea thermometers were attached at intervals of fifty fathoms. Deploying the dredge many times in a single day was impossible; it was so heavy it required all hands to haul it out of the depths. The device likewise took a toll on the specimens collected. As Chermside writes, "any animals unlucky enough to be caught in this are of little value, since they have been pounded to fragments or reduced to become amateur jellyfish...."[61] Hemmed in by ice on the 29th, the crew nevertheless managed to sound and dredge with their "swab" when possible and retrieve what Chermside described as "some fine specimens of coral."[62]

Diana pushed through the ice and into Lomfjorden on the 30th, there to be met by four Norwegian fishing *jakts*. Increasingly unable to maneuver, Leigh Smith made for Heclahamna, where he knew he could gain an elevated view of the ice conditions. Still station-keeping after several days, Chermside writes that "Macawber-like, we wait for something to turn up."[63]

On August 5th, *Diana* made its way offshore to Moffen Island, where they discovered the enormous whale skeleton covered with inscriptions and ship's names the year previous. Chermside described Moffen as a low-lying mass of shingle just a few feet above sea level, with a scattering of granite boulders apparently carried onto the island by the movement of ice grounding on the shoal ground. One group began walking around the lagoon in one direction while a second group walked the opposite way. In just an hour and a half, the two parties completed a circuit that Chermside estimated to be about seven nautical miles and met "at opposite points of a large natural bay or harbor which occupies the greater part of the interior and which had still a great deal of land ice in it."[64]

The moveable entrance to the harbor now lay on the northwest corner of the island, not along the north as shown on their charts. They had been looking for walrus but found only scores of carcasses of walrus killed along the inner edge of the lagoon. "We also saw which was far more interesting the bone-covered sites of what at one time must have been glorious engagements with large numbers of sea-horse. There were three of the sites with immense quantities of bones of the animals evidently all killed at one time & the layers of these was over an acre in extent & I am rather sorry I did not count the number of skulls."[65] If Leigh Smith took this chance to seek out the skeleton he had found the previous year, Chermside does not mention it, or perhaps by this point it had already been carried away as the dramatic souvenir of a passing whaler or walrus-hunter. Chermside does mention a painting hanging in the dining room of the Admiralty, which depicted Moffen Island and an attack on a large number of walrus by men of the Phipps expedition, so it seems clear that the island's connections to British polar history were the subject of a lively discussion amongst the exploring parties.

After two days of exploration around Moffen, *Diana* returned to Lågøya and then continued southeastwards down Hinlopenstretet, arriving at Augustabukta on August 10th. Here Chermside does mention a phenomenon associated with the whale skeleton from Moffen, which had apparently died naturally and been raised by isostatic uplift. The shingle beaches Augustabukta showed the remains of whales "killed perhaps 100 years ago, the dates indeed have been in some cases determined, then the skeletons too heavy to drag above it must have lain in the water & now you find skeletons almost complete at 6, 8 & 10 feet above the sea level."[66]

Chermside does not describe the skeletons in any detail, or how he arrived at a relative death date, so it is not possible to know if the whales died naturally or showed evidence of butchering, but his assumption that the skeletons were left in shallow water, being too heavy to be dragged, makes it clear that he believes the whales were killed by humans. Such evidence at the remote Augustabukta could mean that, absent a shore-based tryworks, the whales were pursued into shallow water by the occasional visit of a pelagic hunting expedition or an expedition operating away from the established whaling stations on the west coast of Spitsbergen. There they could have been flensed alongside a ship, the blubber boiled down on board and the largely intact carcasses left to rot, as opposed to being set adrift as in deep-harbor or open-ocean whaling.[67] The low elevation of Chermside's whale skeletons at Augustabukta, like the palimpsest whale found at Moffen, both suggest human agency.

Perhaps it was while contemplating these maritime mysteries that Leigh Smith repeated his comment about Svalbard to Chermside: "[T]he owner always says it is like Switzerland with the sea."[68]

Returning to familiar waters east of Tumlingodden, near where Leigh Smith had circumnavigated Wilhelmøya in 1871, Chermside recorded a humorous scene when the entire watch gathered around the heavy dredge for a deep-sea sounding in heavy ice, only to lower the instrument and find that the water was but seventeen fathoms deep. *Diana* continued around the southern edge of Nordaustlandet to Vibebukta, which the crew also dredged. They were operating in a fantastically remote area little visited even today. Chermside notes that Leigh Smith wanted to explore "Wiches

Land" [Kong Karls Land], just visible across the pack, but the expedition was stopped by ice near Kapp Mohn. Even so, when added to his 1871 track, with this foray, Leigh Smith came very close to seeing the entire coast of Nordaustlandet. They returned northwestwards up Hinlopenstretet, emerging from the strait on August 23rd with hopes of reaching the Sjuøyane.

With ice still fast to the north, Leigh Smith led the expedition east towards Kapp Platen. There *Diana* anchored in shallow water in an ice-covered "Parry's 'Beverly Bay'" (Beverlysundet), which Leigh Smith – perhaps with an earlier inference from Nordenskiöld, correctly believed to be a channel, or sound, and the land north of the channel to be an island.[69] Nordenskiöld in his chart of Svalbard named this 14 km^2 island after Chermside, and it is now known as Chermsideøya.[70] This is apparently the only new place name added to the nomenclature of Svalbard during the 1873 expedition, and that it was named for one of the youngest expedition member speaks volumes for the impression he made upon Leigh Smith – and perhaps upon Nordenskiöld as well.

With the ice under heavy pressure, the crew spent its time moving from one anchorage to another. In his unpublished account of Leigh Smith's expeditions around Svalbard, Chermside provides an extensive discussion of the ice-breaking methods employed by the crew of *Diana*. Since leaving the southeastern end of Hinlopenstretet, the vessel had made only slow progress in the heavy ice. On the 28th, with the pressure of the ice lessening, the crew, as Chermside related, "set to work in earnest to extricate ourselves from the pack, as further progress seemed impossible and the pack was more or less cemented together by early and very sharp frosts."[71]

On August 28th, *Diana* had managed fifteen nautical miles progress in nine hours through heavy pack, but as Chermside writes, this required that the ice have some 'play.' Now, with three nautical miles of heavy ice separating the ship from sailing ice, the steam engines were run up and the crew warped the ship from its temporary ice dock. Several of the crew were put onto the ice armed with boat hooks. Once the vessel had some maneuvering space and the likeliest spot for the ice to crack was spied from the deck, the ship was rammed into that spot. Loose ice was then pushed aside by the men with the boathooks, or they hopped onto the broken ice and punted the ice out of the path of the ship – appropriate work for Cambridge men like Leigh Smith. While this was carried out, *Diana* was backed to the farthest corner of the cleared area, sometimes as much as two hundred yards. "Then she comes ahead full steam and jumping right on to the ice, succeeds in cracking it. At it she comes again and again and several large piles are by this time smashed. On to these men jump with drills and boring holes. Ice hooks and warps are made fast from the ship and they are towed out of the way, the boathook men removing the smaller pieces. If the floes are nipping fast little is gained, but if not the passage is slowly and gradually cleared...."[72]

The men bobbing about on the ice were then picked up by the dinghy and the ship proceeded to back once more to the farthest end of the cleared area. The bell was rung and the ship lurched forward again, this time with all hands running from one side of the deck to the other to create a rolling motion, "until by the time her head is straight at the obstacle and the Captain shouts 'Steady' from the crow's nest, she is going at full speed and rolling almost to the rail – a crash – and we are through and looking forward to the next obstacle."[73]

When the ice would not crack, Chermside was often at work blasting it with explosives, with varying degrees of success. Yet another method was to jam the bow of the ship into the ice, then place an ice anchor ahead of the ship. A line was run from the ice anchor to the ship, the engines run up, and then the helm thrown hard over, the bow of the ship held in place while the stern forced the ice aside, thereby wedging the floe open further. "When there is no more to be gained over goes the helm the other way, and with the immense leverage gained by the length of the ship, the steam of course, besides giving her the power of pushing ahead gives her also the power of swinging, and thus we force our way through inch by inch, not however without breaking three new warps."[74] Chermside admitted that often each of these techniques would fail in turn and the expedition had to give up and try to find another place to break through. When all the hard work paid off, however, "a grand sight it is as one stands at work on the ice to watch the ship rush bravely at the obstacle at full speed, and how satisfactory as her bow leaps out of the water on to the mass, ere she falls back to feel it groan and quiver and crack under your feet, a dead dull muffled sound perhaps, and a new dark crack telling you that your blast has also done its work."[75]

By August 30th, *Diana* was hooked to ice between Parryøya and Phippsøya, which Chermside saw as a collection of "isolated hills connected by low sea beaches [with] immense quantities of driftwood and some whalebones."[76] Nordenskiöld had cached his small boat and a quantity of supplies on Phippsøya in the spring of 1873 after his aborted attempt to get north of Sjuøyane. Not finding the boat, Chermside wanted to cross to Martensøya and search for it but was stopped by fear of becoming trapped on Martensøya and having to be rescued.

On August 31st, Chermside climbed two peaks, presumably on Phippsøya, of 335 m/1,100′ and 372 m/1,220′ above sea level, for a view to the north. It was not encouraging. On September 1st, before a southeast gale, *Diana* made her farthest north for the summer at lat. 80°54′ N, just beyond Sjuøyane, before being forced to retreat.

The expedition sailed westwards in a heavy gale until the 4th. Finding no possibility of getting further north, they ran for Magdalenefjorden where they rode out the gale for three more days. The seas were so violent that, even as she sheltered in the fjord, *Diana* dragged and broke both of her remaining anchors.

On the morning of September 8th, *Diana* rendezvoused with *Sampson* at Grønfjorden. Captain Walker's crew on August 29th had found a coal mine there at the northeast point of the harbor and taken two boatloads of the stuff on board. Before they parted for the year, *Sampson* passed a spare anchor to *Diana* while Leigh Smith decided on one last late-season attempt to get around the eastern edge of Svalbard.

As *Sampson* headed for home, *Diana* sailed between Edgeøya and Hopen and met pack ice just east of Hopen. The weather was fine and the pack loose enough for *Diana*'s steam power to shoulder it aside. By September 14th, however, severe frost had placed two inches of solid new ice in front of them and cemented the older pack ice together. After a brief exploration of Hopen, *Diana* turned and set sail for Dundee, which the expedition reached on September 26th. The slower *Sampson* returned to Humber Dock early on the morning of Sunday, October 5th. "All well," wrote Walker. "Thus ends the voyage."[77]

After the expedition, Chermside returned home to study coastal defense. He would see service for several years in Turkey, Egypt, and Kurdistan, before returning to Constantinople for seven years as military attaché.[78] He then commanded British troops on Crete and fought in the Boer Wars before being appointed governor of Queensland in 1902. Despite Lady Tennyson's description of him as "a very short plain little general with a biggish moustache," his range of interests and travels and his genial personality earned him considerable popularity.[79]

Although Chermside never returned to the Arctic, his efforts there with Leigh Smith in 1873 must have made a considerable impression. When Nordenskiöld published his revised map of Svalbard in 1875, Chermside's name had been attached to the island discovered north of Beverlysundet. A valley that crosses Chermsideøya was also named for him in the 1920s, but by this point his reputation would have been long secured.[80]

For Leigh Smith, the conclusion of the expedition began a period of evaluation. By the fall of 1873 he had demonstrated a range of skills for geographic exploration in the waters around Svalbard, and his desire to reach the Pole was as strong as ever. He clearly wanted to push further north and put the theory of an open polar sea to the ultimate test of steam power. On September 30th, just as he arrived back in England, Potter summed up his companions: "Mr. Smith was so kind in every way that it was impossible for anyone to help liking him. Eaton was rather a fool and none of us got on very well with him, but I liked Chermside very much although he was rather conceited & always talking of himself [still] he was a very jolly companion...."[81]

Chermside wrote up the results of the 1873 expedition, along with an extended discussion of Leigh Smith's first two expeditions to Svalbard. The manuscript was favorably reviewed by Arctic veteran Admiral Sir Richard Collinson, but ultimately rejected for publication in the RGS's *Proceedings*.[82] Leigh Smith may have charted much of the northwest coastline of Svalbard, but he was still in search of the imprimatur of the arbiters of geographical significance at the RGS in Kensington Gore in London.

It would be seven years before Leigh Smith returned to the north. When he did it would not be in someone else's vessel but in his own specially designed and Peterhead-constructed polar research vessel, *Eira*. His field of operations would shift from Svalbard to new lands being discovered by Weyprecht and Payer even as Leigh Smith was collecting coal in Grønfjorden.

It would be in this new territory where Leigh Smith's method of polar exploration by adapting to local conditions would find both its greatest success in the summer of 1880 and its greatest test, on August 21, 1881, when *Eira* would sink amid ice floes at Cape Flora.

5

THE AWAKENING TO A NEW LIFE, 1874–1879

On September 29th, 1873, the General noted with approval that *The Times* of that morning contained "tidings of the arrival of the *Diana* at Dundee – all well including 21 sailors."[1] A few days later, Leigh Smith returned home. His niece Mabel was putting on an amateur family play, of the kind that Leigh Smith himself had acted in with Barbara and Bella twenty years earlier. The play was rewritten at the last minute to include a scene where a page played by Willy's son rushes in with the news of the return from the Arctic of the famous Benjamin Leigh Smith, to the vast amusement of The Explorer himself.[2] By November, the photographic imagery from the expedition had been developed and Leigh Smith proudly displayed them for his extended family.

After three major forays into the Arctic, Leigh Smith now made an attempt to return to his former life as a wealthy squire, dividing his life between his estate at Glottenham in East Sussex and his townhouse on Gower Street in London. Much of this duty – for now it must have seemed – revolved around parties and politics. When Mabel had her birthday in December of that year, it was Leigh Smith as head of the family who decreed that she should have her grandmother's watch. In May of 1874, Leigh Smith gave a ball for his nieces and nephews at Gower Street. At another gathering later that year, the General noted that Leigh Smith was "the spirit of our party," letting a governess know that he was "game for anything."[3] He attended another ball as the escort of Herbert Chermside's younger sister, an age difference that must have fallen somewhere in the range of two and a half decades. He made a trip to California and returned with a bagful of seeds from the giant Wellingtonia trees of

Yosemite. These he planted on his estates as well as on the property of the General. The giant sequoias, extremely tall though still in their relative infancy, can be seen there today.

He was asked to stand again for Parliament but did not. It seemed that the more Leigh Smith tried to focus on a return to his former life, on the gardens and trees at Glottenham and the political arguments in London, the more matters in the Arctic refused to sit still. For a man who had watched as a ghost ship drifted towards the North Pole from the Sjuøyane, politics must have by now lost whatever attractions they once held.

Moreover, those events in the north were moving rapidly, and they involved both new expeditions and Leigh Smith himself. In the spring of 1874, in recognition of his relief of Nordenskiöld, Oscar II, the King of Sweden and Norway, conferred upon him the knighthood of the Order of the Polar Star. The General, who would have clearly understood the transcendent magnitude of such an international honor, wrote to Barbara asking whether Leigh Smith would ask the Queen to recognize his Swedish knighthood. Such a request, however, was never on the cards, not least given Leigh Smith's reticence to accept public accolades for his work. In the end, there was no ceremony accompanying the decoration: the medal and brooch were simply mailed to Leigh Smith from the Swedish Legation in London.[4]

The royal honor must have touched a nerve, as it was one his own country would never bestow upon him and his pioneering work. Soon thereafter, to make matters worse, a more serious threat to Leigh Smith's work arrived by way of a cutting review article in the influential quarterly, *Edinburgh Review*.[5] This anonymous essay took an easy shot at Leigh Smith's oceanographic results from the 1872 expedition, "in a way," noted the General, "that cannot fail to displease him."[6] The startling observations that showed higher temperatures in the deep-ocean than at the surface were dismissed as the failure of instrumentation. This jab ignored the fact that Leigh Smith noted such results in two consecutive years, data corroborated by similar observations by Weyprecht and Payer. But with all else it was enough to keep one away from medal ceremonies.

Some of the sting of this criticism must have been ameliorated later that same summer. Jane, Lady Franklin, who had spent the last thirty years of her life successfully agitating for one expedition after another to go in search of her husband and his crew, passed away in mid-summer, 1875, and Leigh Smith, as a newly and internationally recognized polar explorer, was asked to serve as one of the pallbearers. Once again, the General recognized the importance of the request and the event. He was quick to note that such a request, given Lady Franklin's enduring fame in British society, was a high compliment indeed.

As in all such commemorations, great and small, there was an unspoken subtext at work. In a greater context, the *Edinburgh Review* article, combined with the death of Lady Franklin, highlighted what had been obvious for some time: the British Government had abandoned the field of Arctic exploration and the pursuit of the North Pole for more than twenty years. Robert McClure, who led the HMS *Investigator* on a search for John Franklin in 1850, was awarded credit for the discovery of the Northwest Passage. Though he did not actually sail through the passage and, moreover, lost his ship in the process, McClure's subsequent sledging work near Banks Island confirmed its existence. In the view of many, there were no remaining objectives in Arctic exploration worth the price that would have to be exacted to gain them. With the passing of Lady Franklin, a three-decade saga of British misery in Arctic exploration seemed at last at an end.

As the Royal Navy left the field, explorers from other nations took up the challenge of the North Pole. While Leigh Smith explored the northern coast of Svalbard in 1871, Charles Francis Hall followed Kane's route between Greenland and Baffin Island. Throughout the years of the American Civil War, Hall had lived with Inuit in Arctic Canada, hoping to learn from them the fate of Franklin. Through his ground-breaking ethnographic studies, Hall made several major discoveries by way of local knowledge, including the location of the remains of an encampment from Martin Frobisher's Northwest Passage expedition of three hundred years earlier. And by interviewing Inuit on King William Island, Hall came as close to certain knowledge of Franklin's fate as any explorer before or since.

In recognition of his expertise, Hall in 1871 was placed in command of a U.S.-sponsored vessel called *Polaris*, with the express mission of reaching the North Pole. Unlike Kane's difficulties in the same area,

Hall breezed through Kennedy Channel and on into a wider basin beyond that he named after himself. Hall and *Polaris* eventually reached the very northern shores of Greenland, the highest point attained by any ocean vessel to that date. At this point, as a highly experienced Arctic traveler, Hall was poised for a meaningful strike for the Pole in the spring of 1872.

At the moment of his expected triumph, however, Hall was taken violently ill. Before he died that October, he complained that he was being poisoned by, among others, the Smithsonian Institution scientist on board the ship. In fact, nearly one hundred years later, a Dartmouth College English professor and biographer of Hall's by the name of Chauncey Loomis, decided to test Hall's suspicions. He received permission to exhume Hall's body from the frozen shoreline of Polaris Harbor, in far northwestern Greenland, where the explorer had been buried. From the frozen corpse, Loomis took small clippings of Hall's hair and fingernails. When these were tested, the world learned that Hall had indeed been poisoned. Unfortunately, the results were not dispositive, as Hall could have done the deed himself, overdosing on the arsenic that was used at the time as both medicine and poison.[7]

For Leigh Smith, as interesting as these events were, they paled next to a new polar expedition being launched from northern Norway. Just as Hall lay dying in Greenland, the Austro-Hungarian North Pole Expedition on board the three-masted ship *Tegetthoff* departed from the fjord at Tromsø. The expedition was led by his old friends Julius Payer and Karl Weyprecht, the same men who had dined on fresh cod on board *Sampson* with Leigh Smith in Tromsø harbor in 1871. The day after the crew of *Sampson* discovered the coal lying about Grønfjorden, Weyprecht and Payer made the much more stunning discovery of a previously unknown landmass east of Svalbard. They immediately named it for their emperor: Kaiser Franz-Josef's Land. As Payer later wrote: "That day brought a surprise, such as only the awakening to a new life can produce."[8]

At the time of this momentous discovery, in August of 1873, Weyprecht was thirty-five years old and had served in the Austrian navy from the age of eighteen. The *Tegetthoff* had been named after a prominent admiral in that navy, under whom Weyprecht had served. Weyprecht had volunteered in 1868 to lead the first German North Polar Expedition, but ill-health forced him to pass command to Captain Karl Koldewey.

Koldewey then led the small expedition around Svalbard in the vessel *Grönland*, but did not succeed in advancing further than Parry in 1828. The following year, with two vessels, *Germania* and *Hansa*, Koldewey made another attempt to reach the pole, this time along the coast of northeastern Greenland. *Hansa* was caught and sunk by the ice, and the *Germania* reached only a bit north of Shannon Island at lat. 75°30′ N in mid-August. There the expedition was forced to overwinter. But Koldewey's surveyor, a twenty-eight-year-old from the spa town of Teplitz in Bohemia by the name of Julius Payer, succeeded in mapping Shannon Island and much of the surrounding coastline, including an inlet later named Kaiser Franz-Josef Fjord.

In the spring of 1871, after Weyprecht had regained his health and was placed at the head of a new Arctic expedition, Payer joined him as a kind of co-commander and geographic surveyor. The failure of Koldewey's expeditions to penetrate very far toward the pole from either the north coast of Svalbard or the east coast of Greenland, led Weyprecht and Payer to seek a new way northwards much further to the east, along the coast of Novaya Zemlya. This is how they came to be in the same harbor in Tromsø as Leigh Smith in June of 1871, while following much the same plan as the Englishman, being based on the prevailing and influential geographical ideas of August Petermann.

Petermann had written hundreds of articles on the development of polar exploration and as a result became known as the father of German polar exploration. Like U.S. Navy oceanographic researcher Matthew Fontaine Maury, Petermann was both a nineteenth-century expert in the study of ocean currents and an indefatigable theorist on the causes and effects of such currents, especially in the Arctic. Petermann esposed these theories through the geographical research journal he founded, the *Mitteilungen aus Justus Perthes' Geographischer Anstalt über wichtige neue Erforschungen auf dem Gesammtgebiete der Geographie* (Reports from Justus Perthes' Geographical Institution upon Important New Investigations in the Whole Subject of Geography) – known ultimately and more popularly as *Petermann's Geographische Mitteilungen*. Though his reputation in his later years and after his suicide in September of 1878 suffered as it became clear that his support for such ultimate Arctic chimeras as an "Open Polar Sea" was mistaken, he is credited with advancing polar research not only in Germany but in Russia, Sweden, Norway, America, France and, in the case of Weyprecht and Payer, in Austria-Hungary.

After training as a cartographer in Germany, Petermann worked from 1845 to 1848 as a mapmaker in Edinburgh, coincidentally the same three disastrous years of the Franklin expedition. The search for Franklin became the touchstone for many of Petermann's ideas and hypotheses about the Arctic, and his *Historical Summary of the Search for Sir John Franklin* (1853), typified Petermann's collation of vast amounts of data – much of it collected by the captains of Norwegian *jakts* – in an apparently neutral essay, which he then diverts in support of Arctic expeditions designed to test his hypotheses.[9] The *Summary* is nominally a history of all the attempts to find Franklin between 1848 and 1853. But it moves at length from the primary object of these relief expeditions, to a discussion of the immediate geographic and future expeditionary benefits of the search. These are defined as the location and character of newly discovered coastlines and Arctic Ocean currents, as well as the seeming paradox of the survival of relatively small overwintering vessels like the American Grinnell expedition ships *Advance* and *Rescue*, as compared to the mounting evidence that Franklin's much larger ships *Erebus* and *Terror* had been destroyed.

The Franklin disaster eventually led Petermann to conclude that the North Pole would not be reached from the American side of the Arctic, where the highest latitude reached by any of the Franklin searchers was Inglefield's lat. 78°35′ N. He proposed instead a route to the pole from the European high Arctic. There, in the ice-covered seas north of Svalbard, Parry had already pushed beyond the 82nd parallel. Petermann also made the rather fantastic suggestion that the search for Franklin be extended further west from the Canadian Arctic to the north coast of Siberia, and this became one of the few suggestions regarding polar exploration that the British Admiralty wisely tabled.

Petermann, who after Edinburgh worked as a cartographer in London for several years, returned to Germany in 1854 to become director of Perthes Geographical Institution in Gotha. It was there, a year later, that he founded the *Mitteilungen*. His view of polar geography, in particular of a warm ocean current flowing into the Arctic Ocean from the Gulf Stream as well as his notion of a far northern extension of the landmass of Greenland, were published on his map, *Karte der arktischen und antarktischen*

Regionen zur Übersicht des geographischen Standpunktes in J. 1865, der Meere strömungen (Map of the Arctic and Antarctic Regions Reflecting the Geographical Points of View in 1865, [and] the Sea Currents)[10]

Petermann's belief in an Open Polar Sea derived from more than his study of ocean currents. Early nineteenth-century expeditions such as those of the Finnish-Russian Matvey Hedenström and the Baltic-German Ferdinand Wrangell had discovered areas of open water, so-called *polynya*, in the Arctic Ocean north of Siberia. It was this term for an area of open water within an ice pack, borrowed from the Russian полынья, that Captain Wells used when he wrote that Leigh Smith's 1872 expedition was in search of *The Gateway to the Polynia*.

Elisha Kent Kane's account of the Second Grinnell expedition in search of Franklin describes how two of his men stood at lat. 81°22′ N, a point Kane later named Cape Constitution, and heard "the novel music of dashing waves; and a surf."[11] Petermann did not believe in an Arctic Ocean completely free of ice, as Kane did after he heard this oceanic music, but Petermann did suggest that explorers would find a sea around the pole that was at least partially filled with manageable levels of navigable ice, broken by wind, storms, currents, rain, fog, and especially by the continuous summer light.

Petermann divided his polar sea into two roughly equal sectors. He created isothermal maps, traced the drift of glass bottles around the polar basin, and followed the reported presence of animals on various islands. All these data allowed him to hypothesize a far northern extension of Greenland. This extension, which he thought might exist as either an undersea ridge or as a land bridge into the central Arctic, bisected the polar basin and created in effect two polar oceans, one north of Canada and eastern Siberia, and the other north of Svalbard, Franz Josef Land and western Siberia. To the barrier of ice discovered by expeditions like Kane's that searched north from Baffin Bay, Petermann ascribed the name "Pack-Ice Sea." The route to the pole, he was convinced, would be found in the sea north of Svalbard, which he fashioned as the "Floating-Ice Sea."

To investigate these hypotheses, Petermann had personally sponsored the 1868 German geographic expedition led by Koldewey on board the *Grönland*. The following year, the track of the second German polar expedition led by Koldewey with the *Germania* was based on Petermann's belief the ice northeast of his imagined Greenland extension might loosen enough to allow a passage to the North Pole. Instead, this same ice pinned *Germania* to the East Greenland coast for ten months in 1869–70.

Petermann extended his dual-sea theory to anthropology, arguing that the East Greenland Inuit must have migrated out of Asia westwards, not eastwards. In his later years, even as he came to question many of his own ideas, Petermann clung to the idea that peninsulas leading northwards from both Greenland and Franz Josef Land converged somewhere near the North Pole. Indeed, an Arctic mirage that Payer mistook for a landmass north of Franz Josef Land he named for Petermann. By the time polar explorers discovered the non-existence of Petermann Land, Petermann himself was long dead and so was the theory of the *polynya* and the Open Polar Sea.

In the spring of 1871, Petermann had placed his blessing upon the first expedition of Weyprecht and Payer in the *Isbjørn*, an Austro-Hungarian effort financed by Count Johann Nepomuk Wilczek. Payer stressed that this initial journey was to be "a voyage of reconnaissance" and "a pioneer expedition to the seas of Novaya Zemlya."[12] It was in fact a kind of proving expedition that had to be undertaken before any kind of serious request could be undertaken to the Austrian government for a major expedition involving multiple years in a more powerful vessel. The governing objective would be Gillis' Land, that mystical island somewhere in the eastern sector of Svalbard, but the rationale for choosing the eastern coast of Svalbard was Petermann's belief that a warm tendril of the Gulf Stream would clear the way for any expedition adopting this route. No attempt would be made to reach the North Pole, because the budget the expedition had at its disposal would preclude the charter of a vessel large enough for any such ambition. But they would be able to study the prevailing environmental conditions to see if a larger ship and more ambitious plan might be seized in 1872.

The ship Weyprecht and Payer settled on, the *Isbjørn*, was a new, 55-foot cutter commanded by an experienced Norwegian skipper named Johan Kjeldsen. With bows protected from pack ice by a four-foot band of sheet iron, the vessel drew six feet of water. Like *Sampson* in 1871, she sailed with an all-Norwegian crew from the Arctic port of Tromsø. The Norwegians would run the ship, while Weyprecht and Payer gave general directional desires and then stood back and made their geographical observations with instruments supplied by the Imperial Geographical Institute. The Tromsømen warned the nominal expedition leaders that, Petermann notwithstanding, approaching Gillis' Land from the south was a losing proposition. They had sailed in that area and let the Austro-Hungarians know that the seas there were as unfavorable as they were unforgiving. To compound matters, the spring of 1871 had been a harsh one, and when Weyprecht and Payer arrived in Tromsø in June they found northern Norway still covered in snow. Rumor had it that the ice was pressing down on mainland Norway itself, as close as twenty nautical miles from North Cape.

But the lure of Gillis' Land would not be denied. The expedition would try to reach the southern coast of Hope Island (Hopen) and then sail eastwards, probing the ice barrier in hopes of finding Petermann's Gulf Stream-induced corridor northwards.

The expedition left Tromsø, appropriately enough, in a snow-storm on June 20th. The ship ran aground on the way out of the fjord and soon met with vessels that had preceded *Isbjørn* by several weeks but because of unfavorable winds had yet to reach their sealing grounds. Payer thought the area was "indescribably bleak … secluded … lonely."[13] He describes fishing villages of magnificent isolation whose impoverished inhabitants looked upon modest towns like Tromsø and Hammerfest as the two great cities of their world. It was not until June 26th that *Isbjørn* shook free of this remote world of rocky outports and reached the sea proper, and just two days after that came into the ice. For the seasoned Payer, the sight of the ice was like coming home.

Isbjørn sailed through forty nautical miles of drift ice before hitting the main pack at lat. 74°30′ N, southeast of Bjørnøya. The small sailing vessel was quickly beset and, in heavy seas lasting more than a week, as the ice continued to press in, one of the small boats was destroyed and the rudder was made fast to prevent it from being torn loose. Then, just as suddenly, the skies cleared and the seas softened.

Payer writes:

The day broke: what a change in the ice! The sea was calm, and a long swell died out on its outer edge. Piles of ice all around us – a weird and deathlike calm! The heavens were cloudless; the countless blocks and masses of ice stood out against the sky in blue neutral shadow, and the more level fields between them sparkled like silver as they shone in the sun. The movement of the sea beyond the ice abated, "leads" within the floes, hitherto scarcely perceptible, widened out.[14]

By the 10th of July, just as Leigh Smith on *Sampson* was reaching the west coast of Svalbard for the first time, *Isbjørn* put on all sail and for several days pounded through a variable sea of young ice. Ten days later, the expedition had gained the 75th parallel. As their respective Norwegian sailing vessels struggled with the ice throughout the summer, Payer and Leigh Smith were having many of the same ideas about future exploration. As Payer writes: "Though drift-ice lay on every side, a steamer would have found nothing to arrest her progress."[15] And both were ready to ditch their recalcitrant Norwegian crews in favor of their own countrymen, who would both speak the same language and respond to the demands of authority when ordered to pursue a nebulous geographic target.

Realizing the hopelessness of maneuvering very far northwards given the weaknesses of *Isbjørn* and its crew, Weyprecht turned northwestwards in hope of finding a harbor on the eastern coast of Svalbard that might serve as a future staging area for a proper expedition. They cruised along the coast of Hopen, again trying to reach Gillis' Land, before being blown westwards. They made for Walter-Thymen's Straits (now Freemansundet), at the same moment that Leigh Smith was almost directly north of them and beginning his penetration into Hinlopenstretet. Winds blew them past South Cape (Sørkapp) and into Hornsund. There the expedition was trapped for the better part of two weeks before *Isbjørn* escaped and again attempted to sail northwestwards.

They were off Edgeøya on August 14th and six weeks of grinding in the ice had taken a toll on the ship. As Payer writes, *Isbjørn* "was in so bad a condition, that part of the bows under the water-line was shattered, and some timbers of the hull were forced in.... [The iron plating] had been broken off like so many chips."[16] An attempt to cruise along the southeastern coastline of Nordaustlandet until they found a harbor (perhaps Vibebukta) where *Isbjørn* could be anchored and the surviving small boat launched in search of Gilles' Land was abandoned when the expected ice-free coastal waters along Nordaustlandet never materialized. There was no warm tendril waiting to carry them north.

Hoping to salvage something of what had been to that point a rather desultory effort at pioneering the icy seas east of Svalbard, they retreated to the unknown western coast of Storfjorden and began a geological investigation of that area. Turning southwestwards, they landed the whale boat at Hopen, where they found equal measures of brown coal and Siberian driftwood. They tried to explore Kong Karls Land but adverse winds forced them back. Weyprecht and Payer wanted to press on, even as the sun set for the first time on August 24th, and it was clear that Captain Kjeldsen and his men had had enough. The Austro-Hungarians prevailed on them to push eastwards for a few more days, and it was then that they at last found some open water which they sailed through all the way to long. 42° E, and all the way north to the 78th parallel. By August 31st, they had penetrated deeply into the Barents Sea, farther than any ship before them in those longitudes and, at lat. 78°38′ N, saw no serious ice before them. A run along the ice brought them on September 5th to long. 56° E. They were groping in the right area for new lands in the Arctic, for there was an unseen and undiscovered Arctic country just over their northern horizon.

But the new land remained out of their vision. The lateness of the season, the increasingly battered condition of *Isbjørn*, and the opposition of Kjeldsen to going any farther in such high latitudes soon to be filled with ice, compelled them to turn southeast. Had they possessed a steam vessel, Weyprecht and Payer likely would have discovered Franz Josef Land during their 1871 reconnaissance expedition, instead of the following year as they did. Instead, they veered southeast until *Isbjørn* was off Novaya Zemlya on September 12th. Once again unfavorable winds kept them from a landing, and at last they were compelled to make for Norway, much to the relief of Captain Kjeldsen, who now had a heavily damaged ship and a sick crew, including one man suffering from scurvy.

On September 20th, *Isbjørn* regained Nordkapp in northern Norway, where Payer and a Lapp sailor who could speak Norwegian left the vessel so he could journey overland back to Tromsø, using a small boat to cross shallow rivers and a reindeer sleigh to cross open ground. The heavily damaged *Isbjørn*, carrying its remaining polar explorer Weyprecht, was towed back into port at Tromsø on October 4th.

In Tromsø, Weyprecht again met Leigh Smith and shared his disappointment at the meager results of the Austro-Hungarian efforts. For Payer, the results were not a complete loss. The observed variability of the ice encouraged him in the belief that a route to the North Pole from the seas east of Svalbard was still a possibility. The seas around Novaya Zemlya, especially, seemed a favorable ground for further exploration. Payer believed they could maneuver as far as lat. 78° N without encountering serious opposition from the ice. In a year otherwise marked by horrendous ice conditions in and around Hopen and Storfjorden, the open areas in the longitudes between 42° and 59° E were a revelation. On the other hand, if Gillis' Land existed, it seemed by now that it was only an island – and perhaps a small one at that – and not the continental land mass some had long suspected.

In all, the results were just enough to organize a new and much larger expedition the following year. On June 13th, 1872, twenty-three expedition members arrived at the docks at Bremerhaven to stow their gear on board the *Tegetthoff*, a 220-ton three master with an auxiliary steam engine. The crew was made up of Croatians from the Dalmatia. The supercargo consisted of Germans, Italians, Slavs, and Hungarians; the common language of the expedition became Italian.

The progress of the expedition was exceedingly slow. *Tegetthoff* dropped anchor in Tromsø only on July 3rd, where divers examined the leaky hull and the seams were re-caulked. A Norwegian named Elling Carlsen came on board as harpooner and icemaster. A French priest conducted a Saturday morning mass for the crew on July 13th, and *Tegetthoff* slipped out of Tromsø the following morning. It was, as Payer writes, "the first and last voyage, which the *Tegetthoff* was destined to make...."[17]

After ten days of lolling in unfavorable winds, the ship encountered the ice on July 25th, far south of even where it had lain in 1871. It soon became clear that 1872 would not be a repeat of 1871 in the Barents Sea. For ten days, the crew warped *Tegetthoff* through a belt of pack ice more than one hundred miles thick. Open water along the coast of Novaya Zemlya allowed the expedition to sail northwards until, on August 8th, they ran into ice so thick that the ship could not move even under its auxiliary

Fig. 27. Tegetthoff *and* Isbjørn *amid the ice, summer, 1872 (from Payer 1876).*

steam power. The ice shifted and moved from day to day, and allowed *Tegetthoff* to slowly crab its way northwards.

The crew received a welcome if somewhat embarrassing reprieve on August 12th, when out of the mist the creaky *Isbjørn* appeared with the maligned Captain Kjeldsen at the helm. He was sailing from Svalbard with yet another Austro-Hungarian charter, this time Weyprecht and Payer's expedition patron, Count Wilczek. When they came upon *Tegetthoff, Isbjørn* was en route to lay in a relief cache for Weyprecht and Payer at Cape Nassau on Novaya Zemlya. Together they sailed northward, and together on August 18th they celebrated the birthday of the Austro-Hungarian emperor and king, Franz Josef I. Two days later, and not a moment too soon, *Isbjørn* parted company with *Tegetthoff.*

Weyprecht and Payer continued on their meandering way through the ice northwards but their progress soon came to a halt. *Tegetthoff* was completely hemmed in by ice and, as Payer later wrote, the ship would never again see open water. On Christmas Eve, even as they were sharing out presents brought for the occasion and enjoying the bottles of wine that had not frozen solid, Weyprecht and Payer could only look back on "a year of disappointments."[18]

The outlook was bleak indeed. The ship was trapped in the middle of nowhere and the only recourse was to wait on the summer of 1873. The crew read a lot: Milton, Shakespeare, a collection of romance novels, and, according to Payer, a run of Petermann's *Mittheilungen*, which seems to have been last on the reading list.

Across the mess table spilled a Berlitz of languages:

> The clatter of the tongues of so many vehement Southerners was like the sound made by the smaller wheels of a machine, while the naïve simplicity of the grave Tyrolese came in between times, like the steady beat of a great cog-wheel. It was a miniature reproduction of the confusion of tongues of Babel. Lusina speaks Italian to the occupants of the officers' cabin, English with Carlsen, French with Dr. Kepes, and Slavonic with the crew. Carlsen has adopted for the 'Slavonians,' as he called our people, a kind of speech compounded of Norwegian, English, German, Italian, and Slavonic. The crew, with the exception of the two Italians, speaks Slavonic among themselves.[19]

When the summer of 1873 finally arrived, it carried no hope. The ship remained stuck fast. Then, at midday on August 30th, just as the men despaired of another winter trapped in the ice, they received a jolt of excitement. *Tegetthoff* was drifting in a seemingly perpetual and disorienting mist at 79°43′ N, 59°33′ E, when for a moment the mist lifted to reveal a startling land of Alpine peaks and enormous glaciers. All of the men shook off their torpor and raced on deck to see the miracle with their own eyes.

Even trapped as they were and for the moment unable to reach the new land before them, they now knew that, no matter what else happened, the expedition would be considered a success. As Payer writes: "For thousands of years this land had lain buried from the knowledge of men, and now its discovery had fallen into the lap of a small band, themselves almost lost to the world, who far from their home remembered the homage due to their sovereign, and gave to the newly-discovered territory the name Kaiser Franz-Josef's Land."[20]

The dramatic headland they had seen Weyprecht and Payer named Cape Tegetthoff after the ship, but for a month the new land remained tantalizingly out of their grasp as northerly winds blew *Tegetthoff* away from its namesake point. The wind turned in late September, pushing the ship to its farthest north at lat. 79°58′ N, where the crew spied a small piece of land they named Hochstetter Island. Six of the men made a mad rush at the island in the hopes of stepping ashore before the ice pushed them too far away. Halfway there, after running and crawling across broken floes, a heavy mist descended and threatened to cut them off from the ship, to which the were forced to reluctantly return. Throughout the fall, as *Tegetthoff* remained fast in the ice, the unexplored Franz Josef Land remained out of reach. As if taunting the men, the high cliffs were illuminated by the aurora.

Finally, on November 1st, 1873, the ship drifted close enough to an island that the men felt safe in making a dash for solid land. Scrambling over barriers of ice fifty feet high, they raced ashore. There, the men stood at last upon "a land more desolate [than any] on earth…. [yet] To us it was paradise; and this paradise we called Wilczek Island."[21] The men rejoiced even in the island's utter bleakness. It was, after all, a totally new experience after months of boredom on board *Tegetthoff.* "We had become exceedingly sensitive to new impressions," writes Payer, and so the following day they trooped back to the crenellated shore to build a cairn around a pole and place a flag atop it.[22] The Norwegian crew member Carlsen was so taken with the solemnity of the occasion that beneath his fur coat he made sure to wear the medal from his decoration with the Royal Norwegian Order of St. Olav.

On November 6th, another flying expedition brought the men to the northwest corner of Wilczek Island. From there they could see larger landmasses to the north. Throughout the winter that followed, Payer contented himself with frequent visits to the nearby island, all the while laying plans for a sledge expedition into the country to the north as soon as conditions allowed in the spring. In February, Weyprecht and Payer concluded that the ship would have to be abandoned as soon as they concluded the sledging expedition. The men would then attempt to escape through the ice pack in the ship's small boats.

Was the land to the north a continent-sized landmass, an island split by glaciers, or a group of islands? It certainly offered at least the possibility that Petermann had been correct, that a northwards-setting landmass could take one all the way to the North Pole. Payer set out to answer these questions with a party of six men and three dogs on March 10th, 1874. In two hours they had reached the southwest corner of Wilczek Island. The temperatures hovered around –14° F. Payer set a course toward what turned out to be two islands.

In discovering what would become a tangled paradise for Arctic nomenclature, he began a series of generous nods towards the international fraternity of polar explorers. The first island he named for Charles Francis Hall and the second for the Royal Navy officer and polar explorer Francis Leopold McClintock, the man who had finally answered the Franklin mystery with the *Fox* expedition. The fjord adjacent to Cape Tegetthoff they named for Adolf Erik Nordenskiöld. Another small island was named for Koldewey, and then a broad sound after the imposing secretary of the Royal Geographic Society and itinerant supporter of polar exploration, Clements Markham.

From the tallest point on Hall Island, Payer could see more mountainous land to the north, a glacial landscape split by a large body of water he named Austria Sound. It was increasingly clear that they had discovered an Arctic land at least as large as Svalbard, and the urge to learn its extent was overpowering. The lands to the east Payer named, again, after Count Wilczek, perhaps fearing that the small Wilczek Island the expedition had originally discovered simply did not match the Count's generosity. The land to the west they named after another expedition patron, Count Ödön Zichy. They returned to the ship from this preliminary reconnaissance on March 15th, in time to hear the final wheezing breaths of the ship's engineer, Otto Krisch, who died from scurvy the following day and became the first human to be buried in Franz Josef Land, on a high cliff on the southern edge of Wilczek Island.

With his experiences from his week of explorations, Payer drew up a plan for an extended foray northwards. He left the ship again – this time with a party of seven men and three dogs – on March 26th, with the thermometer reading –6° F. By April 1st, Payer's team was running up the ice-filled Austria Sound, along the coast of Wilczek Land on their right and Zichy Land on their left. A small island at lat. 81° N Payer named for Elisha Kent Kane, while a small cluster of islands was named for Kane's compatriot and fellow Pennsylvanian, Isaac Israel Hayes.

By April 5th, they were nearing the northern terminus of the scatter of islands along Austria Sound. It was a bleak prospect. Ascending the highest point of Becker Island, Payer recorded a scene to the north of "indescribable waste, more utterly desolate than anything I had ever seen, even in the Arctic regions.... The whole, at a distance, presented the appearance of a chaos of icehills and icebergs scattered over a frozen sea."[23]

Four days later, at Hohenlohe Island, Payer divided his small band in order to mount a flying expedition to a seemingly large landmass to the north, which he named Crown Prince Rudolf's Land. With three companions and two dogs, Payer started off with enough supplies to last eight days. He soon realized that Rudolf's Land was in fact another island, the whole western coast of which was alive with flocks of little auks. Passing a cape that Payer named for the birds, he came into an indentation in the western shoreline that he named Teplitz Bay after his hometown.

On April 12th, Payer reached the northern terminus of his march, a spot on the northern edge of Rudolf Island he named Cape Fligely after an Austrian general and geographer, August von Fligely. From this impossibly bleak spot, Payer's eyes deceived him and he made a massive geographic error. He thought he saw an extension of Rudolf Island to the northeast, toward a cape he named after Sherard Osborne, another prominent Royal Navy figure from the search for Franklin. Payer then thought he saw a series of blue mountain ranges even further to the north, the first he named King Oscar Land. The second chimera he named, appropriately, Petermann Land, and there is every chance that Payer's judgment was affected by what Petermann had led him to believe *ought* to be there, in a theoretic way. The furthest point of "Petermann Land" Payer named Cape Vienna, "in testimony of the interest which Austria's capital has ever shown in geographical science, and in gratitude for the sympathy with which she followed our wanderings, and finally rewarded our humble merits."[24]

As Payer stood atop the icy, stony soil of Cape Fligely, gazing north-wards, he knew he was experiencing the most important day of his life. His small band had reached the limits of their supplies, and this was for-tunate indeed. While Payer was irritated that all the points he thought he had counted north of Cape Fligely were out of his reach, every one of them was in fact a mirage. Had they attempted to march further north, they would all soon be cut off from land on a lethal sea of shifting ice. In the event, they had to be content with planting the Austro-Hungarian flag and leaving behind a message testifying to their achievement, a feat that – Nansen and Johansen coming from the north notwithstanding – would not be bested in Franz Josef Land for thirty years, and then only by a few steps. Then they turned for the south.

The *Tegetthoff,* if she was still floating, lay in the ice 160 nautical miles due south of Cape Fligely. Even suffering from exhaustion and snow-blindness and with their dogs played out, with their sledge fractured and split and the snow turned to spring slush, the men were sky high. And despite the misidentification of lands north of Rudolf Island, they had every reason to feel immense pride in what they had accomplished. As Payer writes: "The utter loneliness of our position could not suppress the satisfaction we felt."[25]

Ten days later, they had regained the ship. With the ship still im-mobile in the ice and with the snow still firm, the indefatigable Payer immediately set out on a third sledge journey, as he sought to fill in some of the archipelago's geographic details to the west of Wilczek Island. On April 30th, Payer and three men and two dogs set out for one final week of exploring.

Payer and his companions sledged to the island he had named for Mc-Clintock and climbed to the highest peak at Cape Brünn. From there they surveyed the land that fell off toward the northwest. These lands included the southern reaches of Zichy Land and they included a Matterhorn-like mountain Payer named Richthofen Peak. It was so impressive that Payer wildly overestimated its altitude as 5,000 feet. Payer desperately wanted to explore this vast land "intersected by fjords and covered with glaciers" since he was sure that it must extend close to mythical Gillis' Land and then to Svalbard.[26] His guesses in this direction were as conservative as his estimations of "Petermann Land" had been generous. He suspected that

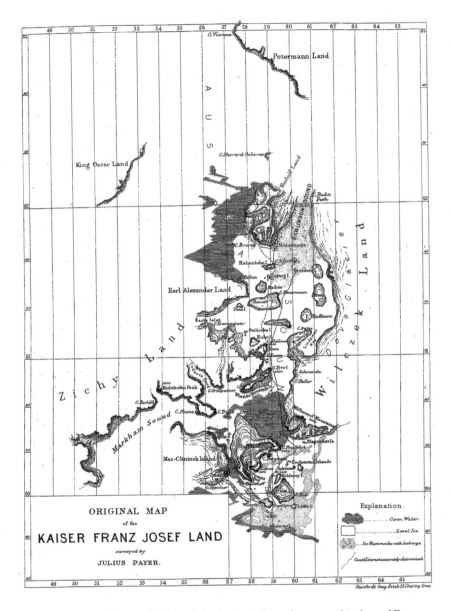

Fig. 28. *The state of geographic knowledge in 1875 about the new archipelago of Franz Josef Land (from Payer 1877).*

Franz Josef Land extended westwards to long. 50° E, maybe even as far as 48° E. What he could not know, from his cold perch atop Cape Brünn, was that the archipelago extended all the way to long. 45° E, a fact that Leigh Smith would demonstrate six years later when he cruised to the islands on board his oceanographic research vessel *Eira*.

Payer and his small team reached *Tegetthoff* again on May 3rd after sledging 450 miles through entirely new lands. The view to the south, however, was still dismal. *Tegetthoff* was still stuck fast and not going anywhere. There was only one thing to do and that was to abandon the ship to its fate. Payer made copies of all his records and put them in a sealed trunk. Weyprecht took the ship's logbooks and the originals of Payer's hard-won records and placed them in a tin-lined sea chest, and then soldered it closed. The chest is now in Vienna.

The men were divided into three groups, with three small boats and three sledges between them. On May 20th, 1874 – which, as Payer with his excellent knowledge of polar history noted, was the same day Elisha Kent Kane abandoned his ship in 1855 – they left the *Tegetthoff* to its fate. A week later, during which time they crawled southwards as little as half a mile a day, they reached an islet Payer named Lamont Island – likely for Leigh Smith's wealthy Scottish contemporary and Arctic sailor. But there the progress ceased. Two months later, they could still see Cape Tegetthoff behind them and Payer calculated that in all that time they had advanced less than ten miles from the ship.

Only by mid-August had the men advanced far enough so they could hear the sound of the open ocean beating against the line of the pack ice. Launching into the swell, they shaped a course for the cache of supplies that Count Wilczek on board *Isbjørn* had left for them at Novaya Zemlya. On August 17th, 1874, the men watched the sun set for the first time that summer and, the next day, they stood at last upon solid ground. They located a small freshwater pond and bathed. Soon after, sailing southwards, they came upon two Russian schooners. After producing official letters that required any inhabitant of the Russian Empire to assist them, Weyprecht and Payer and their men received their first proper food in the ninety-six days since they had left the doomed *Tegetthoff* behind.

News of the triumphal Austro-Hungarian expedition quickly found its way to the savants of the Royal Geographic Society. Clements Markham included a long chapter on the discoveries and implications of the expedition in his 1875 history-*cum*-British-national-polar-expedition-promotional *The Threshold of the Unknown Regions*. An Arctic landmass of potentially massive proportions had just been discovered – Payer himself even hinted strongly that it held every possibility of reaching to the pole itself, since to him "Petermann Land" appeared to extend at least to the 83rd parallel.

The Austro-Hungarian success built momentum for a new national expedition in the United Kingdom. Britain had not mounted a major expedition to the Arctic in thirty years, despite the more or less constant agitation for one by the RGS. On October 24, 1874, Henry Rawlinson, President of the RGS, sent a letter to Prime Minister Benjamin Disraeli, pointing out Weyprecht and Payer's success and asking after the status of the Society's 1873 application for a new polar expedition.

A report from the Hydrographer of the Royal Navy for Parliament pointed out that the government had organized six polar expeditions between Phipps in 1773 and Franklin in 1845. After 1848, another fourteen expeditions, give or take, were sent after Franklin, and once they had learned "of the fate of Franklin's expedition in 1859, Great Britain withdrew from the field of Arctic research. Not so other nations; emulous of the knowledge so honourably gained by British enterprise...."[27]

Even so, and despite the success of the Austro-Hungarian expedition, no nation had yet to best Parry's 1827 mark. And because Payer's report was completely unfavorable to the operations of large naval vessels in the pack ice of Franz Josef Land, the Admiralty chose to put its faith in the musical sound of open water Kane heard north of Smith Sound between Ellesmere Island and Greenland, as well as a description from Charles Francis Hall's crew, which noted that Hall's *Polaris* had sailed through an ice-free Smith Sound all the way to lat. 82°16′ N.

All that was required to successfully push through Smith Sound to the North Pole was the application of steam power to whaling vessels, vessels manned by competent Royal Navy tars and not the "undisciplined crews" employed by the foreigners, especially the Americans.[28] The formula was simple: Smith South + steam power + Royal Navy crews = North Pole. You could have the whole lot for about £56,000. The port of Dundee, with its jute mills and their reliance on whale oil from the Arctic, was all for it. So were the other Scottish and Yorkshire ports of Peterhead, Aberdeen, Whitby, and Hull, which promised to offer up their "most intelligent among the experienced mates, harpooners, and foremast men.... Take this course," the report confidently concluded, "and the safety of a Government expedition is thus assured."[29]

The report dismissed the efficacy and efficiency of mere private attempts at polar exploration, which were invariably "undertaken with totally inadequate means and resources...." Only a national expedition would as a matter of course concern itself not only with the geographic and hydrographic problem of the North Pole but with gathering the latest data regarding Arctic geodesy, meteorology, magnetism and physics, geology, botany, and zoology. Nor was anthropology forgotten: "The condition of an isolated tribe, deprived of the use of wood or metals, and dependent entirely upon bone and stone for the construction of all implements and utensils, is also a subject of study with reference to the condition of mankind in the Stone age of the world...."[30]

With a sanguine disregard of why the British government had not launched an Arctic expedition in a generation – and no doubt to the amusement of men like James Lamont – the report concluded that:

> Under Dr. Kane and Dr. Hayes and Captain Hall, the sufferings, the hardships, insubordination, and small results, in comparison with the expenditure and expectations of these American private expeditions, fully confirm the opinions of all British Arctic authorities as to the necessity for the officers and seamen in such expeditions being always under naval control and discipline, and strengthen us in saying that no amount of private enterprise, enthusiasm, or funds will justify the risk to lives or the success of an expedition, such as the Royal Geographic Society contemplates, except under Government auspices and Government control. That conceded, the safety of an expedition is comparatively guaranteed....[31] (Admiralty Arctic Report 1875: 14)

Faced with such a barrage, and with an array of Germany, Austria-Hungary, Sweden, and the United States all challenging the British sense of priority in the Arctic, the government finally relented. Disraeli wrote to Rawlinson on November 17th, 1874, that he would have his polar expedition through Smith Sound. Two vessels, *Alert* and *Discovery*, both five times the displacement of *Tegetthoff*, were fitted for contact with ice. Placed under the command of George Nares and Henry Stephenson, the ships and their crew of 120 men left England the following May.

Nares succeeded in besting Hall's farthest north for a ship, reaching lat. 82°27′ N, before placing *Alert* into a winter harbor. There, surrounded by firm ice and with little indication of open water anywhere to the north, Nares spent the winter nurturing extreme doubts as to the existence of an open polar sea. The following spring, to settle the matter, Nares organized a sledge expedition under the leadership of twenty-five-year-old Albert Markham, younger cousin of Clements. Half a century after Parry, Albert Markham led a group of fifty-three officers and men in dragging two heavy boats mounted upon sledges towards the North Pole.

Compared with Parry's difficult experience, Markham's sledge expedition was a living nightmare. Clothing, food, gear, all were substandard, and the toll on the men was rapid. By the time the sledge expedition managed to crawl back to *Alert*, only nine of the original party were fit for duty. The rest were suffering from the accumulations of snow-blindness, scurvy, frostbite, and malnutrition. The ships were extricated from the ice later that summer and the 'guaranteed' government expedition beat a blessed retreat back to Portsmouth.

The failure of the Nares expedition was so discouraging to the Royal Navy that it turned away from the North Pole for nearly a century, until the arrival at that very spot of the nuclear submarine HMS *Dreadnought* in 1971. But the exploration of the poles was not abandoned altogether. By the end of the nineteenth century, again largely at the instigation of Clements Markham, the Royal Navy would begin dragging their heavy sledges towards the South Pole, leaving several more sailors and a soldier dead on the ice. But after the return of Nares, British exploration of the Arctic would be left to the private explorer.

One of those private explorers was none other than James Lamont, who by 1876 had become James Lamont, F.G.S., F.R.G.S. In that year he published his second volume of Arctic hunting and scientific banter, *Yachting in the Arctic Seas*. Subtitled *Notes of Five Voyages of Sport and*

Discovery in the Neighborhood of Spitzbergen and Novaya Zemlya, the book was designed not only to document his explorations in the *Diana* but to "stimulate many men of leisure and means to continue the exploration" of the north.[32]

Making no secret of his views of the Government's evident bumbling, he remained a determined advocate for private exploration:

> A Government expedition may happen to hit off an open season, and will then accomplish a great deal. But any Government is with difficulty persuaded to increase the estimates for the mere discovery of valueless regions of sea and land; and it is only by the pressure of public opinion, headed by the Scientific Societies, that they are at last compelled to do something for the honour of the nation. Finally, after much writing in the newspapers, much agitation in the scientific world, and much contemptuous criticism of the opinions of whalers (who alone really know something about the matter), an Arctic expedition under Government auspices is resolved on. Double pay, liberal rations, and the chance of excitement, attract crowds of volunteers – a Royal personage or two wave their hands as the ships, gay with flags, weigh anchor – a great many guns are fired, and the nation for a year or two forgets all about the Arctic expedition.[33]

That Victorian naval explorers backed by the full weight of the British government could do no right has become a familiar refrain since the end of the (later) Heroic Era of polar exploration in the late nineteenth and early twentieth century. Fergus Fleming's description fits here. The Victorian explorer was, he writes, "a brave, patriotic chap, steadfast but daring, manly but emotional, confident but modest, willing to carry the banner of queen and country to the furthest reaches of the world; ready not only to face the void but to stare it down, and do so in blind, cheerful ignorance."[34]

For Lamont, the private explorer was a different breed altogether; he possessed "means, inclination, and courage to give this object ten or twelve years of his life" and absolutely no ties to the government of the United

Kingdom.[35] It is certainly possible that much of Lamont's venom toward government-sponsored exploration derived from his service as laird of the Lamont clan. He would have known all too well of that clan's destruction by the Campbells and its abandonment by the government during the civil wars of England two hundred years earlier. Even so, as if suddenly realizing his churlishness, he made clear that he was not impugning the massive British government *Alert* expedition that was underway even as he was writing his Arctic memoirs in 1875.

As if to prove his point, the next disastrous attempt on the North Pole was a quasi-governmental operation sponsored by a newspaper. In 1869, James Gordon Bennett, publisher of the *New York Herald*, had sent his reporter Henry Morton Stanley to Africa to locate the British missionary Dr. David Livingstone, a man many considered long dead. When Stanley found Livingstone, alive and well, in 1871, his dispatches from Africa triggered a rise in the circulation of the *Herald*, just as Bennett had hoped it would. Having found a formula for gaining readership for his news-paper, Bennett in succeeding years exploited it at every turn.

Bennett was even more fascinated with the Arctic than he was with Africa, having already sent two of his reporters on board a vessel that went to look for the survivors of Hall's expedition in 1873. Five years later, Bennett sent a reporter along with an American Geographic Society ex-pedition that went to the Canadian Arctic on a rumor that John Franklin's diary would be found on King William Island. No diaries were found, but the expedition did retrieve several relics and skeletal remains of Franklin sailors who had died on the island. Once again, *Herald* circulation re-ceived a boost from the stories published about these finds.

In 1879, Bennett sponsored his greatest venture in the Arctic, an at-tempt by U.S. Navy Captain George Washington DeLong to reach the Pole in a vessel called *Jeannette*, and named after Bennett's sister. DeLong and Bennett, like Weyprecht and Payer, were heavily influenced by the ideas of Petermann. Bennett thought that the way to reach Petermann's open water around the pole was through the Bering Strait separating Alaska from Russia. A warm Pacific Ocean current flowing north from Japan would carve a path north through the ice, and meet with the warm waters of the Gulf Stream, flowing north between Greenland and Sval-bard. Where these two currents met, at the top of the world, there, at long last, DeLong would find the Open Polar Sea. The captain and many of the U.S. Navy sailors who signed on to the expedition would die bitter deaths disproving this theory. That the U.S. Navy agreed to man the ship, while Bennett paid for the expedition and issued what amounted to orders to the U.S. Secretary of the Navy, speaks as well to the enormous power that a newspaper publisher could command when the subject was geographic exploration in the late nineteenth century.

At the same moment, Adolf Erik Nordenskiöld was searching for a Northeast Passage across the top of Russia. When a few months passed without word from him, Bennett decided that Nordenskiöld, like Livingstone, was in dire need of rescue, just as he had been in Svalbard in 1873 when Leigh Smith came to his rescue. In this scene, DeLong would play the part of Stanley and Leigh Smith.

DeLong sailed from San Francisco in the summer of 1879, but before the *Jeannette* even reached the Arctic, Nordenskiöld and his ship *Vega* broke through the ice and reached the Bering Sea. With no dramatic rescue to report, DeLong turned north towards the Pole and a search for Petermann's open sea.

Two months out from San Francisco, *Jeannette* became stuck in the ice north of the Siberian coast near the Lena Delta. After two years of drifting in this trap, the ice crushed DeLong's ship once and for all. He and his men took to their small boats and made a desperate retreat toward the Siberian coast. One of the three boats reached safety; one vanished with all hands; and DeLong's own small boat made it to shore where he and all but two of his men starved to death as they waited in vain for relief. To intensify the disaster, a U.S. Navy vessel sent to find DeLong, the steamer *Rodgers*, was itself abandoned after it burned while keeping winter quarters at St. Lawrence Bay, Siberia. Bennett had not solved the polar problem, but the dramatic publicity became oxygen for his newspapers.

Leigh Smith spent the second half of the 1870s as a witness to these cascades of incompetence. Combined with the Austro-Hungarian triumph in Franz Josef Land and Lamont's exhortations ringing in his very wealthy ears, these all set the scene for Leigh Smith's return to Arctic exploration in 1880. David Gray had written to him in the fall of 1876 with the wish that Leigh Smith would soon "have another chance of getting a ship and that you will try once more to get north if you do not receive favorable news from the Arctic expedition this month [the disastrous government-sponsored Nares expedition, which would return to England in November having fallen far short of the North Pole]. I think it would be well worth your trouble to try again."[36] Gray advised Leigh Smith that if the Peterhead-built Arctic vessel *Windward* came up for sale he would let him know.

In the summer of 1876, just as Lamont published his *Yachting in the Arctic Seas* and Nares' British Arctic Expedition limped homewards, Leigh Smith offered £4,500 for the vessel *Norvegen*, owned by the Deutsche Polar Schifffahrts Gesellschaft in Hamburg.[37] For unknown reasons the transaction did not come to pass and so Leigh Smith went back to the drawing board. The General wrote in his diary in early June that Leigh Smith had even traveled to Hamburg intent on buying the steamer, with which he wanted to explore the coast of Greenland.[38] But by the first week of July, he had changed his mind, evidently fearing he was being swindled.[39]

Other contacts would send letters to Leigh Smith whenever a potential vessel for Arctic exploration came onto the market. In 1877, Gray sent along a note that new engines installed on his *Eclipse* were giving more than nine knots and that he was ready "for a dash at the Pole should a favorable opportunity occur...."[40]

On March 8th, 1878, Leigh Smith suffered a badly cut left hand when a Hansom cab he was riding in overturned and his hand went through the window. It was many weeks before he was feeling up to receiving visitors or taking a draught of Bass beer with his lunch. When the General finally saw him in London in mid-April, Leigh Smith was surrounded by potted flowers sent him by his cousin Florence Nightingale.[41] The General's notes suggest that Leigh Smith may have suffered from a bacterial infection, if not typhus, following this injury, since he was forced back into bed throughout the summer of 1878. By August, the General found Leigh Smith increasingly impatient with his enforced confinement and "pining for sea air."[42]

Leigh Smith began to feel better again in early 1879, though he still had only limited use of his injured left hand. From his Gower Street townhome in London, he escorted his niece Mabel to several plays, including HMS *Pinafore* and *She Stoops to Conquer.*[43] By September he was in Glasgow looking at ships,[44] and in November contemplating another run for Parliament.[45] But the pain in his hand continued, until in October he finally despaired and had his wrist opened and the tendons cut. He told the General that "he was tired of no amendment in the usefulness of the limb."[46]

He was now fifty-one. With his body starting to betray him, he was beginning to see that the chances to get back to the Arctic and to do some meaningful work would only grow longer each year. After the operation, he made up his mind. Word spread quickly around the family at the end of the year. On New Year's Eve, 1879, the General records in his diary that Leigh Smith had decided to build his own ship for Arctic exploration.[47]

In the end, Leigh Smith had decided that a charter would not do, nor would the purchase of an existing vessel satisfy his requirements. What he needed was a purpose-built oceanographic research vessel, one built to his specific needs and based on his experiences with *Sampson* and *Diana*. The ship, he decided, would be constructed by a yard in the whaling port of Peterhead and supervised by his close Arctic confidant David Gray. It would not be a hand-me-down from one of his wealthy countrymen; it would be his and his alone. With the Royal Navy gone from the field and all the talk of national polar expeditions at an end, with Lamont content to manage his estates and Payer now working as an artist in Vienna, and with his injury healed, his time had come. The door to the north, maybe even to the North Pole itself, had opened for him once again and possibly for the final time.

6

EXPEDITION FOUR: FRANZ JOSEF LAND, 1880

Clements Markham, as secretary of the Royal Geographic Society, had aptly described Leigh Smith's approach to Arctic exploration at a meeting of the society on the evening of January 17, 1881. Leigh Smith, Markham intoned, had always believed that "discoveries are to be made, in the icy seas, by perseverance, and by watching for and promptly seizing opportunities."[1]

In the summer of 1880, this meant a plan to steam and sail across a wide swath of the northern seas while observing where openings in the ice might present themselves, and then trying to exploit these. It was the method Leigh Smith had used since the first voyage to Svalbard in 1871. Now, as a result of the vessel that took shape in a Peterhead shipyard over the winter of 1879/1880, he could realize his vision of scientific reconnaissance in the Arctic. Leigh Smith would finally have the Arctic exploration platform he had always desired.

North of Aberdeen, at the easternmost Scottish fishing port of Peterhead, he contracted with the firm of Stephen & Forbes to build a robust exploring vessel. The port had been a major shipbuilding area for the first half of the nineteenth century but by the time of Leigh Smith's order both whaling and the shipbuilding that enabled it were in permanent decline. In 1850, more than five hundred local carpenters had been employed in building ships for the one thousand men working the Greenland whaling grounds. David Gray's whaler *Active* had been built at Peterhead in 1853. By the time of Leigh Smith's first expedition to Svalbard, however, the Peterhead fleet that counted more than thirty vessels in 1857 was down to just eleven.[2]

Fig. 29. Clements Markham, ca. 1870s (courtesy of the Royal Geographic Society (RGS-IBG)).

A few sea hunters like John and David Gray and others tried to survive by pioneering the use of steam engines on their vessels and focusing their efforts on seal populations. The *Windward*, a three-masted vessel that would serve as supply vessel for the Jackson-Harmsworth in Franz Josef Land in the 1890s, was launched from the yard of Stephen & Forbes in Peterhead in 1860 and that very same summer killed over 5,000 seals off the coast of Greenland[3]

Windward was 118 feet long and constructed from oak, teak, and greenheart, its bows reinforced with iron. Steam engines that generated 30 horsepower to drive a single screw propeller were installed in 1866. In its general configuration, *Windward* can be seen as an early version of *Eira*, the three-masted, steam-equipped screw barquentine Stephen & Forbes built for Leigh Smith in the winter of 1879–80.[4]

At 360 tons and 125 feet, *Eira* was forty tons larger and about a bit longer than *Windward* but otherwise a very close copy. David Gray helped Leigh Smith draw up the specifications for *Eira* and likely acted as Leigh Smith's eyes at the Stephen & Forbes yard during the winter months when Leigh Smith was not present for the construction. The hull of the new ship was three feet thick, with the bows built out to an astonishing thickness of eight feet.

By early May, 1880, *Eira* was launched at Peterhead and towed to Aberdeen to have a 50 hp steam engine installed. David Gray's daughter did the honors of christening the new ship.[5] Using Buchan's estimate of the value of *Windward*, the cost of *Eira* would have been in the area of £10,000, or more than £780,000 in 2010 currency.[6] An 1881 note from Leigh Smith's agent in Peterhead, William Baxter, placed the fire insurance policy on *Eira* at £8,000.[7]

At the same time, according to the General, who lunched with him in London on May 4th, Leigh Smith was looking fit and had regained almost the full use of his injured hand.[8] And, as the General's diary makes plain, he was acting much as one might expect from a fifty-one-year-old man about to embark on a risky adventure. After the lunch in London, he gave the General a bottle of White Hermitage. He then handed his collection of *Wellington's Despatches* to his eighteen-year-old nephew Harry.[9] He gave to his brother Willy a rowboat that he had in Portsmouth, apparently expecting Willy to go to Portsmouth and row it back to Hastings.[10] He spoke of selling his estate at Glottenham; he was losing £2,000 a year by not having the value of the estate invested in the markets – a figure that must have stuck in a man who just spent £10,000 on his own research vessel.[11] He thought about breaking up his property at Scalands and selling it off piecemeal.[12]

By the end of May, preparations to get *Eira* underway were in full swing. Provisions were loaded for a voyage that was anticipated to last more than two years. On June 11th, 1880, Leigh Smith left London for Margate with W.J.A. Grant, a photographer with previous exploring experience who was tapped to record the expedition. At Margate, they boarded *Dobhran*, his cousin Valentine Smith's luxury steam yacht, and sailed for a rendezvous with *Eira* in Peterhead.

The day after their departure, his niece Mabel began a portrait of Leigh Smith, for a gallery of Arctic explorers being assembled by a relative of Lady Franklin's.[13] Another niece, twelve-year-old Milicent, sent her uncle a parting message that read: "I hope you will find the north pole, if there is such a place, for I don't quite see how anybody can know as nobody ever seems to have been there; and bring back the old man with the lantern who sits upon it for us to see."[14]

Leigh Smith and Grant found *Eira* "in a rather backward state ... carpenters and painters were still hard at work."[15] Grant did not think they could be away in less than a month, but in the end they were on their way on June 19th. As for their ultimate destination, Grant writes that he had no idea: "no one on board knew – not even Leigh Smith himself, for he wisely determined to be guided entirely by circumstances, and if the ice prevented him from getting far north, or finding anything fresh to do in one direction, he could then try somewhere else."[16]

Eira was launched from Peterhead with a crew of twenty-one. Besides Leigh Smith and Grant, there was William Neale, who joined the complement as surgeon. He would go on to act as a kind of colleague and majordomo for Leigh Smith for the rest of his life. Forty-two-year-old Captain William Lofley of Hull was *Eira*'s ice master and it was Lofley who hand-picked most of the crew, which included two mates, two engineers, and seventeen men. On June 20th, the ship called at Lerwick and took on board four Shetlanders who would be responsible for hunting as many whales on the voyage as possible.

The announced goal, as mentioned in a brief notice in *The Times* on June 23rd, was a voyage to Svalbard. First, Leigh Smith shaped a course toward Jan Mayen, which the expedition missed on account of fog. Continuing north by west, *Eira* attempted to close on the coast of Northeast Greenland but found the way blocked by a loose fringe of ice. From

Leigh Smith's notes, Markham estimated that *Eira* had steamed some 140 nautical miles through the ice for ten days without getting more than seventy nautical miles closer to the Greenland coast itself. Giving up the attempt to force a passage, the ship was veered off toward the northeast and Svalbard.

On July 11th, *Eira* met with two other vessels from Peterhead: David Gray's steam whaler *Eclipse* and John Gray's steam whaler *Hope*. The brothers related to Leigh Smith that ice was pressing down hard on the north coast of Svalbard and he would be well advised to explore in another direction. It was during this brief encounter that a photograph taken by Grant on the quarterdeck of *Eira* shows the cohort of owner/captains, David Gray, Leigh Smith, and John Gray, along with Neale. Then, standing somewhat awkwardly between Leigh Smith and John Gray, is a twenty-one-year-old medical student from the University of Edinburgh by the name of Arthur Conan Doyle. In the last year of his studies, Conan Doyle was serving that summer as surgeon on board the *Hope*. Within three years, Doyle would use his Arctic sailing experiences as the basis for a novel, *The Captain of the Polestar*, and in short order his medical practice would be overtaken by a new career as a writer.

Taking leave of his Peterhead colleagues, Leigh Smith directed *Eira* towards the northwest corner of Svalbard to have a look at the ice for himself. Going ashore at Smeerenburg on Amsterdamøya, he confirmed for himself what the Grays had told him: there would be little chance of exploring the northern coast of Svalbard in the summer of 1880. He and his companions walked over to a collection of whaler's graves and found the hallowed site in a state of disarray. Grant found the graves "in a most dismal appearance, for bones and skulls were strewn about in all directions, nearly all the coffins having been broken open."[17] But even in 1880, the centuries-old site had already gained a measure of historical recognition. Grant noted a granite historical marker brought to the site two years earlier by the Dutch exploring schooner *Willem Barents*, "and here it now stands in memory of the gallant men who had discovered Spitzbergen in 1596, and others who had died on this very spot."[18]

After a few days spent anchored in Magdalenefjorden, *Eira* moved off towards the south, rounding Sørkapp on July 31st. From here, Leigh Smith had a couple of options. He could have followed Lamont in hunting his

Fig. 30. On July 11, 1880, Eira meets up with the Gray brothers. Front row: David Gray (at helm), Leigh Smith, John Gray, and Dr. Neale leaning against the stay. Between Leigh Smith and John Gray is twenty-one-year-old University of Edinburgh medical student Arthur Conan Doyle (courtesy Hancox Archive).

way around Storfjorden or sailing directly east towards Novaya Zemlya. Instead he made a daring decision to follow the Austro-Hungarians, and see how *Eira*, a true steamship, would fare in an attempt to reach the new islands of Franz Josef Land.

After the experiences of Weyprecht and Payer, three other expeditions had attempted to reach the new lands they had discovered. In the summers of 1878 and 1879, a Dutch expedition in the *Willem Barents* and led by an officer named A. De Bruyne, had sailed across the Barents Sea towards the archipelago, getting close enough to sight it in the latter year. Albert Markham, sailing with Sir Henry Gore-Booth in the Norwegian schooner *Isbjörn*, got close enough to the islands to convince himself that a steam vessel could reach Franz Josef Land nearly every year, if the attempt was made late in the season, when a steamship would be able to

Fig. 31. Leigh Smith ashore at what appears to be Smeerenburgfjorden, Svalbard, in 1880. An apparently abandoned and pillaged small boat lies in the foreground (courtesy Hancox Archive).

penetrate the loose pack ice. *Eira* would be the first such vessel to test this proposition.

On August 6th, *Eira* met the ice again at about 77°10′ N, 40° E and commenced steaming along the edge of the pack. Two days later, the ship was made fast near an iceberg grounded in forty-eight fathoms. The soundings showed them that they were close to the coastal shelf of the new land. Leigh Smith attempted to force a way north, but a storm soon pushed the *Eira* southwards. It wasn't until early in the morning of the 14th, after the weather had moderated and *Eira* was steaming northeast-wards at about six knots in the 54th meridian east of Greenwich, that Leigh Smith saw Franz Josef Land for the first time.

It turned out to be a small island, and *Eira* was maneuvered in towards it. Their position was well west of the furthest western spot explored by the Austro-Hungarians, so the men knew that they were seeing entirely unknown lands for the very first time. That same afternoon, the ship was

Fig. 32. Eira *working through the ice, 1880 (courtesy Hancox Archive).*

made fast to coastal ice fixed to the island, which was later named after a Royal Navy officer and watercolor artist by the name of Captain Walter Waller May (1830–1896). W. W. May had served on two Franklin search expeditions before retiring from active service soon thereafter to take up painting full-time. He published a series of sketches from his Arctic expeditions and made a living illustrating the accounts of other explorers.[19] He did the same for Leigh Smith, producing some fine sketches of *Eira* maneuvering in and around the ice of Franz Josef Land for Clements Markham's account of the expedition in the *Proceedings of the Royal Geographical Society*. Markham, who was given over to habitual enthusiasm whenever a potential new route to the North Pole presented itself, was exultant: "Franz-Josef Land was reached! The problem was solved, and

Fig. 33. Skinning walrus off May Island, 1880 (courtesy Hancox Archive).

the route was proved to be easily navigable, which will surely lead future explorers to new and important discoveries in the far north."[20]

Leigh Smith and his crew had entered a world of huge, flat table bergs twice as tall as *Eira*'s masts. W.J.A. Grant, along with one of the Shetlanders, landed on the basalt rock of May Island and, picking their way around the driftwood on shore and the nests of ivory gulls on the cliffs, made the brief climb to its 61 m/200′ summit. From this vantage point, Grant had a view of *Eira* moored to the fast ice (ice formed along the shoreline) while, nearby, Leigh Smith, Captain Lofley, and Dr. Neale in the small boats maneuvered for clear shots at walrus.

More vitally, to the north, across a strait strewn with loose ice, lay another unknown island. This was later named for Sir Joseph Dalton Hooker (1817–1911), the director of the Royal Botanic Gardens at Kew and the closest confidante of Charles Darwin. Hooker, a fellow of the Royal

Society, had been the youngest crew member of the *Erebus* and *Terror* expedition to Antarctica in 1839–43 and, for the twenty years after 1865, director at Kew. After the expedition, it was Hooker who examined and classified the specimens of flora returned to London by the expedition.

Grant and his companion trapped seven of the cliffside gulls in hopes of returning them alive to the Zoological Gardens in London (only one survived the voyage), while Leigh Smith and his party killed seventeen walrus.

The following day, the loose ice closed in around the ship so Lofley quickly retreated ten nautical miles south in order to moor to a massive ice floe that was so large the spotter in the crow's nest could not see over the top of it. When conditions improved, *Eira* returned to the area of May Island, where another, longer island was discovered and named after Robert Etheridge (1819–1903), a paleontologist who had made a career out of identifying fossils from a succession of British expeditions and who became the president of the Geological Society of London the following year. The geological specimens returned by the expedition were turned over to Etheridge for analysis.

Leigh Smith, along with Grant, Neale, and a boatswain, landed on the island and climbed its summit, where they left a record of their arrival. Descending to the shore, the party watched as their small boat was carried away by the ice. They saw a way to intercept the boat by running along the edge of another floe. Hurrying along the ice, they caught the boat just as they were about to be stranded.

A snow squall blowing strongly from the east obscured visibility that night, but the following morning the skies cleared and the crew witnessed a berg being flipped over after a collision with an ice floe. It was a sharp reminder of the treacherous waters in which they were sailing. As Grant writes, at 4 a.m. they had to "shift our position to avoid being smashed up by a large flat berg against which our floe was driving."[21] At 10 a.m., *Eira* steamed around Etheridge Island and made for a point to the west that had been seen by the Dutch on September 7th during the previous summer and named Barents Hook (now Cape Barents).

Eira reached Barents Hook that same evening. From this point westwards, they would be sailing where no other expedition had ever explored. Pausing offshore, Leigh Smith and Grant left the ship and went ashore on

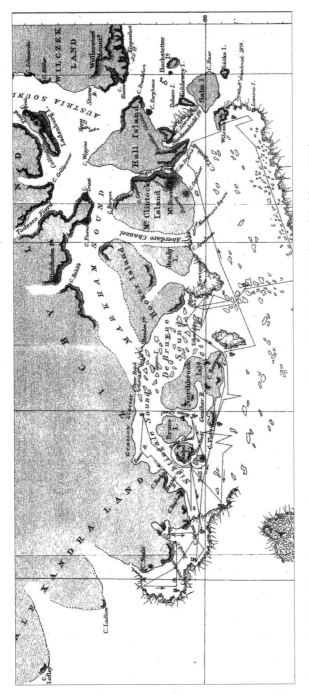

Fig. 34. Leigh Smith's explorations along the southern reaches of Franz Josef Land, 1880 (from Markham 1881).

Northbrook Island, walking westwards in a landscape of thousand-foot cliffs towering over low swampy land holding just enough soil to support a carpet of grasses and moss. Stopped by a glacial wall, the two returned to *Eira* and continued exploring westwards under sail. During this, the men on board ship were dredging the sea bottom, making collections of marine animals for the British Museum which would be studied by Albert Günther.

They came to the western end of the land at a point Leigh Smith named Cape Flora. Despite the presence of "luxuriant vegetation" in the form of grass and Arctic flowers, this spot is almost certainly named not for its greenery but after Leigh Smith's cousin Flora Smith, the sister of the extremely wealthy and generous Valentine Smith, though the possibility cannot be dismissed that the landscape and his cousin's name made for a happy coincidence.[22]

The same can also be posited for the small island with a hill on it that *Eira* passed on the 18th. The hill reminded the men of a bell, and afterwards it was so named, but it can also be seen as a play on the name of Leigh Smith's sister Bella.[23] Rounding the corner of Bell Island, *Eira* entered a fjord that Leigh Smith named Nightingale Sound after his famous cousin Florence. Further north on the western side of Nightingale Sound lay an enormous glacier which Leigh Smith named for "Uncle Joe" Gratton. On the back side of Bell Island he found a small harbor framed by Bell and a second small island named Mabel Island after his favored niece Amabel, daughter of the General and Bella. His discoveries in Franz Josef Land were becoming a true family affair.

They were at 80°4′ N, 48°40′ E, in a spot never before seen by human eyes. On the north side were high cliffs that formed a kind of natural amphitheater, and below this lay a wide flat plain more than a mile long. On the east was the dramatic visual landmark of high basaltic peaks, "running up like needles," the only peaks of their kind seen on the whole cruise from May and Etheridge islands.[24] There were plants growing in the soil accumulations at the bases of the cliffs and the cliffs themselves were full of nesting little auks. With a good holding ground in five to seven fathoms, it was a rare protected anchorage in a landscape especially hostile to ships. Leigh Smith named it Eira Harbour.

Fig. 35. In Leigh Smith's papers, this dramatic feature on Mabel Island was named 'Cathedral Point' (courtesy Hancox Archive).

From the deck of the harbor's namesake on the morning of the 20th, the men spied a mother polar bear with two cubs sniffing around a box that had been left on shore. Leigh Smith deployed one of the small boats to land a party to kill the mother while a second small boat waited off-shore in case any of the bears escaped the first party. As the first group approached, the bears made it to the water where the mother was shot and, as Clements Markham writes, "her two children were [doomed] to an aimless life of inactivity at the Zoological Gardens."[25] The mother was shot through the head and the small bears lassoed and towed by the small boats back to the ship. There they were imprisoned in casks and in retribution howled for the remainder of the expedition until being offloaded at Peterhead.

The following day, *Eira* got underway to explore north from Eira Harbour along Nightingale Sound. The chart of Franz Josef Land based on Leigh Smith's 1880 cruise and published with Clements Markham's article shows that north of Mabel Island they found another island. This was later named Bruce Island, likely after Henry Bruce, 1st Baron of Aberdare (1815–1895), who in 1881 was elected president of the RGS.

(The waterway separating McClintock and Brady islands was also named Aberdare Channel – Clements Markham was apparently taking no chances in his tributes to the hierarchy of the RGS.) Mabel and Bruce islands were separated by a waterway named Bates Channel, likely after the estimable English naturalist Henry Walter Bates (1825–1892).[26]

Rounding the northern point of Bruce Island, they found another channel, this one north of the land Leigh Smith had walked with Grant a week earlier. That land was now found to be an island and named for the 1st Earl of Northbrook, Thomas Baring (1826–1904).[27] Northbrook had previously served as president of the RGS and in 1881 was First Lord of the Admiralty. The channel north of Northbrook Island was named after the Dutchman De Bruyne, since this sound flowed southward towards Cape Barents, the point seen by De Bruyne's expedition a year earlier. A small island in De Bruyne Sound was named for Leigh Smith's old comrade from the 1873 expedition to Svalbard, the Reverend Alfred Edwin Eaton. A bay north of Cape Flora was named for the biologist Albert Günther.

To the north was Markham Sound, so named by the Austro-Hungarians seven years earlier. Markham Sound at the moment they reached it was impenetrable on account of ice, and Leigh Smith named the headlands on either side of the ice front after the home ports of many of his sailors: Dundee Point and, cleverly, Peter Head. Dundee Point was seen as the corner of Hooker Island, so they had now come in a circle from where they had started their explorations of the western reaches of Franz Josef Land.

While cruising off Gratton Glacier, an attempt was made to capture a young walrus for the zoological collections of England, but this failed when the mother attacked the small boat coming for her offspring. The mother was killed and the offspring dove to safety. The damaged small boat was sinking by the time it made its return to *Eira*.

The ship returned to Eira Harbour by sailing back down Nightingale Sound. The large territory to *Eira*'s starboard, the northern segment of which was dominated by Gratton Glacier, was named Alexandra Land after the Princess of Wales, Alexandra of Denmark (1844–1925). *Eira* tried to reach this land west of Eira Habour but the ship was soon stopped by ice. The whole coastline was dominated by a series of glaciers flowing down to the sea. At regular intervals, these glaciers were split by headlands of black basalt. These headlands were successively named after the Peterhead shipyard that had built *Eira*, as Leigh Smith added Cape Stephen and Cape Forbes to the map. These in turn were separated by two bays, Essen and Baxter, the former named for *Eira*'s chief engineer and the latter for Leigh Smith's agent in Peterhead, William Baxter. As Markham writes, the landscape was "wild and desolate in the extreme."[28]

Returning to Eira Harbour, W.J.A. Grant went ashore on the 22nd to make a collection of plants. The day, as he described it, was dull and misty, calm and warm.[29] He found nine species of flowering plants, mostly varieties of saxifrage, two grasses, and a lichen. None were new to the Arctic: all had been found in Greenland during previous expeditions and all but one seen in Novaya Zemlya. Grant also found a length of a ship's spar along a shoreline full of natural driftwood and, nearby, the vertebrae and jawbones of two whales. Climbing to the highest point above the harbor, at an altitude of over 305 m/1,000′, Grant took photographs of *Eira* anchored down in its namesake waters. On the 23rd, Leigh Smith circumnavigated the two islands that formed his natural harbor.

Returning to sea level, Grant collected samples of Cretaceous petrified wood and fossilized plants and, lying beneath these, 175-million-year-old fossils of extinct marine cephalopods of the Jurassic period called belemnites. From his vantage point, Grant had seen pack ice lying heavy to the south and southwest but none in the immediate area of the harbor. Leigh Smith took this as a chance to take *Eira* around the land to the west of Eira Harbour and attempt to define the western limits of Franz Josef Land, just as in 1871 he had discovered the eastern limits of Svalbard. *Eira* departed on the 24th and rounded a cape to the west and opposite of Bell Island that was named for Grant.[30]

From Cape Grant, *Eira* put on full steam westwards, with every nautical mile a new addition to the geography of the Arctic. Pushing aside a belt of loose ice, they gained a second headland that was named for John Crowther of Peterhead, *Eira*'s first mate.[31] Following along this coastline northwest for another twelve nautical miles, they came upon a third headland and named this for Dr. Neale.[32]

Eira was eventually stopped by ice late in the evening of the 24th, off a headland Leigh Smith named Cape Ludlow after his brother-in-law,

Fig. 36. Eira, *in likely the only photograph taken in its namesake harbor. The unmistakable Bell Island is to the left (courtesy Hancox Archive).*

the General. A distant headland, seen some forty nautical miles off to the northwest, was named for his captain and ice master, William Lofley.[33] They were at 80°19′ N, 44°52′ E. Sounding, they found no bottom at 175 fathoms. Unable to proceed further, Leigh Smith had come very close to linking his explorations in Nordaustlandet in 1871 with his new discoveries in the extreme west of Franz Josef Land in 1880. From Cape Barents, the spot seen by the Dutch under De Bruyne in 1879, Leigh Smith had come 110 nautical miles further westward along previously unknown territory. From the decks of *Eira*, he had seen another forty nautical miles further west, virtually the limit of the archipelago. It was a remarkably daring reconnaissance.

Soon after spotting Cape Lofley in the distance, the weather closed in, with driving snow and mist. Icebergs lay close nearby as the ship was moored to a floe drifting southwards. Early on the 25th, *Eira* was cast out

Fig. 37. Eira *in Franz Josef Land, 1880. This image shows the ice conditions encountered near the limits of* Eira's *exploration of the western reaches of Franz Josef Land (courtesy Hancox Archive).*

from the floe and maneuvered on a return course eastwards. En route they entered a large bay with a small island in it. In another of Leigh Smith's plays on familiar names, the island was named 'David' and the bay 'Gray' in tribute to his friend and colleague, the whaling master from Peterhead. *Eira* was moored to a land floe at the head of the newly discovered bay. Walrus and seals were in the waters, and Arctic fox and ivory gulls ashore. In the end, they would kill more than two dozen walrus and thirteen polar bears.

In Gray Bay, *Eira* was surrounded on all sides by glaciers, one of which, two miles off, suddenly split in a deafening series of cracks and thunderous booms. The whole bay became a mass of rolling waves of ice as *Eira* clung to her mooring at the head of the bay. This was followed by a two-day gale that blew in from the northwest, pinning the ship in Gray Bay. As soon as it lessened on the 28th, *Eira* steamed out of the bay, past two Greenland whales, and then eastwards towards the comparative safety of Eira Harbour.

Their 'home' harbor, however, was now full of ice, so they continued on to a small bay on the exposed southern coast of Northbrook Island where they could anchor and ride out the lingering storm. As soon as the gale subsided the following morning, they weighed anchor and continued eastwards to May and Etheridge islands and the larger McClintock Island, all of which were surrounded by ice. They reached Cape Tegetthoff on the morning of the 30th, and found their way to the east blocked by ice.

At Wilczek Island, where the *Tegetthoff* had been abandoned, Leigh Smith went ashore and searched for any trace of the abandoned Austro-Hungarian ship, but found only a can on the ground.[34] There was, on the other hand, open water, and with fresh thoughts of the *Tegetthoff* disaster in his mind, Leigh Smith took this as an omen. He ordered *Eira* out of Franz Josef Land waters so that they might make an attempt to reach Kong Karls Land in Svalbard before the rapidly changing weather forced them south for good.

Beginning on September 1st, *Eira* sailed south and west along the edge of the ice in hopes of finding a break in the pack ice where an approach to Kong Karls Land could be effected. By the 10th they were off Hopen, where the weather was "extreme fine and calm" as Grant noted. "Next morning we steamed round the south-west corner of the island, and then steered a northerly and afterwards a north-easterly course" but no opening beyond small bights in the ice could be found.[35]

The weather also made a turn for the worse, and so Leigh Smith shaped a course for Storfjorden, anchoring in Lamont's old Ginevra Bay on the 17th. Climbing a nearby hill, he spied Kong Karls Land in the distance, separated from them by a relatively ice-free sea. But the season was now too far advanced to make another attempt, so as soon as the weather cleared Leigh Smith decided to head for home.

Eira departed from Svalbard on the 22nd and two days later, in a heavy sea, anchored in Hammerfest in northern Norway. The bad weather forced the *Eira* aground, damaging her false keel. She was refloated with some difficulty and only after a passing Norwegian steamer, the *Nordstjerne*, pulled her free. From Hammerfest, Leigh Smith sent a telegram to Clements Markham at the RGS: "Reached Franz Josef Land Aug. 14.

Fig. 38. Eira *aground near Hammerfest, Norway, after the 1880 expedition (courtesy Hancox Archive).*

Explored land to the west as far as 45° E and 80°20′ N and sighted land from that point, about 40 miles N.W."[36] Markham was ebullient. "This is extremely satisfactory, quite confirming Captain [Albert] Markham's view that, with a good steamer, a very advanced position might be reached in that direction, and that it is the best route for future polar exploration."[37]

After temporary repairs at Hammerfest, *Eira* dropped anchor a few days later in Bodø, before leaving Norwegian waters altogether. The expedition arrived in the Shetlands on October 11th, where the Shetland contingent of the crew was discharged at Lerwick. The following day, *Eira* was back at Peterhead, where, *The Times* noted, it would remain until the new year, when Leigh Smith would again take up his explorations of the Arctic.[38]

Clements Markham was appropriately effusive. *Eira*'s first expedition was "the most important summer cruise that has ever been made in the

Arctic Regions. [It will] form a fresh starting-point for future Polar discovery...."[39] This was a radical shift in thinking for the influential Markham, long a champion of large, government-sponsored polar expeditions. Markham even drafted a confidential memorandum for the RGS Council, in which he argued that, with the success of the *Eira* expedition, the Council was now in a position "to advocate the despatch of a suitably equipped expedition for the purpose of reaching an advanced base near the north-western extremity of the Franz-Josef Archipelago."[40]

The massive extent of the glaciers indicated that Franz Josef Land was possibly even larger than suspected by Payer. The marine invertebrates collected in Franz Josef Land were sent to the British Museum. When they were studied and published by Edward J. Miers at the Natural History Museum, he announced a new species of sea spiders, *Pycnogonida*. Miers named it *Anomorhynchus Smithii* after its discoverer. Similar sea spiders had been found in other waters, but Leigh Smith had discovered one that was unique to the seas around Franz Josef Land.

W.J.A. Grant had made the first photographic record of the islands. These Leigh Smith had reproduced into albums to be given as gifts to the senior personnel of the expedition as well as to close family like the General, who made a note in his diary a week after *Eira*'s return to Peterhead. "Ben ... brought a dog to 64 [Gower Street]. 2 bears & a snowbird [ivory gulls captured by the expedition] arr'd on the 15th at the Zoo. Dr. N[eale] says they had a very happy time of it on the ice."[41]

Two days later, under the headline 'Mr. Leigh Smith's Arctic Expedition,' *The Times* carried a column that recapitulated the expedition and mentioned the delivery of the bird and the bears to the Zoological Gardens. The column also noted that Leigh Smith had discovered seven new small islands, along with four large islands, adding to the dozens of new Arctic places and place names he had discovered in Svalbard in 1871. "They are all covered with glaciers and snowfields, with bluff, black headlands on the southern exposures, whereon was vegetation."[42]

The evening of August 24th, 1880, when he stood on *Eira*'s deck and spied the western limits of Franz Josef Land, marked the high point of Leigh Smith's career as an explorer and, perhaps, of his life as well. Dodging the ice rather than confronting it, he had successfully explored further north and east in his new oceanographic research vessel than any other vessel in history. He had opened the door for further exploration northwards from his newly discovered natural harbors in Franz Josef Land.

Albert Markham was ecstatic. "I have only this moment heard of your grand success, and hasten to send you my most sincere and hearty congratulations on the result of your cruise." Markham was the only other Englishman who knew the challenges and risks of taking a vessel into Franz Josef Land waters. "It has quite confirmed my own views on the subject, namely that two years out of three a steamer may, with comparative ease, with of course those two virtues which all Arctic explorers ought to possess, namely patience and perserverance, reach Franz Josef Land."[43]

Unlike 1873, when Chermside wrote his account of Leigh Smith's expedition and it was rejected by the RGS's *Proceedings*, this time Clements Markham himself wrote up the results and and brought the finished article to Leigh Smith's townhouse on Gower Street in mid-November, 1880. The article's peer review by the Royal Navy's problematic polar explorer George Nares lasted all of one line: "This paper is original & should be printed in *Proceedings*."[44]

Markham would read the paper at a meeting of the Society on January 17th, 1881, a reading pushed back by a month when several officers arrived in London on leave with a new survey of Afghanistan and had to present their results at the December meeting.[45] Even with the additional time, Leigh Smith found himself indisposed when the time for meeting arrived. After the reading, George Nares rose to offer his support to further work in Franz Josef Land, and Robert Etheridge followed with a talk on the geological results, illustrating his lecture with fossils brought back by the expedition. Never one to pull a punch, Clements Markham was perturbed that Grant, too, did not show, as he was "hard at work shooting woodcocks with [Henry] Gore Booth."[46]

But these minor quibbles could not deter the fact that in less than ten years Leigh Smith had gone from unknown neophyte to Britain's essential Arctic explorer. The transformation was made complete when a letter arrived from Markham just three months after the January meeting, with congratulations on Leigh Smith's unanimous selection by the RGS Council to receive the Society's Gold Medal, "in recognition of your Arctic discoveries."[47] It would be fifteen years and take Fridtjof Nansen and the *Fram* to best the results of the 1880 *Eira* expedition.

7

EXPEDITION FIVE: FRANZ JOSEF LAND, 1881–1882

The results of *Eira*'s 1880 cruise likely surpassed even Leigh Smith's expectations. During the accounting of his stunning success at the Royal Geographic Society on the evening of Monday, January 17th, 1881, when he was nowhere to be found, the president of the Society, Henry Bruce, Lord Aberdare (who now had two features in Franz Josef Land named after him as a result of Leigh Smith's work) excused the explorer's absence on account of a "temporary indisposition" while noting that Leigh Smith was a man "of a singularly modest disposition, so much so that he had declined to write himself a narrative of his adventures."[1]

Sir George Nares rose after the talk to candidly admit that his own Arctic expedition had effectively closed the Smith Sound route to the pole and that Leigh Smith had very likely opened the route that would be taken in the future, via Eira Harbour in Franz Josef Land. Given the trouble encountered by Nares both in sailing and in trying to establish a secure base in the Smith Sound area, Leigh Smith's cruise to Franz Josef Land and the discovery of Eira Harbour were comparatively effortless. "The question now," Nares asked, "was, would it be possible to get there in future years."

"[I] think it [will] be," Nares answered himself. "But at the same time great caution was necessary in pronouncing judgment on other attempts. Even if Mr. Leigh Smith did not again start for that region, he was certain to have many followers in his footsteps, and if they did not prove so successful, no fault should be found with them. Ice navigation was not to be played with, and success was not always certain."[2]

Fig. 39. Eira *at Cape Crowther. One of W. W. May's sketches to illustrate Clements Markham's talk to the RGS in 1881 (courtesy Hancox Archive).*

Even with these wise cautions, the discovery of the protected maritime shelter of Eira Harbour especially excited Nares. "If a good base could be once established, expeditions might go on in confidence."[3] Leigh Smith's report on the presence of polar bear and walrus meant ready sources of meat, furs, skins, and rope, both for expeditions exploring towards the pole as well as for explorers cut off by ice and forced to overwinter. Bears also indicated the presence of the seals they hunted, another potential source of food for both dogs and men.

Robert Etheridge, president of the RGS (and another individual now with an island in the archipelago named for him), was at that moment attempting to classify the fossil collections returned by Leigh Smith. The fossil wood collected in Franz Josef Land appeared to be a species of pine from the Cretaceous period, and as such some 100 million years old. This new fossil data connected Franz Josef Land with primitive forests that once spanned much of the northern hemisphere.

The big news of the evening, however, was passed along in the discussions by Admiral Sir Erasmus Ommanney, one of the many retired officers with Arctic experience who were regulars at meetings of the RGS.

As interested as he was in the 1880 expedition, Ommanney was equally pleased that Leigh Smith now planned another expedition to Franz Josef Land in the summer of 1881. He then paid Leigh Smith the considerable compliment of expressing his conviction "that the name of Mr. Leigh Smith would be handed down to futurity as one of the great Polar explorers of the Victorian age."[4] Albert Markham was in no doubt of it when he wrote to Leigh Smith the previous November: "I do hope you will follow up your successes of this year, by the achievement of even a greater one next year.... I should like to have a good long talk with you about Franz Josef Land, and better still be your companion in your next voyage!"[5]

By the conclusion of the meeting, the considered opinion of the RGS was that future polar exploration should thereafter be prosecuted from two different directions: from the area of Smith Sound – which even thirty years after Kane's optimistic assessment was still luring explorers into its trap and would soon see the magnificent disaster of the Greely expedition; and from Leigh Smith's newfound Arctic staging grounds of Eira Harbour. With regards to the latter place, Etheridge's concluding remark was also the evening's most prescient: "Without wintering in Franz-Josef Land, it would be impossible to determine whether that route could be followed or not."[6] In due course – but certainly not by design – Leigh Smith would provide the RGS with an answer to that question.

Almost exactly two years later, at a meeting of the society on February 12th, 1883, Clements Markham again provided the written account of a Leigh Smith expedition to the Arctic. This time, however, it was Dr. Neale who stood at the podium to read Markham's words in the place of the explorer himself, who was once again indisposed and unable to attend. The RGS president remarked on how well-known Leigh Smith was to them all – in possession as he now was of the Society's gold medal for exploration – even though several of the members present had never met him personally or had ever seen him at a meeting of the Society. The stated reason for his current absence was an incapacitating cold.

If this struck the members as a bit odd, given that Leigh Smith had just survived one of the great Arctic adventures of all time, no one let on. Perhaps this was because, this time, the expedition to Franz Josef Land that Markham documented and Neale read equaled any adventure to that point in history of polar exploration. It would rival the escape of Nansen and Johansen in 1896 and the voyage of Shackleton and his men in the *James Caird* in 1916.

The expedition began, once again, in Peterhead. Leigh Smith boarded *Eira* at the far northeastern Scottish port on the 14th of June, 1881, along with a crew of twenty-four. His goal was to sail for Franz Josef Land, which he now knew to be a geographic maze. It was his intention to establish a formal base camp at Eira Harbour, and then to follow up the successful 1880 cruise by pushing *Eira* deeper into that maze, perhaps all the way to the North Pole.

It had been a long winter of refitting the ship at the Stephen & Forbes yard at Peterhead, with Leigh Smith supervising the operations by correspondence from London to William Baxter, his agent in the northern port. The 1880 expedition had attached Baxter's name to a bay in Alexandra Land, in between two capes named one for Stephen and the other for Forbes. A small bay further north along the coast had been named for *Eira*'s engineer, named Essen.

In the fall of 1880, Baxter found himself as stuck between these characters as was his namesake bay in Franz Josef Land. Baxter was none too pleased with the condition of *Eira* when Essen left the ship after the expedition. He also complained to Leigh Smith that Stephen & Forbes were not fulfilling their agreement to service the ship.[7] Baxter advised Leigh Smith not to pay Essen's engineer's gratuity. "The ship was left in most abominably bad order as [Captain] Lofley admits and I don't think you should throw away money to undeserving men."[8]

But Leigh Smith presumably paid off the inept and, according to Baxter, inebriated engineer. Whatever his faults, Essen had made enough of an impression to have his name attached to a bay in Franz Josef Land, and its geographic proximity just north of Baxter's own bay must have irked Baxter to no end. "Essen might have been civil when sober but he was a most careless and faithless servant to you," Baxter writes in January.[9]

Baxter went even further – and overstepped the mark – when it came to the results of the expedition. He was adamant that Leigh Smith take full credit for *Eira*'s success at the meeting of the RGS. He wrote that David Gray would even come south to London if Leigh Smith would put in an appearance at the January meeting.

[Gray] quite agrees with me that your achievements in the *Eira* should not be allowed to fall to the ground and kept concealed unless you yourself specially desired. Had Captain [Albert] Markham done half as much he would have proclaimed from the housetops. No fear of his candle being put under a bushel and you, well excuse the liberty I take in saying you do not give yourself justice unless you are represented at the annual meeting of this Society. Everyone admits the importance of the *Eira* cruise, its real work and great results and I for one will feel disappointed if the same is not put prominently before the Public & the world through the Meeting of the Geographical next month.[10]

Baxter seems to have realized that he might have taken too many liberties with these comments. His insult of Albert Markham came at the exact moment Markham was praising Leigh Smith to the skies and Markham's influential cousin Clements was writing up the results of *Eira*'s 1880 expedition for the *Geographical Journal*, as well as readying his talk before the January meeting of the RGS.

There was no response from Leigh Smith to Baxter's plea, although the impertinent letter must have brought forth many of the reasons why Leigh Smith instinctively recoiled from public appearances. When no reply was forthcoming even weeks later, Baxter dispatched a brief note with the "hope that I said nothing displeasing to you in my letter and that your silence is not in consequence of its contents."[11]

Leigh Smith's conspicuous absence from public acclaim was again on display the following spring, when the French Geographical Society voted him a medal for his work in the Arctic. As the General writes in his diary, Leigh Smith "begged to be permitted to decline the invitation of being present on the occasion." Leigh Smith did not give a reason to the society for his wish, but the General made it crystal clear: "he dreads such public ceremonials more than ice...."[12]

W.J.A. Grant had already sent his congratulations on the French decoration, remarking that he was "very glad that the French, at any rate, have come to the fore in the shape of a medal. I fancy the [Royal] Geographical [Society] must feel rather ashamed at letting a foreign country be the first to show any appreciation of what you have done: anyhow they will no doubt give you the Gold Medal after next cruise, whether it be successful or not."[13] And Grant entirely sympathized with Leigh Smith's reluctance to travel to France to receive the honor personally, writing that "nothing would induce me to read a paper in English, much less in French.... It is an awful grind writing those things."[14]

Whether or not spurred on by the French award, the Royal Geographical Society hastened to award its Patron's Medal to Leigh Smith at its anniversary meeting in the hall of the University of London on May 23rd, 1881. The gold medal was awarded "for important discoveries along the south coast of Franz-Josef Land, and for previous geographical work along the north-east land of Spitzbergen."[15] The award placed Leigh Smith in select company in the polar fraternity, alongside such lights as the Rosses, Robert McClure, Elisha Kent Kane, and Leopold McClintock. It also raised him alongside his contemporaries in the discovery and exploration of Svalbard and Franz Josef Land, men who had already received a gold medal from the society: August Petermann, A.E. Nordenskiöld, and Weyprecht and Payer.

Again, Leigh Smith searched for and found reasons not to be around when a high honor was bestowed upon him. Clements Markham accepted the medal on his behalf.

Eira had been dry-docked at Peterhead in mid-November, 1880. Lofley wrote to Leigh Smith that the grounding in Norway would require repairs to the ship's false keel, a new stem plate and repairs to her ice plates.[16] When Lofley got a look at the hull, the damage was not as bad as he had feared. "The main keel was a little chafed, so we have taken a piece out and will let a piece in before the false keel is put on, as we think it will be better in two pieces then putting one piece of thick false keel on. There is no other marks about the ships Hull [*sic*]. I see she will be better with several more ice plates as the ship strikes the ice bow down."[17] In addition to these repairs, Leigh Smith asked Lofley to have another water closet constructed in the forward part of the ship.

In between these routine repairs and throughout the winter and into the spring of 1881, Leigh Smith, Baxter, Lofley, Forbes, and David Gray were in continuous discussion over the shortening of *Eira*'s masts. They were shortened gradually, cut down in stages as the handling of the ship was tested. The bowsprit was left as it was. The final cut-downs were made and the modifications complete in late April. There was, as well, international interest in the design and construction of the *Eira*. The Dutch Royal Navy asked for the ship's specifications to see if a similar ship could be used in their Arctic work.

Throughout March and April, 1881, as Leigh Smith dodged the ceremonies that sought to decorate him, his ship was provisioned as it had been for the 1880 expedition, with hundreds of pounds of compressed beef and mutton to go with nearly half a ton of boiled beef and a ton and a half of vegetables in tins and a full complement of spirits. Besides the 200 tons of coal to be carried, there was only one more major item to load on board the ship, a custom-made storehouse. The storehouse was built by Forbes along the lines of similar huts placed in the Davis Straits by whalers in the event of a shipwreck and forced overwintering in Greenland or Baffin Island. Leigh Smith planned to erect the storehouse at Eira Harbour, the first permanent structure at a place he now clearly intended to demonstrate as the best base for all future British attempts to explore northwards from Franz Josef Land.

Part of that demonstration would revolve around the killing of as much wildlife as possible to show the riches of the new base camp. Lofley was arming *Eira* to the teeth and shared his strategy with Leigh Smith in April: "I am also getting six rockets the same as the Dundee ships uses for killing whales.... I think with the two whale boats and the two walrus boats we shall manage very well and be able to take a whale if we get the opportunity. I am getting seal clubs, and I think we should be better with another rifle or two – do you think we shall require any more Henry Cartridges there was only about two hundred used the last voyage."[18]

Baxter and Lofley also replaced Essen with a different chief engineer, an Aberdeen man by the name of William Robertson. This was a fortuitous hire on many levels, as Robertson possessed a long-held desire to visit the Arctic and when he finally returned home two years later wrote an extended account of the expedition. Though Robertson's account of the second *Eira* expedition would not see the light of day until the twenty-first century, it serves to confirm the impression of Leigh Smith as an even-tempered leader set on scientific exploration but not at the expense of the health of his crew.[19]

Robertson came on board *Eira* on June 9th, 1881, having signed for an Arctic exploration cruise of four months. He found the ship less a yacht than a kind of hybrid whaler, "a trim-built steamer of one hundred and eight tons register – fully rigged and equipped with all the boats required for whaling and walrus-hunting. It was propelled by a pair of engines of 50 NHR, with ample boiler power, a great consideration in vessels for Arctic travel."[20]

As the final preparations were made on board *Eira* in early June, and prior to his departure to meet the ship at Peterhead, Leigh Smith called on the General and his family. "He looks stout and well – but is getting grey and slightly bald," the General writes of the now-fifty-three-year-old man. He was looking for a place of peace and quiet before the expedition, so no dinner party was thrown for the suddenly well-known and decorated explorer. He stayed for two days, "full of kindness and geniality."[21] And then he was off.

On Tuesday, June 14th, *Eira* slipped from Peterhead Harbour, as Chief Engineer Robertson recalled, "amid ringing cheers from the crowds on the quays and jetties."[22] *Eira* fell in with the ice at 72°45′ N, 17°20′ E. By the end of June, the ship was off Novaya Zemlya, cruising along the edge of the ice, searching for an opening to the north. Finding no ice-free corridors, an attempt was made to pass through the Kara Straits and enter the Kara Sea, but this also failed.

Not until July 13th did an opening present itself at long. 46°08′ E, where *Eira* found some maneuvering room in an area of rotten ice. As they progressed north, the ice became thicker and many large floes were left in their wake, including a fifteen-nautical-mile-long behemoth that took the ship three hours to gain. When their passage was blocked, the crew broke out cotton gunpowder to break through.

Ten days of constant battle with the ice brought *Eira* to its destination. On July 23rd, Leigh Smith once again saw the Franz Josef Land cape he had named after the General. They had arrived back in Franz Josef Land along the southwestern shore of Alexandra Land. The coast to the west was open, so Leigh Smith wasted no time in exploring further west than he had been able to in 1880. They found that Cape Ludlow was indeed connected to Cape Lofley, the furthest point yet seen in Franz Josef Land. Between the two capes, then, was a bay about the same size as

Gray Bay. If they had been able to cruise just a few nautical miles further to the northwest, they would have reached the extreme western limits of Franz Josef Land, at a point Frederick Jackson would name Cape Mary Harmsworth during his polar expedition fifteen years later.[23]

Soon the ice floes around Cape Lofley began to hem in the ship, so Leigh Smith made for the southeast and the relative safety of Gray Bay. Inside the bay, the waters were calm and the sun was out. On shore, above the ship, a prehistoric raised beach could be seen, now nearly one hundred feet above sea level. Columns of basalt rose even higher, nearly one thousand feet above the bay. Flowers could be seen on shore. Nesting birds filled the bay-side cliffs. Neale counted thirteen separate species of birds, including Arctic terns, eider ducks, burgomeisters, kittiwakes, and a snowy owl.[24] Walrus lounged on nearby floes. It was a vision of an Arctic paradise, and the crew of *Eira* wasted no time in transforming it into a butcher shop.

As recounted by William Robertson, the walrus-hunting boats were silently launched and as silently rowed into position as near as possible to where the walrus lounged in the sun "on a piece of ice not larger than the floor of a middle-sized room.... The only vulnerable part of this animal's body, is the back of the head, and if you manage to plant a bullet there, it is instantly fatal. To attempt to shoot them, on any other part of the body or head, is only a waste of ammunition, the thickness of the skin being about an inch, besides the layer of blubber, on an average two inches."[25]

Seventeen walrus were immediately dispatched and the men began the grim work of cutting up the carcasses. The skin, blubber, and ivory tusks were removed and the remainder of the carcass left behind, hopefully to attract polar bears, which would then in turn be shot and skinned. The blubber was then removed from the skin, cut into small chunks, and stuffed into the holding tanks on board *Eira*. The skins were salted and rolled up into the hold and the tusks extracted from the skulls and boiled clean. With a brief excursion to the vicinity of nearby Cape Crowther, where another thirty-five walrus were killed, *Eira* remained in Gray Bay for over a week, until August 2nd. A visit to David Island resulted in the collection of more fossil wood.

Soon after, *Eira* left Gray Bay and steamed towards Eira Harbour, which Leigh Smith found blocked by ice. However, icebergs moving down

Nightingale Sound had cut paths through the fast ice and allowed *Eira* the maneuvering room to explore northwards. The open lanes of water soon closed, and *Eira* retreated to Bell Island on August 6th.

There, on the edges of Eira Harbour, the crew set to work erecting the large storehouse that had been specially prefabricated at the Stephen & Forbes yard in Peterhead. Christened 'Eira Lodge,' the crew celebrated its successful construction with a dinner on board its namesake ship followed by a concert and ball inside the hut itself, where "on that lone bleak spot our songs and choruses rang merrily out."[26] Dinners, concerts, and balls; Leigh Smith had successfully brought his upper-class idyll from the salons of London and the rolling countryside of East Sussex to the most remote corner of the high Arctic.

As *Eira* steamed around Mabel Island and through Bates Channel into Günther Bay on August 15th, the remarkable Victorian idyll was nearing its abrupt end. In thick weather, *Eira* steamed towards Cape Flora, which Robertson called "a better field for the collection of plants and fossils."[27] There, at 9 p.m. on the evening of the 16th, the ship was made fast to the fast ice about three nautical miles east of the cape. Strong breezes swept along the coastline and, on Wednesday, August 17th, the captain ominously notes in *Eira*'s logbook a "number of bergs in sight to the Eastward."[28]

Leigh Smith went ashore near Cape Flora, and then tried to find a path eastwards in the hope of locating any traces of the lost *Jeannette* expedition. The *Jeannette* had been crushed by the ice just as *Eira* was departing Peterhead for the 1881 expedition, and resolving the fate of the men of the *Jeannette* was very much on Leigh Smith's mind as he explored the islands of Franz Josef Land.

Finding the way blocked by ice, *Eira* continued to be moored to the fast ice east of Cape Flora, bows facing westwards, while Neale and Leigh Smith occupied several days in scouring the surrounding cliffs for fossils and plant specimens and the crew dredged the waters off the cape to bring up samples from the bottom sediments. The weather was calm, but there were definite hints of impending disaster. The captain's log on Friday, August 19th, notes the "pack ice close round the ship."[29] Apparently anticipating more of the same station-keeping, he roughed out the entries he expected to make for the 20th through the 22nd. But there were to be

Fig. 40. Eira *foundering, August 21, 1881, off Cape Flora, Franz Josef Land (courtesy Scott Polar Research Institute, University of Cambridge).*

no more entries and by the 22nd the *Eira* was at the bottom of the ocean just off Cape Flora.

On Sunday morning, August 21st, the calm and sunny weather was still holding. Over the course of several days, the fine weather and calm seas had lulled the crew into a false sense of security in their extremely exposed anchorage. When the morning tide turned, it brought with it the offshore ice. Quickly, *Eira* was pinned between the offshore ice and the fast ice to which it was moored.

The movement was so sudden that it took Lofley by surprise, and by the time he realized what was happening it was too late. As Robertson recalled, "some material part of the hull had been opened, which was beyond any pumping power we had to keep the bark afloat."[30] There was no chance to get the ship out of its trap. A grounded berg protected the hull from more damage for a short time, but when it suddenly gave way a plank of offshore ice went straight through the hull below the foremast.

The pumps were started but, as Robertson knew immediately, they would not be able to keep up with the incoming seawater. *Eira* heeled to port as all hands turned to removing everything they could from the ship before it went down. The men used the steam winch to extract hundreds of pounds of stores from the hold before seawater drowned the boilers. "Fortunately," writes Robertson, "the lockers on the cabin floor were full of stores, the aft-hold being in a few minutes filled with water. These places were soon emptied of everything, many willing hands passing the goods along on to the ice, sufficiently clear of the ship."[31]

Ice sheared off the jib-boom as the *Eira* settled into the sea. Everyone was ordered off the ship. For a few moments, the lower yards caught on the surface of the ice and righted the ship, by holding her masts above water. Then they, too, snapped upwards with a loud crack, to be followed by the topsail and topgallant yards. But it was four hours more before *Eira* slowly settled onto the bottom in about eleven fathoms of water. The depth was not even deep enough to contain the entire ship. The fore topmasts continued to show above the surface of the sea.

Looking despondently down through the crystal-clear Arctic waters, the men could see the ship lying on the bottom, almost as if in an aquarium. From this bizarre and helpless point of view, they could see no damage to the hull. But it hardly mattered now. Instead, the profound shock of realization hit the men that their only way home was now close enough to touch the tops of the masts, yet the ship itself was gone forever. "Each man looked at his neighbor, and the strained set looks on the faces, indicated that thoughts were busy, though tongues were silent."[32] As they gathered to look down at their former home, the feelings of the crew were unanimous: "She's awa.'"[33]

And with that, the stranded expedition now faced a winter in a place where no human had ever lived before. It was now that Leigh Smith had perhaps his finest hour. With the ship gone, some of the crew considered that it was now every man for himself. Leigh Smith was having none of it. "What is all this grumbling about I can do better without you than you without me; will you act just as if you were on board ship and I will do my best for you all."[34] With that, a cheer went up from the men and it was

Fig. 41. The sinking of the Eira, *August 21, 1881 (courtesy Scott Polar Research Institute, University of Cambridge).*

resolved that Leigh Smith was still in charge of the expedition and that his orders would still come down to the crew through the captain.

With the paramount problem of discipline overcome, the expedition still faced long odds. If they survived the winter, they would then need to find a way to get their small boats across several hundred nautical miles of broken surface ice and then across a large stretch of open ocean if they wanted to see England again. After "a very meager dinner, and a glass of grog," a tent was put up on the ice, consisting of spars and sails hurriedly cut away from the sinking ship.[35] A floor was made from planks found floating on the surface. The men lit a fire and made tea. Leigh Smith himself sat down on the ice and, for the first time in his Arctic explorations, began to make notes. "Then after a good supper, no one having eaten anything since breakfast, all turned in except those on watch."[36]

The outlook was daunting but far from hopeless. The ship had gone down so slowly that the men had salvaged nearly everything that could be gotten off. The haul was a large one: nearly a ton of cooked and compressed meats, over 3,000 pounds of vegetables, 288 small tins of consolidated soups, 80 pounds of biscuits and another 80 of tea, to go with a cask of sugar and a half cask of molasses, 14 pounds of corn flour, 200 tins of milk, 60 tins of cocoa milk, to go with 75 gallons of rum, 18 bottles of whiskey and another 18 of sherry, 12 bottles of gin and 12 of brandy, 60 bottles of beer and 72 bottles of champagne. Robertson notes as well that a flute, a whistle, a triangle, and a banjo were salvaged. To complete the band, someone soon made a drum.

With the exception of the cabin boy and Leigh Smith himself, all of the other twenty-three men smoked, so when a supply of tobacco was discovered that would allow each of them about a half-pound a month during the winter, there was general rejoicing. Unfortunately, the smoking pipes had gone down with the ship, so the men improvised and, as Robertson writes, "the smoker's ingenuity showed itself, and some of the pipes made were worthy of a place in a museum."[37]

Eira had been outfitted to survive two years in the Arctic. Since the wreck had occurred barely two months out of Peterhead, the ship was still stuffed with supplies. Moreover, they hadn't wrecked in a completely unknown or remote area; instead, the wreck occurred close to Cape Flora, along a shoreline they already knew well. Ice prevented the small boats from reaching the new storehouse at Eira Harbour but, all things considered, they were in comparatively good shape.

There were so many supplies lying about on the ice that Leigh Smith quickly marked all of the compressed meats, along with a quarter ton of soup and bullion, 16 gallons of rum, 12 pounds of tea, and 50 tins of milk for the sea journey they would have to make as soon as the ice began to move the following summer. To these supplies the crew added 800 pounds of cooked walrus meat. All of these would be placed in reserve and, if at all possible, none of it would be touched throughout the winter and instead saved for the escape in the small boats.[38]

The following morning, Monday, August 22nd, the crew rose early from their cold, uncomfortable berths on the ice to begin the process of transferring the tons of supplies lying about on the ice to the shore. Once everything was carried ashore using the small boats, the tent was taken down and then erected on land at a spot approximately three miles to the west and about twenty feet above sea level on the raised beach at Cape

Flora. All of the supplies had likewise to be lifted from the stony shore and carried up onto the raised beach, a back-breaking exercise.

Their new home was covered with moss and flowers. A small freshwater pond was nearby. Robertson thought the yellow flowers looked like buttercups. Two unlucky polar bears wandered past the strange scene and were promptly shot and killed and added to the survival stocks. On Tuesday, the men brought the remaining spars that could be salvaged from the ship and then proceeded to shoot as many guillemots, or looms as Leigh Smith called the ubiquitous birds, as they could.

Five boats had been saved from the wreck: two whale boats, two walrus boats, and a gig, the latter a long and narrow general work boat. On Wednesday, another attempt to reach Eira Harbour in the boats failed. There was now simply too much ice to get the small boats through. The men returned to Cape Flora and continued collecting driftwood and shooting Brünnich's guillemots.

Since the tent would not provide enough shelter to keep two dozen men alive much beyond the end of August – and in any case the wind at the exposed cape threatened to carry it off – a new hut was constructed at Cape Flora. The loose stones in the raised beach formed the walls of what Leigh Smith christened Flora Cottage. *Eira*'s spars and sails provided the frame of the roof as well as the roofing and the abundant turf could be used to chink up the walls. "Everything," writes Robertson, "was done under the personal supervision of our worthy commander, Mr. Smith."[39]

When finished, the interior of the new hut measured thirty-nine feet long by twelve feet wide by four and a half feet high. During the sixteen days required to build the hut, the men lived in the drafty, freezing tent. The winds were now so strong on the cape that in early September one of the boats was blown clear into the water, from which it was just barely rescued from being crushed in the ice. The men were accordingly extremely happy to occupy their new shelter. Eighteen of the crew moved into one end of the hut, while Leigh Smith, the doctor, and the ship's officers took over the other end. They were separated by a central kitchen that served also as the area for the polar bear watch.

As Robertson writes:

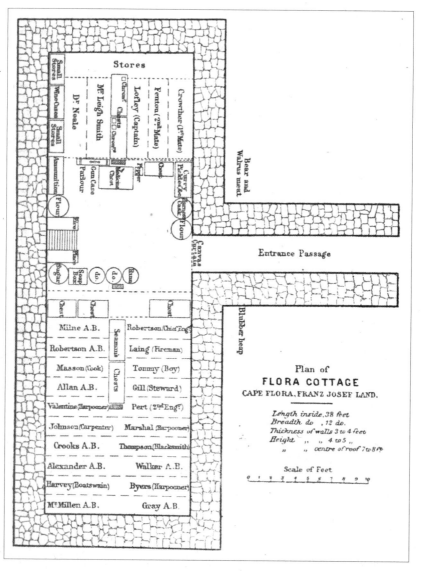

Fig. 42. A sketch of Flora Cottage (from Markham 1883).

It was lit by a sort of lamp called an 'Ekeema,' the construction of which consisted of a tin dish filled with blubber oil, canvas wicks giving the flame. It gave a fair light, but was exceedingly dirty, and afterwards a few small lamps were made, which were more useful for reading, card playing, mending cloths, etc. As there was no seating accommodation, everything had to be done in our beds. The kitchen was about twelve feet square, not a very large place to work in. We had two or three trials of stoves for cooking, but all were failures, being too small and too smoky.[40]

The stove eventually used was constructed from stones and turf blasted from the now-frozen ground with guncotton, and then fortified with planks and sheet iron. Besides the foodstuffs and boats saved from the ship, the men had also managed to salvage virtually all of their bedding, along with three chronometers, two clocks, two sextants, a thermometer and barometer, six rifles and two guns with ammunition, and the seaman's chests and a medicine chest. Surveying his predicament in early September, Leigh Smith knew that there were much worse ways to settle in for a winter at lat. 79°56′ N.

Leigh Smith instituted a daily regime designed to keep the men both well-fed and active throughout what promised to be a long and sunless winter. His writings during this period of shipwreck and excitement are some of his rare extended words to come down to us, and they reveal a man completely free of drama, at ease with routine, and content only when everyone had a satisfying daily ration of deep-fried dough, rum, and walrus stew:

We breakfasted at 8 A.M. and had about 10 lbs. of bear & walrus meat cut up small and made into soup with some vegetables, it was boiled for about 4 hours. Each man had about a pint of tea with sugar & milk. We dined at 12:30 and had about 15 lbs of bear & walrus meat boiled up with vegetables made into soup. Each man had a "dough boy" made with a ¼ lb of flour & boiled in the soup. Each man had a small glass of rum at 4 P.M. except on Saturdays when he had a large one at 6. We had tea at 5 P.M. which consists of 10 lbs of bear & walrus meat made into soup with vegetables and a pint of tea for each man. We used about 10 lbs of vegetables a day. When we could afford it we increased the quantity of bear & walrus meat. The meat was cut up and weighed or measured out in the afternoon. The water for cooking was got by melting ice or snow during the night. The ship's cook (one man, named Masson, along with a cook's mate, a boy of 16 from Peterhead "both capital fellows") did all the cooking and worked from six a.m. to six p.m. He was assisted by the cook's mate, who cut up the blubber, wood, etc. Captain Lofley made the "Dough-boys." The Doctor served out the food into 25 tins made from old provisions tins. The men's tins were handed in to them & they sat up in bed & eat their food like a lot of blackbirds in a nest. On Sunday morning at 9:30 the ship's bell rang for prayers. The Doctor officiated.[41]

The calculations here suggest that each man was taking in over a pound of stewed fresh meat and about three-quarters of a pound of vegetables a day. Combined with tea, milk, sugar, and rum, the fare was excellent and stands in stark contrast to the starvation and misery that would attend the last months of the U.S. Army's First International Polar Year expedition (1881–84). That sad episode, an attempt to reach the North Pole and conduct extensive scientific research led by U.S. Army Lieutenant Adolphus Greely, had just settled into its winter quarters on the north shore of Lady Franklin Bay on the northeastern coast of Ellesmere Island, a polar desert about two degrees further north than Cape Flora, when Leigh Smith and his companions were shipwrecked in Franz Josef Land.

The only writings from Leigh Smith himself that could be described as proper diary entries are contained in a tiny *Blackwood's Penny Pocket Book and Diary* for the year 1881.[42] It is a small daybook filled with advertisements for jewelry, hair restorer, soap, and washing machines, all evidence for the growing obsession with personal appearance and cleanliness, along with monthly mini-almanacs containing essential notations on British history, culture, and society. On June 14th, as *Eira* was readied to sail from Peterhead, Leigh Smith could be reminded that this was the same day that the Trinity law sittings began; on July 23rd, the day *Eira* made landfall in Franz Josef Land, it was the anniversary of the taking of

Fig. 43. 'The Hut' (Flora Cottage), one of four pencil sketches by Benjamin Leigh Smith made during the 1881–82 expedition (courtesy Scott Polar Research Institute, University of Cambridge).

'Ghuznee' [Ghazni] in 1839, during the First Anglo-Afghan War; and on August 21st, the day *Eira* was nipped by ice at Cape Flora, it was the tenth Sunday after Trinity.

Leigh Smith's own notations in the tiny book are both sparse and terse. A list of Her Majesty's Chief Officers of State shows a series of tick marks after some of the names, such as W. E. Gladstone, Lord Selborne, W. V. Harcourt, and J. G. Dodson. Leigh Smith could have been marking off people he had met, or were these people seen as possible names to be added to the nomenclature of Franz Josef Land in the event any new lands were discovered? In all the monthly almanacs, only December has a few days ticked off, these being December 12–17, the 16th being noted as the day the term ended at Leigh Smith's alma mater of Jesus College at Cambridge.

There are no notations in the daybook proper until May, when Leigh Smith writes down the occasional name and time, such as "Adamson, 7.30" on Tuesday, May 10th, or "Lady Belcher" on Wednesday, May 25th. On Tuesday, June 7th, Leigh Smith writes: "To be in Peterhead," followed by an "x" on Monday, June 13th, apparently to mark the anticipated day of sailing. There is nothing more until Friday, August 19th, when Leigh Smith writes: "Went on shore at Cape Flora with Dr. [Neale]" followed by "Went on shore with captain [Lofley] at C Flora" on Saturday and what looks to be "Ship lost" on Sunday, August 21st.

After this, Leigh Smith records the crew's progress in their winter survival in staccato phrases, for example:

August
22, Monday: "Getting things ashore. 2 bears."
23, Tuesday: "Killing looms. Bringing [indistinct] from ship."
24, Wednesday: "Killing looms. Getting fire wood."
25, Thursday: "Killing looms. Getting fire wood."
26, Friday: "Began house."
27, Saturday: "Building house."
28, Sunday: "Peat. 2 Seahorse."[43]

By the 29th, they had finished building the walls of the house, part of which had to be rebuilt during a snow storm the following day after it collapsed in the night. On September 1st, one of the small boats finally managed to thread a pathway through the ice and reach Eira Harbour, where more supplies were gathered up and brought to the new camp at Cape Flora, while the next day two other boats set out for more walrus and returned with "2 old 2 young." Four more walrus were killed on Saturday the 3rd. A two-day gale then came up from the west and north as the men gratefully moved into their new accommodations.

September
7, Wednesday: "Fine day"
8, Thursday: "Calm & Warm. 6 walrus, 1 bear. Plenty of water now to go south."
12, Monday: "Stacking wood. Flensing walrus."

The entry for Thursday the 8th carries some sentiment, with its hint of reproach that if only they still had *Eira* they would now be on their way home through excellent seas. After this, the days were noted only by the tempo of Arctic survival: when a bear was shot or ice was fetched or a new fireplace built, or whether it rained or snowed or the direction of the wind or whether the ice was in or out. Bob the dog was only allowed into the hut in the evening. As Robertson recalled, Bob would wait for Leigh Smith and Dr. Neale to retire, at which moment he would bolt to his favorite spot in the corner and sleep all night, usually with Tibs the kitten lying curled up on his back. In the morning he would be turned out once again.

On October 26th, Leigh Smith writes that the bay ice has broken up and then the next day he records that there is plenty of open water. But he did not trouble about the state of the sea at such a late date. He knew better than most that they could not have made a run for it after September. The next day, Friday, October 28th, his crew brought in five walrus killed on the edge of the ice; the following week they killed two more bears. The last bear seems to have been brought in on November 11th, and Leigh Smith's last entry is on Tuesday, November 29th, the same day his tiny daybook reminded him to "Order *Blackwood's Diary* for 1882."

Putting down his *Blackwood's*, Leigh Smith took to keeping a new 'logbook' for *Eira*. Perhaps he felt compelled to keep a faithful logbook since every time he emerged from the small hut he could see the tops of the masts of his ship sticking above the ice-covered waters, a bizarre and constant reminder of her presence as well as her absence. Captain Lofley had made the last proper journal entry on August 19th and now, three months later, Leigh Smith began what he called his "hut log." On November 28th, he recorded that the temperatures had actually risen, and were warmer than at the beginning of the month. The temperatures ranged from 17° to 51° F. The small hut with its twenty-five occupants plus a dog, a cat, and a canary suddenly felt too warm.

They were using about twelve pounds of coal each day to cook their food, and another two gallons of walrus blubber was burned to heat the hut. When the weather turned for the truly cold, the carpenter's saw had to be employed to cut the walrus and bear meat into pieces for the boiling pot. Robertson found the cold "intense. It seemed to pierce to the very core of life, compelling us to shelter ourselves as often as possible. No amount of exercise could overcome it, the natural heat of the body gradually evaporating."[44]

They had begun by using wood to do all the cooking, but the smoke threatened to choke the crew out of the hut when the fires were lit for breakfast. The decision to switch to coal was made when the wood supply ran low in early November. Always watching the levels of his supplies, Leigh Smith noted that they began using their coal supply for cooking on November 10th and at a regular rate would exhaust it in mid-January. There was a ton of blubber still on hand, and Leigh Smith thought it might last until March when, if worse came to worst, they could collect peat from the surrounding swampy ground.

By the end of November, the stove in the hut had to be rebuilt, as it had begun to fall down and was taking down the wall behind it. Walrus blubber was now used to melt ice for drinking water. But they had shot two bears, and on the first day of December, Leigh Smith writes confidently: "All well. No one has any doubt that we shall get home all right."[45]

At home in England, however, Leigh Smith's family and friends were increasingly desperate at the lack of news from the Arctic. In mid-September, the General noted in his diary that he had just ordered half a dozen copies of Clements Markham's pamphlet on the 1880 expedition: *The Voyage of the Eira*. The next day, at a moment when *Eira* had been at the bottom of the ocean for three weeks, he noted that Leigh Smith's sisters Nannie and Barbara had been in contact over whether they should ask Markham's opinion whether their brother's ship could be successful, given the conflicting accounts of the state of ice in the Arctic that summer. By the end of the month, the General writes plaintively that: "We look in the newspaper in vain for tidings of Ben & the *Eira*."[46]

A few days later, the General writes that he was starting to get anxious. When the anniversary of Leigh Smith's 1880 arrival at Lerwick passed on October 11th, the General was certain something had gone wrong: "He has I fear met with obstruction of some sort – either from the ice or from injury to the machinery of his vessel."[47]

By the end of October, when still no word had arrived from the north, the family and its influential friends moved into action. His cousin Valentine Smith, a man who was orders of magnitude wealthier than Leigh

Smith himself, began to make inquiries. He telegraphed Baxter in Peter-head for an informed opinion as to the chances for survival of *Eira* and her crew. Sir Henry Gore-Booth, an avid explorer who was also 5th Baronet of a family of landlords in Sligo in Ireland, offered to make a search for Leigh Smith the following summer. Gore-Booth had apparently made the pledge after a dinner with Leigh Smith in the spring of 1881.

Gore-Booth was true to his word. The General writes that Gore-Booth "wanted to go with Ben on his present voyage but failing in this he built up an ice-going vessel of his own."[48] Gore-Booth telegraphed Mack Giæver, an agent in Tromsø, to ask whether any of the walrus hunters had seen *Eira* around Svalbard or Novaya Zemlya over the course of the summer.

The absence of *Eira* was also beginning to make national news. The day after Gore-Booth's offer, the General noted a story in the *Athenaeum* remarking on the non-arrival of the ship. A few days later, Baxter's reply to Valentine Smith arrived and included the thoughts of David Gray. Gray believed that a vessel loaded with provisions should be sent to *Eira*'s relief the following spring. Willie Leigh Smith left his farm the next day to confer with Valentine Smith on the best way to proceed.

In the meantime, Gore-Booth received a reply from Tromsø. The only sea hunter to have seen *Eira* that summer was Captain Isak N. Isaksen of the *jakt Proven*. On June 30th, the *Proven* had come across *Eira* off Matochkin Shar, a strait that splits the Russian archipelago of Novaya Zemlya in two. Isaksen learned that, despite the condition of the ice, Leigh Smith intended to force his way northwards. At the place where the two vessels met, the ice was lying six miles off the coast; further north, it was lying even further offshore, some fifteen to twenty miles. When he had returned to the coast of Novaya Zemyla later in the summer, in early August, the ice had moved off and the coastline was clear. On August 16th, *Proven* was twenty nautical miles north of Novaya Zemlya and saw no ice at all. On the other hand, the east coast of Novaya Zemlya was jammed solid with ice, with heavy seas running from the north-northeast. Isaksen recalled that the ice had vanished so completely that he thought the seas between Novaya Zemlya and Franz Josef Land must have been nearly free of ice in that month and into early August.

As Giæver wrote to Gore-Booth: "If the *Eyra* [*sic*] had not got into the Pakice [*sic*] so that she has got stuck fast into it in the month of July, [Isaksen] feels certain that he has reached Franz Josef Land unhindered. He nearly thought one might reach the North Pole this year."[49]

Fortunately for Leigh Smith, Gore-Booth interpreted this letter perfectly. He discounted any suggestion that *Eira* might be stuck somewhere on the east coast of Novaya Zemlya, and did not jump at the magnificent possibility that Leigh Smith might be shivering at the North Pole at that very moment. Instead, he focused on the notion that Leigh Smith was most likely wintering over somewhere in Franz Josef Land, and would be planning to make his way south via the ship-gathering spot at Matochkin Shar the following summer, probably in July when the surrounding seas would again see a large-scale break-up of the ice.

As Gore-Booth assembled the state of the geographic problem he would have to deal with the following summer, Valentine Smith, working behind the scenes, had arranged for a letter to be sent to Lord Aberdare at the RGS, urging him to push the government to send a national relief expedition in search of *Eira*. The General was thrilled: "It is the best thing that could have happened – and now we shall I think hear of Allen Young offering to take command of the relieving vessel – but of such the naval service would be jealous – which is wrong for Allen Young knows all about Arctic exploration which is not the case ordinarily with men of the R.N."[50] Allen Young, a life-long merchant mariner and a contemporary of Leigh Smith, indeed had long experience in the Arctic, having served as sailing master on board *Fox* during Leopold McClintock's expedition in 1857 that retrieved the only written record of what had happened to Franklin. He later purchased an ex-Royal Navy gunboat, *Pandora*, and used it to explore the Arctic on his own before selling it to James Gordon Bennett, Jr., who renamed it and thus sealed its fate as the *Jeannette*.

The General wrote that it was Willie Leigh Smith who persuaded Valentine Smith to go to Clements Markham and ask Markham to write the memorial for Aberdare to deliver to the government on behalf of the RGS. In order to push the government into action, Valentine Smith agreed out of his own massive fortune to guarantee the money required to effect the rescue. That sum was thought to be anywhere from £8,000 to over £14,000, the latter sum even more than the *Eira* itself had cost to build.

"The newspapers have leaders about the *Eira* and her brave crew," the General writes on the first of December. "Nothing can be known regarding them till next summer – a weary period of suspense."[51] The following day, the General wrote to Valentine Smith himself, with his view that if the government failed to come to the rescue of Leigh Smith and his crew then all the results of his 1881 expedition might be lost and with them any discoveries he had made, discoveries which might now go to the credit of some other country exploring the same area in the future.

The General's winter of suspense was not eased in late December, when word spread in the newspapers of the terrible fate of the crew of the *Jeannette*. To ease his mind of such horrors, the General wrote again to Valentine Smith and to Willie. He proposed that the rescuers send up pilot balloons and carrier pigeons. Both could carry messages that revealed the rescuers position and their progress, so that Leigh Smith and his men would not lose heart, as it appeared had happened to the men of the *Jeannette*.

The General need not have worried. On the same day he was composing this letter, Leigh Smith and the crew of *Eira* were enjoying a Christmas Eve sing-song that included liberal rations of grog to wash down a treat of hot biscuits and butter. Lamps and candles were lit in every corner of the hut. Robertson writes that Leigh Smith gave a short, cheering speech to the men. But in his own log of Christmas Day, Leigh Smith writes only two words: "Big feed."[52] Robertson writes that New Year's Eve was more of the same but with "even greater zeal … being more of a Scotch holiday."[53] They were, as James Lamont might approvingly say, surviving an Arctic winter as proper men of leisure and means.

Throughout December, as he had since the moment of the sinking, Leigh Smith continued to keep a close watch on the food supplies. The men had consumed the last of over a thousand guillemots shot over the course of the fall and into the start of the winter. The birds were now gone from the islands, but there was enough bear and walrus meat on hand to last until March. And they still had the 900 lbs. of canned meat and 800 lbs. of tinned soups being held in reserve for the escape southwards the following summer. Chief Engineer Robertson writes that these had been "carefully stowed away, and in the days to come, even when in our direst need, the idea of touching that sacred store, never entered our heads."[54]

In addition to these, there were still plenty of vegetables along with 300 lbs. of bread and 500 lbs. of flour. The animal mascots were doing equally well. The canary was hale and singing, Tibs the kitten had grown into a cat, and the retriever Bob was busy hunting Arctic foxes while judiciously avoiding polar bears. On December 6th, Leigh Smith noted that three months had passed since the men moved into the hut. "I have never been cold in bed since we have been in the hut although the temp has been down to 22, but in the tent I was very cold. Men playing and singing."[55]

On Wednesday the 21st, there was general rejoicing that the shortest day of the winter had passed and the days would now begin to lengthen. The significant events in their Arctic sojourn all seemed to be marked on the 21st of each month: the *Eira* had been lost on August 21st; the fall equinox passed on September 21st; the sun rose for the last time a month after that; and now they passed the shortest day of the year in a light snowfall. Robertson noted that there was little to do except talk and play cards and keep the doorway to the hut free of snow and ice. The whalers were the best story-tellers, with tales of narrow escapes and great hunts. Every Saturday after supper, all of the musical instruments came out and, along with a double ration of grog, a week-concluding music festival was held. "The last item, sung in chorus, was always 'Rule Britannia,' which was lustily gone through by all."[56] Sundays were given over to Dr. Neale, who led divine services, followed by a large breakfast of walrus or polar bear curry.

On January 4th, they counterintuitively observed open water as far as the horizon, in the same month as they recorded the lowest temperature of their stay at Cape Flora: −42° F. It might have been even colder, but the thermometer was not constructed to record anything below that mark. Their bodies, however, recorded the air was so cold that you could breathe out and watch your breath fall as snow.

By Saturday, January 21st, they passed five months since the loss of *Eira* and a month since the shortest day. Leigh Smith recorded "three or four hours of very good light" and, simply, "All well."[57] Robertson writes that he had never experienced such prolonged and sustained high winds as in the two months of January and February at Cape Flora. "For the greater part of these two months, we were house-prisoners. There was nothing to invite us out, and even if there had been such, the darkness would have rendered walking dangerous."[58]

On the 25th, they killed their seventeenth polar bear since the shipwreck, their fourth bear killed in January to go with three walrus. They now had enough meat on hand to survive until the boat journey without breaking into any of the reserve supplies they would need for that long voyage.

One Saturday night during the end-of-week sing-a-long, the laughter and noise stopped as the men heard Bob engaged with a polar bear just outside the hut. When the dog retreated toward the entryway, the men dispatched the bear and dragged it through the opening where it was carved up and skinned on the spot. On another occasion, one of the men was almost killed as he emerged from the entryway and just ducked out of the way of the massive paw of a lurking bear. Robertson also recorded the time when a bear got onto the roof of the hut and the men in the crouched bunks watched the massive paws depress the canvas roof as the bear padded across it. It was soon shot and added to the larder.

Their spirits were lifted further in early February with the arrival of the first bird, which Leigh Smith recorded as a snowy owl. This lone traveler was followed ten days later by a flock of dovekies and another snowy owl. On Tuesday, February 21st, another milestone day, Leigh Smith wrote "Sun back today but the sky was cloudy & we could not see it. 6 months since the ship lost.... All well."[59] As the dim sun began to return to the north, Bob the dog silently led the men to a hummock where they found and shot three walrus, providing food and fuel for weeks. After a long day on the ice butchering the walrus, the men "spent the rest of the evening very pleasantly, our worthy commander giving us the means to spend a few jolly hours, which showed us that for a time his anxiety was at rest."[60]

It was only now, more than six months after the sinking, that Captain Lofley began to express his remorse at the loss of the *Eira*. On February 24th, Leigh Smith writes that the captain had remarked: "I never thought the ship would go or I should not have stood on the floe looking at the after stern post." A week later, Leigh Smith writes that the captain told him that the *Eira* "would have been quite safe if the berg had not given way & the ice come in from the east."[61] The captain had clearly been turning the whole event over in his mind throughout the long winter. Yet only now did he begin to give voice to his feelings of regret and professional responsibility for the safety of a vessel anchored in as exposed a position as a ship could be.

In March, female polar bears began wandering into the encampment. All of the bears killed over the winter had been males. By March 16th, it was warm enough for one of the men to begin entertaining the others by playing a cornet. Indeed, the temperatures took a dramatic turn upwards in March. Leigh Smith had been recording the monthly means since the establishment of the hut, and they read as follows:

Oct:	+8.95
Nov:	−1.25
Dec:	+4.79
Jan:	−25.1
Feb:	−26.7
Mar:	−1.4
Apr:	−1.25

Leigh Smith recorded the sun falling warm on his face on March 19th. Two days later, the spring equinox arrived, seven months after the loss of the ship. Another snowy owl paid a visit, then another. The men put a skylight into the hut. All was well.

Throughout March and April, the men killed more and more guillemots as they began returning to the Arctic. The arrival of the birds allowed the harpooners to climb the cliffs behind the hut and scour them for birds. At the same time, there were no walrus, and the bears had become scarce and those that showed near the camp were emaciated. On April 19th, the crews' twenty-ninth bear, a very thin male, was shot and found to have canvas in its belly. By the end of the month, the men ate the last of the doughboys. With twenty-five mouths to feed, the men were going through two polar bears and an assortment of birds each week as they dutifully continued to save the tinned and preserved supplies for the boat journey.

With the first of May at hand, all eyes were on the lookout for clear water. The boats were dug out from the snow. Two of the walrus boats and two of the whale boats were now readied for a long journey through ice and open seas. None of the sails for the small boats had survived the sinking, so new sails were sewn from some table cloths – the table cloths being much lighter than the surviving canvas sails from *Eira* that had served as roofing for the hut over the winter. When the tablecloths were used up, spare shirts, bed sheets, "anything strong enough to hold wind," as Robertson writes, was pressed into service.[62] Tents were sewn from the remaining canvas to be used to cover the boats when they had to be drawn up on the ice during the boat journey.

Three of the boats were in good condition, but the fourth was worse for the attack by a walrus the previous summer. All were reconditioned by *Eira*'s carpenter, who overhauled the hulls and re-caulked the seams. "He also had to make masts and other spars out of what was handiest; the engineers and blacksmith doing everything required in the iron or brass way."[63] When the work was finished, Robertson looked at the boats and decided that "they presented a queer and motley sight."[64]

On Sunday, May 14th, Leigh Smith marked eleven months since they had departed from Peterhead. With fresh meat a constant source of concern, the men worked to make everything ready to launch the small boats at the first sign of open water channels that would lead them homewards. On the 20th, Leigh Smith noted that this was the day that the Austro-Hungarians had started for the south. He had three weeks of fresh meat left and was extremely happy when the men brought in a new bear kill, their thirty-third of the winter. On the 24th, the water was running nearer to their hut and meandering off to the southwest as far as the eye could see. It was the Queen's birthday, so the men put up flags and drank her health with champagne.

In late May, the optimism faded somewhat, as spring snow storms blanketed Cape Flora, as the open water was seen only five to ten miles offshore, and the last of the firewood was used. For the month, they had used 121 cartridges to kill three bears and 366 guillemots. By June 3rd, they were left with about two weeks of fresh meat, so they continued to scour the cliff face above the cape for more birds, shooting one hundred guillemots with thirty-one shots on Sunday, June 4th.

The following day, the captain told Leigh Smith that the boats could be launched across the ice into open water in three more days. Leigh Smith sent three men across the ice to find a path, but he was not convinced they were ready. The captain himself walked the ice in search of a road on the 6th but found no safe passage to open water. The hummocks of ice were still too rough to risk dragging the boats across them.

By the end of the week, the boats were nearly fitted out and ready to be hauled to the water. Leigh Smith hiked across to Günther Bay and found the ice there decaying rapidly. On Tuesday, the 13th, a gale blew onto the small cape, breaking up the surrounding ice. A crack in the ice appeared directly in front of the hut and the men watched as it widened to more than a mile. It was as if the door to the south was suddenly yawning open. "Now we are free," exulted Leigh Smith in the log.[65] He now planned to get underway, with admirable precision, on June 21st, another milestone day and ten months from the day of the loss of the ship.

With the ice breaking up, the harpooners were now free to bring in more walrus. Bear and walrus meat was boiled and then soldered into tins by the blacksmith. The supply of salt had run out three weeks previous, and Robertson writes that eating the unsalted walrus meat made the men nauseous.

On the 14th, a year to the day since they departed Peterhead, one of the boats was sent across to Eira Harbour to retrieve a final load from the storehouse of supplies there. It brought back a sledge and four walrus shot along the way. The boats were then stowed with the forty days' worth of provisions salvaged from the sinking *Eira*. The crew had left these alone for ten long months, even through a long winter when the temptation to sample a few treats must have been considerable. With the addition of the preserved walrus meat, Leigh Smith calculated that they had enough food to last for two whole months.

A man was now sent each day to climb the cliffs behind the hut and survey the horizon to the south. Ice was continuously breaking away from the fast ice. Belugas were observed transiting past Cape Flora. The Arctic Ocean and the skies above it were alive with life and ice in motion. The cooking pot was in continuous use boiling walrus meat for the journey south. One of the men found a 14 lb. sounding lead that had gone missing. It was melted down to make slugs for cartridges. Others climbed back to the cliffs to collect more eggs. The whole operation, from the moment of the sinking to this day when escape was finally at hand, had been a masterful accomplishment.

The true celebration, however, waited for Sunday morning, June 18th. The previous night, a hard wind blew down from the northwest. Early in the morning, one of the men, out attending to his morning business, returned to the hut with what Robertson described as "the symptoms of having received a great shock. In broken sentences he gasped forth the joyful tidings that the sound was a sea of water, and the ice before our door was fast disappearing. 'Hurrah' after 'hurrah' ran through our dingy dwelling...."[66]

On the appointed day, Wednesday, June 21st, the boats and the stores were taken down to the edge of the ice. Each of the small boats was christened. Leigh Smith's whale boat was named, appropriately, *Phoenix*. The other whale boat received the name *Flora*. The two walrus boats were named *Advance* and, with a nod to Leigh Smith's famous cousin, *Nightingale*. "Each boat had besides, nailed on her bow the name '*Eira*' cut out of tinplate, so that if a boat had to be abandoned, and afterwards was picked up, its identity would be known."[67]

The men sealed the hut against polar bears, leaving a few bottles of champagne inside, and on a shoreline where no humans had previously wintered, gave three cheers to the hut that had allowed them not only to survive but lay the plans for their escape. At half past nine on the evening of the 21st, Leigh Smith ordered the boats into the sea. They were 400 nautical miles or more from Matochkin Strait, the spot where Leigh Smith thought they would find the greatest chance of rescue, where the summer whalers and walrus hunters would meet to exchange information on their various courses in and out of the Arctic. A good wind was blowing, and the small fleet made off briskly away from Cape Flora.

At home in England, since the beginning of the New Year, matters had likewise not stood still. In mid-January, Valentine Smith hosted a dinner for all those concerned with the fate of *Eira* and its crew. A month later, the General noted that an acquaintance was working with the Royal Society's Francis Galton to compile lists of supplies that would be required for any rescue vessel. A few days later, he wrote despairingly that the Admiralty would not commit a single government vessel to any planned rescue; it was only prepared to offer £5,000 towards a mission that was estimated to cost as much as £14,000. "I think that Lord Northbrook's stinginess will be attacked in Parliament by the opposition," scoffed the General.[68] Had he known it at the time, Ludlow could have added irony to injury with the fact that *Eira* had shipwrecked off the very island Leigh Smith had named for the distinguished First Lord of the Admiralty a year earlier.

By the end of February, the General along with two of Leigh Smith's surviving sisters, Barbara and Nannie, had each contributed £1,000 toward the relief expedition. By early April, Allen Young had been named its commander. He possessed of all the right qualifications: he was experienced in the Arctic, upper class, and had replaced his former vessel *Pandora* with a new vessel named *Hope*. The whole effort was given the name of "the *Eira* Search and Relief Expedition" and, with the exception of the government grant for about one-third of the cost, it would be a private affair.

On June 1st, *The Times* ran a two-column article on "The Missing Arctic Ship *Eira*," reminding its readers that Leigh Smith was still missing as he attempted to follow up his discoveries in Franz Josef Land from 1880. The note brought the public up to date with the saga, while not letting them forget the "smallness" of the government grant. For *The Times*, there were two possibilities: the *Eira* had been unable to reach Franz Josef Land and instead had been beset and carried off "into unknown space." Or, having reached the islands, the expedition had in fact reached the archipelago "and been frozen up in some bay or harbor, and compelled to pass the winter there."[69] If the ship was beset, there was every possibility that it, too, like the *Jeannette*, had been similarly crushed. "Such has been the fate of many of the early ice navigators, and, in recent times, of the *Fox*, the *Tegetthoff*, the *Jeannette*, and possibly that also of the *Eira*."[70]

If they were alive, the likeliest route for Leigh Smith and his men to escape was to take to their small boats and make for either Svalbard or Novaya Zemlya. The relief expedition would find their greatest potential for success if they waited at the edge of the ice pack for the twenty-five men to emerge from the north. The mission of the *Hope*, therefore, would be to sail for Novaya Zemlya and lay in provision depots and erect message cairns at various points along its western coast. In all events they were to avoid the pack itself lest they fall victim to it as well.

Young would be aided by Sir Henry Gore-Booth, who along with W.J.A. Grant from the 1880 expedition, would be sailing in Gore-Booth's new yacht *Kara*. Gore-Booth had found the vessel under construction at Wivenhoe in Essex, had the planking doubled and the bows reinforced with iron, and named it after the remote sea east of Novaya Zemlya. With a crew of Scottish whalers and provisioned for as much as a year at sea, *Kara* sailed in early June, bound for its namesake waters.

In fitting out the *Hope*, Young was offered the considered opinions and suggestions of some of the best-informed Arctic hands of the time, including Nordenskiöld in Stockholm, Payer in Munich, and Commodore M. H. Jansen of the Dutch Arctic Committee. The list is noteworthy for its implicit recognition that none of the old British Arctic hands knew anything about the conditions around Franz Josef Land or Novaya Zemlya. Payer insisted that, given Leigh Smith's probable location, he would have to save himself. No ship could help him without risk to itself. Payer correctly assumed that Leigh Smith was at that moment "making preparations for leaving his ship in order to retreat to the south by means of sledges and boats."[71] Jansen, who in the survey vessel *Willem Barents* had seen the ice conditions in the area for himself in 1879, cautioned that even he did not have enough experience to know for certain what was usual and what constituted the exceptional. But from the reports of the winds and ice conditions in the fall of 1881, he did not believe that *Eira* could have reached the coast of Franz Josef Land. If it had, it had likely been grounded or crushed.

Nordenskiöld, on the other hand, having spoken directly with the Norwegian walrus hunters who operated in the area, knew that the ice west of Novaya Zemlya had largely cleared by the late summer of 1881. He was convinced that, not only had Leigh Smith made it to Franz Josef Land, but that the conditions were such that he had been able to explore much of its western coast. If *Eira* had in fact been wrecked, everything depended on exactly where that unfortunate event had taken place. If still in Franz Josef Land, Leigh Smith could try to retreat via Novaya Zemlya. If *Eira* was sunk further to the west, near the mythical Gilles Land, then the retreat would be via Svalbard, where Leigh Smith was "well acquainted with every cove, and where he knows a large and excellent house, built for the Swedish expedition under my command, 1872–73, is to be found at Mossel Bay, latitude 79 deg. 53 min. north. This house was afterwards given by Mr. O. Dickson to the Norwegian hunters, who employ it for a common rescue depot."[72] Nordenskiöld thought it not at all impossible that the upcoming Swedish expedition to Mossel Bay would arrive to find Leigh Smith tucked up snugly in the station of his old friend. But he was equally convinced that, if *Eira* went down in Franz Josef Land, the rescuers would find Leigh Smith in Novaya Zemlya. There simply were no other escape routes.

Unbeknownst to Leigh Smith and his men as they made their final preparations for the departure from Cape Flora on the weekend of June 18–19, 1882, Allen Young was at that very moment sailing from England in the *Hope*. Henry Gore-Booth in the *Kara* had left for the Arctic as well. The General had sent a note to Young with "a few valedictory lines."[73] By July 3rd, the *Hope* had arrived safely at Hammerfest in northern Norway and procured a small sloop named *Martha* that would be used as a tender for *Hope*.

The two vessels departed Hammerfest on the 9th, coaled for two days at Tromsø, stopped at the northern telegraph station at Honningsvåg for one last communication with England, and then sailed through a gale towards the Russian Arctic. Young paused at the Russian observatory at Karmakuli on Novaya Zemlya, but when the expected officer in charge of the station still had not shown himself by July 25th, Young proceeded northwards, but not before he left behind a depot of supplies in case Leigh Smith retreated that way.

With the *Hope*, the *Martha* and the *Kara* now en route to Novaya Zemlya, it remained for Leigh Smith and his two dozen men in four small boats to navigate through several hundred nautical miles of broken pack ice and reach the edge of the ice. There they would have to cross an expanse of open ocean before picking their way through the treacherous fast ice attached to the coastline of Novaya Zemlya. And then they had to pray that someone would be there waiting for them.

On the first day out from Cape Flora on June 21st, the small fleet ran southwards for twenty hours before the pack ice forced them to stop, haul out of the boats, set up the tent, and wait for more favorable conditions.

The wait turned into more than a week until at last a narrow opening appeared in the ice. In the meantime, the bored men took out the cornet and the melodeon – a small nineteenth-century cabinet organ – and the sound of music again rang out over the ice.

By June 30th, the men were still waiting on the ice, unable to move. A rain storm drove them under their tents on one day, a gale on another. "We are all weary of this waiting," writes Leigh Smith, "and yet we can do nothing as it knocks our boats to pieces to attempt to drag them over the ice."[74] Without sledges or proper boots, any kind of serious exploring of the pack was out of the question. So they sat.

The first of July brought the first good news in more than a week. It was a bright clear morning and at 4 a.m. the boats were launched into a narrow channel in the ice and went zigzagging through the pack. The ice was nearly five feet high above the surface of the sea, and these walls often threatened to close and pinch the small boats between them. When the ice did block their way again, the men set to work cutting a passage while pushing the loose ice out of the way and, if all else failed, dragging the boats back up onto to ice to await a new lead.

On July 2nd, the men were stranded again. A survey of the boats found them much the worse for the wear of the previous day. They were banged up and leaking badly. Monday, July 3rd, dawned clear and beautiful and at 9 a.m. the men dragged the boats to a hole in the pack and began maneuvering through "very hummocky & hoary ice" before stopping for dinner.[75] Bellies full, they followed the edge of a large floe for a mile or so before pulling the boats onto the ice. July 4th was also bright and clear, but the leads in the ice were running east to west and not in the north–south direction they needed to go. Leigh Smith writes that they had "not gained much by all our labour and our boats are getting very shaky."[76]

It went on like this for another week. They would launch the boats and row and punt through narrow lanes of water between walls of ice, perhaps coming to more open water where the sails could be put to use, before the whole exercise was stopped by an impassable ice barrier. If no way could be found around or over it, they hauled out the boats, made tea, and waited. Leigh Smith's own boat hit a sharp ice edge on the July 8th and had to be hauled out onto the ice for repairs.

Fig. 44. The crew of the Eira *dragging their boats across the ice. Engraving by C. W. Whyllie from a sketch by Benjamin Leigh Smith made during the 1881–82 expedition (courtesy Scott Polar Research Institute, University of Cambridge).*

On Monday, July 10th, which Leigh Smith described as a very hot day, the fleet made its first significant progress to the south by southeast, coming into a large body of water and following it for a dozen nautical miles. But in the days that followed, this kind of progress became the exception. It was a little to the east, then the west, crabbing southwards, dodging around ice, a mile here, two miles there, and occasionally hauling one of the boats out of the water when it got too close to a floe and a plank stove in.

A heavy rain blew in on the 14th, obscuring the way ahead so that the leads could not be seen through the thick weather. The men hauled out the boats, waited around their mugs, launched, found the way blocked, hauled out again. If there was any consolation in their struggles, it was the concentrated knowledge that they could not turn back and that guiding the small boats through the labyrinth of increasingly rotten and slushy ice was the only way forward.

On Monday, July 17th, as they approached one month out from Cape Flora, the men found good leads in the ice and large gaps of open water, only occasionally being squeezed through narrow channels or having to haul the boats over the ice. The character of the sea had changed dramatically. The ocean was now awash in tiny fragments of sea ice, or brash ice. The following day, a gale kept the men sheltered on the ice in the morning, but by late afternoon they were on the move again. They sailed past narwhals and belugas and even managed to shoot a polar bear to add to their food supply. Wednesday saw good navigation as well, the boats maneuvering down a long lane of open water. Another bear and a seal were killed.

They tried to make a start on the 20th but thick weather drove them back onto the ice. They tried again the following day, only to have the boats nearly sunk in collisions with the ice in heavy rain and poor visibility. The wind intensified during the night, with ice and spray whipping about. In bitter cold they stayed put until late at night on the 22nd, when they launched again for just two hours, the wind and seas being too high for the boats.

On Sunday, July 23rd, the waterways opened once again. It was still overcast but the men could see open pools of water reflected in the sky. They sailed and rowed all day, maneuvering first west, then south, and then southeast. Finding themselves trapped once again just after midnight, they finally hauled the boats out onto the ice at 1 a.m. on Monday morning. They were on the move again seven hours later, sailing through a light covering of ice to the southeast. As Leigh Smith writes, it was foggy at times, "but sun shining & a fair wind & we sailed along delightfully. In the afternoon ice got more open and we could feel & see the swell of the sea."[77]

They were getting close to escaping from their ice prison and they knew it. They sailed through the night and by Tuesday, July 25th, they crossed an expanse of open water until they arrived at the fast ice of Novaya Zemlya. Three times they found a lead in the ice and attempted to follow it in to the land, sailing and rowing some thirty nautical miles, and each time the ice closed and they were forced back. They continued heading south, probing the fast ice.

By now the men were approaching their breaking points, hanging on for dear life after more than a month in the small boats. They were further depressed when Tibs, the cat, who had taken to jumping onto the ice for a walk whenever the boats were drawn up, was found missing after they had set sail and was never seen again.

They continued working inshore along the jagged edge of the fast ice, hauling the boats onto the ice each night to get some rest. A heavy swell began rolling in from the south-southwest, warping the ice on which they had to sleep each night. Their destination was close, but it was now a race between the durability of the boats, the solidity of their nightly ice encampments, and their personal hardiness.

On Monday, July 31st, the men awoke to find the ice so closely packed and grinding together that the boats could not be launched. As Leigh Smith surveyed the scene, there was not much to take heart in. "The floe on which we hauled up has been broken into pieces & the bit on which our boats are is not more than 50 feet by 100 feet."[78] When the boats finally got away, the men rowed through the night and into following day, the first day of August, 1882. They hauled out at 3:30 in the morning, but as they slept, the ice on which they rested broke in two and threatened to carry off the boats.

They quickly launched again, and the small fleet rowed continuously for nearly seven hours, before stopping for tea at five. Three hours later, they finally penetrated to fast ice and got into open water along the coast. As Chief Engineer Robertson writes: "Hard work and short rest were beginning to tell on all, and while finally retreating, we took a long semi-circular course through the much slackened ice, when quite unexpected, there appeared in the distance, an open ocean clear of ice."[79]

They cleared a point of land and rowed east for the rest of the night. When dawn came on the morning of August 2nd, they set sail through a heavy thunder storm. The seas were high and the boats were taking on water when land was sighted at three in the afternoon. As Chief Engineer Robertson remembered:

Early on the second of August, as the weather gave every sign of being dirty, it was resolved that the two walrus boats should keep together, as they could sail much closer to the wind; the whale boats, being better sailors on a wind side only, had also to keep company, each taking their own course toward the desired haven. It was now blowing a fresh gale, and to make matters worse, a very severe thunder storm came on. The wind, rain, hail, thunder and lightning not only made us very uncomfortable, but rendered our positions extremely dangerous. The rain and water shipped made baling almost a continuous operation, and rest was out of the question. Certainly we did lie down on a heap of wet clothes every now and then, getting the full benefit of spray as it swept over our little craft. It was very cold; cramp seized all our limbs, and with no warm food to heat us, it was the very essence of misery, the storm continuing well into the afternoon. The two whale boats had not been seen since morning, they having been lost sight of during the first thunder squall.[80]

Robertson and his fellows in the walrus boats sighted land soon afterwards, eventually coming into a small bay. The whale boats arrived soon thereafter and the whole party reunited. They set about to build a fire and dry their soaked clothing, but no sooner had the flame caught before a fierce rainstorm drowned it out. The men were too exhausted to care. They slept like dead men until the sun broke through the following morning, when they finally had a chance to dry themselves and their clothes. It was while the men were engaged in this happy task that one of them chanced to look up and see a schooner coming round the point leading to their small bay and the cry went up: *"A sail! A sail!"*

Sir Allen Young, accompanied by three officers and a surgeon from the Royal Navy in the *Hope*, had arrived off Novaya Zemlya on July 26th. They were trailed by Sir Henry Gore-Booth and W.J.A. Grant in *Kara*. Near Matochkin Strait they met up with two Russian schooners and the Dutch Arctic surveying vessel *Willem Barents* and laid a series of depot along the coastline for Leigh Smith and his men.

Staying inshore with a sharp lookout for any activity they might observe on the remote shorelines, the *Hope* proceeded into Matochkin Strait and promptly struck a sunken reef. The water was high at the time, and as it ran out the *Hope* was soon fast aground. When a swell began running over the reef that evening, it pounded the ship until Young ordered the *Hope* lightened by removing the stores to the *Martha*. Gore-Booth also came alongside to take some of the burden onto the *Kara*. Not until a high tide on 27th, and only then by putting on all steam and canvas, was the ship warped off the reef. They anchored a mile to the east in a dense fog.

Surveying the damage, Young found the rudder post knocked away from the keel and hanging by some loose bolts. A jury-rigged lever on the rudder trunk allowed the ship to maneuver the following day into a small inlet, where all weight was moved forward to the bow in order to raise the stern and effect more permanent repairs. Young could be thankful that the hull had sustained no serious damage and the relief expedition could proceed without itself becoming a casualty. He still expected to sail northwards along the Novaya Zemlya coast all the way to Franz Josef Land if necessary.

At 10 a.m. on the morning of August 3rd, as he was contemplating his next move, Young saw the *Willem Barents* return to the bay with all colors hoisted. The *Barents* had just weighed anchor earlier that morning, so Young knew that good news was at hand. Soon after, a small boat from the *Barents* arrived with Leigh Smith on board. Young scarcely recognized him. Instantly he ordered all of his own four small boats away to collect the remaining men of the *Eira*, and by 3 p.m. that afternoon they were all on board. As Chief Engineer Robertson writes, the men were "met with a very hearty welcome, and everything was done for our comfort; then, and all the time we were on board. A good meal, a good wash, a change of clothes, and a sound sleep worked wonders with us. We never expected an organized relief to be sent out for us, yet needless to say we were delighted to see our own countrymen, and to be landed direct on British soil."[81]

All that remained was for *Hope* to be reballasted, take on coal from the *Martha*, resupply the fresh water, and hoist up the small boats. The fleet sailed for Scotland on the morning of August 6th. The makeshift rudder assembly performed well and the *Hope* was off the northern coast of Norway by the 9th. Fighting through south and southwest winds along

Fig. 45. Rescue of Leigh Smith and the crew in Matochkin Strait, Novaya Zemlya (courtesy Scott Polar Research Institute, University of Cambridge).

the Norwegian coast, they arrived to a tumultuous welcome at Aberdeen on August 20th.

In Aberdeen, Leigh Smith and Sir Allen took up residence at the Douglas Hotel. The crew was paid off and sent home, the Peterhead men taking a tug back to their home port and the crew members from Dundee taking a train for home. The exception was second mate Thomas Fenton, a native of Dundee, who passed away at the Aberdeen Infirmary from cancer, just four days after the return of the expedition. He was forty-four and left behind a widow and children.

Apart from the second mate, who had endured ill-health throughout the expedition, the remaining two dozen men quickly returned to their former selves. And they had a monumental story to tell. They had been thrown ashore at Cape Flora on August 21st, 1881, with barely enough fresh meat to last for two months. By carefully marshaling the stores saved from their destroyed research vessel, they were able to make a comfortable life for themselves in an impossibly remote spot on the planet. For ten months, they foraged and hunted and butchered their way through an Arctic winter, boiling meat stew thickened with the blood of polar bears.

As Neale surveyed the men after the journey, he found them remarkably fit. "The effect of living on the meat of the country was (I am certain) that there was not the slightest symptom of scurvy among us; when the daylight returned, instead of everyone looking pale and anæmic, it was a surprise to all old wintering hands to see every one with rosy cheeks."[82] From October 1st to May 1st, every man had enjoyed an ounce of rum each day, about half of the traditional half a gill served in the Royal Navy. There had been little sickness and no severe cases of frostbite. Snow blindness affected them all with the return of the sun, but none had been permanently affected. The mate had sustained an injury to his right forearm in July of 1881, but he neglected to tell Neale until it became infected. Apart from this and second mate Fenton's cancer, they had lived as inactive hermits for nearly a year and come out largely intact.

The scientific results of the expedition, apart from Neale's notes on the Franz Josef Land wildlife, had gone to the bottom in the laboratory room on board the *Eira*. Even so, Clements Markham used Neale's notes to write twenty-three pages which, again, Sir George Nares recommended for publication in RGS's *Proceedings*.[83] And the crew had survived in such a positive way as to shame many of the larger government Arctic expeditions of the nineteenth century. Through *The Times* reporter in Aberdeen, Leigh Smith expressed the gratitude of himself and his crew for the blessing of the relief expedition. It was noted that he would travel to London, "and will then put his notes of the voyage and the sojourn on Cape Flora into permanent shape."[84]

But he never did. Leigh Smith never got around to putting his notes into any shape, permanent or otherwise. In his defense, the loss of his fine new ship and the ordeal, however well-managed, at Cape Flora, would have taken a large toll on any man. And, unlike most explorers before and since, he had no financial need to publish, and the very idea of publicity mortified him.

He was about to return to his extended family an even larger presence than when he left. But the Arctic, which had dominated his life for twelve years and afforded him a kind of self-knowledge, even as he sought to avoid the recognition that came with his successes, would now begin to fade in importance in his life. He was getting too old for the kind of immense adventures his five expeditions had brought. By the fall of 1882, his brief, brilliant career as an Arctic explorer was over.

8

BENJAMIN LEIGH SMITH AND HIS TIMES, 1883–1913

A telegram from Leigh Smith in Aberdeen arrived in East Sussex on August 21st and the news of his safe return spread instantly around his family. His niece Milicent in her diary writes: "What do you think? We got a telegram from Uncle Ben! He is all right, he says, I think, 'Got back all safe but *Eira* is awa' or something like that."[1] For what it's worth, Milicent also received a different story about the doomed Tibs than the one relayed by Robertson. "When they started from Flora Cottage they were obliged to drown the cat because the sailors said they would never get home (I suppose) safely if they had a cat on board."[2]

However Tibs met his end, that story never made the papers. *The Times* welcomed Leigh Smith and his crew back heartily, since there "had been much reason to fear that the crew of the *Eira* had met with the fate as overtook most of the crew of the unfortunate *Jeannette*…. Mr. Smith's theory of Arctic navigation was pretty well known to the experts in such matters. It is that an explorer should cruise summer by summer in the Arctic seas ready to seize any opening which the break-up of the ice, the winds, or the currents offer to carry him northwards. This was the maxim on which he had conducted his previous voyages; but it was naturally feared that he might have pushed his theory too far."[3]

One gets a sense of the anxiety felt over Leigh Smith's fate – and the joy at his return – from a letter written by Isabella Blythe, the partner of Leigh Smith's sister Nannie. She records the response of David Gray as he witnessed Allen Young's *Hope* bypassing Peterhead on its return from Novaya Zemlya: "Capt Grey [*sic*] saw the *Hope* steaming past & put off in a steam tug after her & the moment he was near enough he shouted 'What news of the *Eira*?' Sir Allen Young 'Gone to the bottom' – Capt Grey 'And the Crew?' Sir A Young 'Here on board' Capt Grey 'and Mr Smith?' Sir A Young 'Safe on board' Capt Grey 'Stop, let me up; I *must* see him I *must* hear his voice....'"[4]

Leigh Smith's geographic successes, signified by his gold medal from the RSG in 1881 and magnified in the public mind by his miraculous emergence from a Franz Josef Land winter in 1882, were now solidified. It was the irony of his life that he gained the two things he most despised – fame and recognition – at the very moment he lost the magnificent *Eira*, which was perhaps the one thing he had always desired more than any other in his life.

So, too, within the bedrock stratigraphy of Victorian England, his honors would only go so far. Whether from his own illegitimacy or his family's long history of dissent or his sibling's problematic natures, somewhere in his mind Leigh Smith had to know that any and all of these would forever keep him at arm's length from royal Britain. Unlike his world-famous cousin Florence Nightingale, whose nursing work in the Crimea earned her the first Royal Red Cross from Queen Victoria, the exploration of Svalbard and Franz Josef Land would not lead to any royal honors. There would never be a Sir Benjamin Leigh Smith.

Even as he shied away from public acclaim, there is still the conundrum of Leigh Smith's domineering of his family. His triumphant return and justly earned fame did nothing to loosen his iron control over them. With Amy banished from his affections as a result of her marriage to Norman Moore ("I am very glad I am not your father," he had venomously written to his one-time favorite after her engagement[5]), Leigh Smith returned to his estate at Glottenham and the chance to reward his other nieces for their affections. Fourteen-year-old Milicent writes in her diary that just a month after his arrival from Aberdeen, Leigh Smith was back in Scotland, exploring Loch Lomond with his new favorite niece, her sister Mabel.

Both girls would soon come under his direct supervision. The General, who had provided so many details of Leigh Smith's life across two decades, passed away at the age of eighty-one on November 30th, 1882. Following Bella's death eight years earlier, the three surviving children, Mabel, Milicent, and Harry, were now orphaned and Leigh Smith took

Fig. 46. The estate at Glottenham, ca. 1890 (courtesy Hancox Archive).

them under his care. Less than two years later, Harry died at the age of twenty-two while returning from a journey to India.

The succession of funerals, the necessity of managing the estates and seeing to the upbringing of his nieces, to say nothing of the loss of the *Eira*, all provide indications as to why Leigh Smith did not immediately return to the Arctic. Still, as a public figure, he was expected to contribute in other ways. *The Times*, in an extended editorial on the upcoming International Polar Year, all but demanded that Leigh Smith sit down and write an account of his expeditions, "since the opinions of such a competent authority cannot fail to be of permanent importance. His last two voyages materially strengthen the arguments which have already been brought forward in favour of Franz Josef Land as a basis for further exploration towards the Pole...."[6]

No such account was ever forthcoming from the halls at Glottenham. The closest *The Times* would get to an exposition on Franz Josef Land by Leigh Smith came two weeks later, when Dr. Neale read a paper on the 1881–82 expedition at the February 12th meeting of the RGS. The hall at the University of London "was filled and several distinguished Arctic explorers," including McClintock and Nares.[7]

The man of the hour himself, survivor and leader of one of the great escapes in the history of polar exploration, stayed at home with a cold. *The Times* again implored Leigh Smith to go north in an editorial in April, with the same result.[8] Leigh Smith did take part in an International Fisheries Conference presided over by the Prince of Wales in London in June, 1883, and was made an honorary fellow of his old college at Cambridge, but otherwise remained out of public view.[9]

At the end of 1886, Milicent, now 18, began to study for her college examinations. Her tutor had an attractive younger sister by the name of Charlotte Sellers, who was also 18, a woman without means of her own and a strict Roman Catholic into the bargain. Leigh Smith, forty years her senior and now gray and balding, took notice. "To everyone's amazement and most people's dismay," as Charlotte Moore writes, Leigh Smith proposed the following June and was accepted.[10]

Charlotte Moore also uncovered, tucked away in one of Norman Moore's many scrapbooks, a series of bitter quatrains composed on the occasion of The Explorer's engagement to her namesake Aunt Charlotte:

"Benjamin Leigh Smith"

My name is Ben and I can hate
In love I'm no adept
To die of want once seemed my fate
Unmoved mid bears I slept.

I lived upon the wild beasts' blood
Tenderer were they than I
And miles around the frozen flood
Wearied my dauntless eye.

I neither cared for God nor man
For sister nor for friend
Yet love such as I have I can
Give you till my life's end.

Though years have passed since I was young
I feel my frame is tough
And when my passing-bell is rung
I'll leave you wealth enough.

I'm grey & old & have no heart
But offer you my hand
And gold & store [or stone?] I can impart
And well with men I stand.

I have shown constancy in hate
And that I can in love
If you will trust me with your fate
You may yet live to prove.[11]

One wonders if these lines returned to Norman Moore when, two decades later, he was called in to judge Leigh Smith's competency. Whatever the truth of the poetry, two sons followed the marriage, Benjamin Valentine in 1888 and Philip in 1892, the latter in the year that Leigh Smith turned sixty-four. The family heard whispers that The Explorer was looking into a new vessel and another trip to the north in 1890, but any thoughts of a return to active exploration were now the daydreams of a new father living inside the body of an old man.

By the 1890s, Leigh Smith's Arctic explorations were confined to commenting on the expeditions of others. When a young British artist, photographer, and traveler named Frederick W. W. Howell submitted a manuscript for RGS's *Proceedings* on his travels in Iceland, it was rejected for publication after a review by "B. Leigh Smith, Esq.," who found "little that is new in the paper."[12] Now a gray eminence, Leigh Smith could cast the same critical eye on the neophyte expeditions of others that twenty years earlier had been thrown his way.

Fig. 47. Leigh Smith and his young sons at Scalands, early 1890s (courtesy Hancox Archive).

Fig. 48. Charlotte Leigh Smith at Scalands, 1898 (courtesy Hancox Archive).

Fig. 49. A hunting party at Scalands (Charlotte sitting in front of Leigh Smith; Richard Potter on right) (courtesy Hancox Archive).

Credland has noted that Leigh Smith took "particular pride" in the temperature recordings he made in the waters around Svalbard, while Jones claims that it "was one of his regrets that fuller credit was never given to this oceanographical work."[13] Indeed, by the time his place had been secured in the first comprehensive history of oceanographic research, published in 1912, Leigh Smith was in an advanced state of dementia and just months from his death just after New Year's Eve 1913.[14]

On this first Arctic cruise, Leigh Smith had combined a bit of daring with the good fortune of beginner's luck. Ice conditions north and east of Svalbard, which looked so forbidding in August, 1871, suddenly cleared in early September. It was during this bold flying expedition eastwards during the first two weeks of September when most of the geographic features associated with Leigh Smith's Svalbard expeditions would be scouted. Eventually, this quick foray would lead to thirty-three new place names in northeast Svalbard, including twenty-two new islands. It was also in this moment when he would reach his personal farthest north, on a quick dash north of Rossøya.

August Petermann, who did not lightly pass out exclamation points in his *Mittheilungen*, had thrilled to Leigh Smith's collection of new islands and his expansion of the limits of Svalbard. "After the observations and measurements of the Smyth-Ulve' [*sic*] expedition, we now know that northeast Spitzbergen has a width of 10.5 degrees of longitude instead of, as on the best past maps, only 7.5!"[15] Leigh Smith had shown as well that new islands could be found north of this newly expanded Svalbard, so Giles Land might still be discovered somewhere east-northeast of Nordaustlandet. Equally, Leigh Smith's observations of open water east of Nordaustlandet and north of Rossøya, along with his ocean temperature recordings with their suggestion of potential inversion layers of warmer polar waters, were seized upon to support Petermann's notion that an open polar sea might surround the North Pole.

The turning of the northeast limits of Svalbard at what became Kapp Leigh Smith, along with the location and definition of Brochøya, Foynøya, Schübeleøya, and thirty other new Svalbard place names, these together would have made the expedition a success. When combined with the geographic work at Tumlingodden on Wilhelmøya, the bathymetric survey at Vestfjorden, and Leigh Smith's pioneering deep-sea temperature recordings and scientific approach to solving the ice and ocean current dilemmas presented by Svalbard's unique geography and location, the 1871 *Sampson* cruise comprised a considerable triumph by a neophyte explorer. Leigh Smith himself would not enjoy such success again until his 1880 expedition to Franz Josef Land.

While Leigh Smith kept a journal of his 1871 voyage to Svalbard, and asked others to keep journals of his other voyages, to the end he avoided any publication of his own. When he left such work to others, the results were uneven at best. Markham's accounts of the Franz Josef Land voyages are detailed and written with precision, but Wells's account of the 1872 expedition was hastily written for a general audience and offers constant and nonsensical shifts in time and place, randomly tacks on accounts of other expeditions, and mixes the chronology of the 1872 expedition with little regard for continuity. His 350-page volume agrees roughly with the chronology contained in Chermside's three-page summary of the expedition, but events and places are frequently confused. This is perhaps not surprising given the state of knowledge of the geography of Svalbard in the nineteenth century, but it did Leigh Smith no favors.

For his 1873 campaign in Svalbard, Leigh Smith had had the discerning eye to choose the highly intelligent, well-adapted and adaptable twenty-three-year-old military officer Herbert C. Chermside as his expedition chronicler. The 1873 expedition marked the conclusion of Leigh Smith's extensive explorations around Svalbard, during which he had gained vast experience with high latitude sailing, ice navigation, deep-ocean scientific research, and the infinitely complex geography and geographic nomenclature of Svalbard. He had added dozens of new names to the gazetteer of the islands, discovered several new islands and delineated the eastern extent of the archipelago. He had come to the rescue of Nordenskiöld's major Swedish expedition and in the process gained a first-hand sense of the requirements for surviving an overwintering in the north. This invaluable knowledge would be put to the test during his own forced overwintering in Franz Josef Land.

Even with the largely unheralded results from his three expeditions to Svalbard and the enduring notoriety of his overwintering and escape from Cape Flora in 1881–82, it was his spectacularly successful reconnaissance of Franz Josef Land in 1880 for which he will be justly famed. In just two weeks in August, 1880, between the time he sighted and anchored off May Island, to his departure from Gray Bay, Leigh Smith defined the southern coast of Franz Josef Land from Cape Tegetthoff to Cape Lofley. From the point of land the Dutch had named Barents Hook in 1879 to the point where *Eira* was stopped by ice, Leigh Smith charted 110 nautical miles along a previously unknown Arctic coastline. What remained trended off to the northwest, toward the eastern limits of Svalbard, which he had defined in 1871. Leigh Smith had made clear both the western reaches of Franz Josef Land and the eastern extent of Svalbard; what were left were details.

Leigh Smith's nimbleness in adapting his plans to changing conditions was in marked contrast to the overweening government-sponsored expeditions of the era. As Jonathan Karpoff notes, in the nineteenth century, "government expeditions fared poorly. They made fewer major discoveries, introduced fewer technological innovations, were subject to higher rates of scurvy, lost more ships, and had more explorers die."[16]

In this sense, Leigh Smith can be seen to have initiated private oceanographic, biological, and geographic research in polar and sub-Arctic waters, work that would be continued in the twentieth century with, among others, Amundsen's Northwest Passage expedition in *Gjøa*, Albert I of Monaco's early century expeditions to Svalbard in the *Princess Alice*, Alexander Forbes's explorations of the Labrador coast in *Ramah* in the 1930s and even Jacques-Yves Cousteau's Antarctic expedition in *Calypso* in the 1970s. It is easy to imagine Leigh Smith going to the Arctic in the late twentieth century with his vessel carrying a small helicopter and matching submersible. Unlike the similarly equipped modern yachts of the super-rich, however, Leigh Smith would not have sailed without a detailed scientific research program.

Even as his own possibilities to return to the Arctic receded and as a new generation of polar explorers, led by the incomparable Nansen, were successfully exploring the polar mystery, Leigh Smith still clung to the notion of a return to Franz Josef Land, even of being the first to the northern end of the Earth. "I hope we shall have a try at Franz Josef Land, there is much to be done there. From Eira Harbour with a good dog sledge 85° might be reached or as much farther as the land goes. Before talking of going to the Pole, Franz Josef Land should be explored. I don't want

Fig. 50. Professor Julian A. Dowdeswell, PhD, Director of the Scott Polar Research Institute, in his rooms at Jesus College, Leigh Smith's alma mater at Cambridge University. A portrait of Leigh Smith, as painted by J.L. Reilly after a Stephen Pearce portrait, is in the background (courtesy Julian Dowdeswell).

Nansen to attempt this as I think he would do it, and it ought to be done by an Englishman."[17]

Though he was an enthusiastic supporter of other British explorers and adventurers (he advised one that "4000 fur seal skins would pay the cost of a hunting expedition to Antarctica for whales [and] seals"[18]), there is very little in his note about Nansen to suggest that Leigh Smith thought that he shouldn't be the Englishman who stood first at the North Pole, with good reason. Without the national budgets and pressures of pole-seeking and without scores of seemingly expendable sailors, Leigh Smith had nevertheless pioneered a method to collect scientific data by allowing ice and weather conditions to dictate his areas of operations.

There are only two surviving memorials to him.[19] One is a plain cement marker on the exterior of his East Sussex estate at Glottenham. It is affixed in the exterior wall just above the balcony doors of what may have been his study. It says, simply, *BLS 1890*. Appropriately, given the manner of his demise, Glottenham today is an elder home, a munificently peaceful spot from which to transition from this life to whatever comes next. The other surviving memorial to Leigh Smith is the great storehouse erected at Eira Harbour in Franz Josef Land, a lasting tribute not only to The Explorer but to the men of the Stephen & Forbes yard in Peterhead who built the prefabricated structure and the crew of *Eira* who assembled it at that impossibly remote shoreline in 1880.

By the time of his note about Nansen, whether he recognized it or not, Leigh Smith's moment to seize the polar grail had already passed. Another accident with a cab in 1890 had left him seriously injured once again, even as he was learning his circuitous way as the father of first one, then two small boys. When he regained some of his old form he traveled to Egypt, where he "should have done some excavations but could not get the necessary permit in time."[20]

A British polar expedition under Frederick George Jackson, with Leigh Smith's support, was preparing to use his old overwintering base at Cape Flora on Northbrook Island in Franz Josef Land to launch a new attempt on the North Pole. Nansen's transpolar drift expedition in the *Fram* departed the Norwegian capital of Christiania a year ahead of Jackson.

When Jackson, a man half Leigh Smith's age and an archetype of the new era who required both publicity and money, arrived at Cape Flora, he entered through the frozen door of Leigh Smith's winter hut as an archaeologist might enter a prehistoric tomb in search of icons. He would recover items from Leigh Smith's last expedition as if they were the relics of a lost civilization, which in fact they assuredly were. Jackson would build a series of new structures at Cape Flora and relegate Leigh Smith's stone hut to the status of a shrine to British polar exploration. It stood for more than a century until the treacherous cliff on which it was built collapsed and the hut crumbled into the same polar sea that had claimed *Eira*.

Though he wrote several articles and one very long book about his three-year expedition, Jackson failed to best the progress north made by Leigh Smith twenty years earlier. The greatest result of the Jackson expedition in the public mind was, not the three years of patient and painstaking geographic work in the immensely complex archipelago, but the spectacular and dramatic meeting with Nansen and his companion Hjalmar Johansen as the Norwegians made their miraculous way south through the islands in the spring of 1896. Nansen had not reached the pole but, as Leigh Smith had feared, he got closer than anyone before him.

As these energetic expressions of nationalism and scientific exploration gave way to a catastrophically noisy half-century of polar celebrity that followed the conclusion of Nansen's transpolar drift, Benjamin Leigh Smith was managing his fortune and trailing two energetic sons around his estates in the rolling green pastures and orchards of the East Sussex countryside. His marriage inevitably became strained and distant, and given Leigh Smith's preferences in women this was probably not the result of his wife being too young but rather her growing too old to interest him anymore.

He eventually reconciled with Amy, just before her death from tuberculosis at the age of forty-two. She had been very sick for some time and her frailty finally softened him. He would write to her with light questions about how to manage a household or to offer an unminced comment on the opposition to the new station on the local railway to London. The "natives do not seem to care about having a good station or to understand how to lay it out. They are stupid, stupid, stupid as Barbara used to say."[21]

His form of geographic exploration, discrete, patient, even gentile, would have precious few equivalents in the twentieth century. The new century was seized by those explorers who could combine dramatic geographic goals with clever mass communications strategies, and it very soon became difficult to discern which was the more important. A boisterous American journalist named Walter Wellman loudly and proudly attempted to reach the pole in 1894 along the route north of Svalbard that Leigh Smith had charted in 1871. Like Frederick Jackson, Wellman would not get nearly as far north or east as had the nimble Leigh Smith, but he would generate considerably more publicity.

A Swedish engineer and dreamer named Salomon August Andrée launched a balloon towards the pole from Svalbard in 1897, in an elegant and, perhaps, quasi-suicidal attempt to evade the requisite punishment of an over-ice sledging expedition. When his frozen body and those of his two companions were finally discovered alongside the glacial dome of Kvitøya in the late summer of 1930, complete with intact diaries and

Fig. 51. Summer, 2009. Polar historian Huw Lewis-Jones with Leigh Smith descendant and novelist Charlotte Moore, near the whale jaw brought from the Arctic to Scalands by the explorer (photo by the author).

undeveloped photographic film, the resulting media spectacle was immediate, enervated, international, and profound, as had been the initial launch thirty-three years earlier. Andrée generated more publicity just in the month of July, 1896, when he could not even get his balloon off the ground amid contrary winds blowing against the north shore of Danskøya, than Benjamin Leigh Smith did in twelve years of determined and creative polar exploration.

Walter Wellman ventured into the second of Leigh Smith's Arctic patches in 1898, when he removed one of Jackson's buildings at Cape Flora and relocated it to an open expanse of shoreline at Cape Tegetthoff on Hall Island. There Wellman created his own polar base camp for an expedition that was remarkable for its manifest ineffectiveness. His published chart of the expedition shows one large island and three small islets he discovered, along with four other islands he thought he had discovered that turned out later to be mirages. It was the mistake of a man beholden to publicity, one who had not attained the North Pole that he had promised his financial patrons, and who now had to distract them with something other than the polar grail, in the hopes they would write him another check.

Benjamin Leigh Smith, who wrote all his own checks, never experienced the need or the pressure to produce such imaginary results, and certainly not data he could falsify while still in the field with just a little extra effort. Yet, within a decade, while attempting unsuccessfully to fly a dirigible to the North Pole, it was Walter Wellman who would be sending wireless messages from the Arctic to the president of the United States. It was a triumph of public style over scientific substance at the start of a long century of such victories. But, for all his publicity, Wellman would not get any further north in his airship than he had in a plain Norwegian steamer in 1894, nor match Leigh Smith's farthest north in the small Norwegian schooner *Sampson* in 1871.

Such instant communications technologies like wireless, and the balloons and dirigibles, aeroplanes and submarines that carried them, all would come to dominate polar exploration. They would become as famous if not more so than the explorers who employed them. And the idea that polar experiences could be written in the form of cliff-hanging episodes to be fed to newspapers to be consumed in turn by a rapacious public is one that would have appalled Leigh Smith. It is impossible to imagine Leigh Smith representing himself as a polar hero by donning sealskins and standing amid stuffed Arctic fauna for a posed photograph in a London studio.

Benjamin Leigh Smith approached polar exploration from the perspective of a carefully opportunistic gatherer of data, not a seeker after a predetermined grail. He would cruise about in search of a momentary opening in the ice of the polar seas, one that might lead to a new station from which to take deep-ocean soundings. If a crack in the polar pack suddenly yawned open and offered a gateway to the pole, well that was just the good luck one enjoyed as a result of careful planning combined with a lot of patience.

It was more likely that he would be content to step ashore on a stretch of rocky Arctic beach never before seen by human eyes. He would pause, and then perhaps name the place after any one of dozens of esteemed scientific explorers or favored relations. He would arrange for photographs to be taken, engage in some hunting, and then share stories over a well-cooked meal of a guillemot enjoyed with a glass of wine. Or a doughboy drowned in butter and washed down with half a gill of rum. And even in shipwreck, he and his colleagues and his crew would all return home alive.

ACKNOWLEDGMENTS

First and foremost, I would like to thank Charlotte Moore, whose fine sense of family history has enabled her to see the enduring value in preserving the letters and images of her singular assortment of ancestors, including her great-great uncle, the explorer Benjamin Leigh Smith. Her own intensely interesting *Hancox*, a history of her family and her family home, along with her transcriptions of the Leigh Smith portions of the General's diary and her welcome to me when I visited Hancox in July of 2009, September of 2010, and again in June of 2012, allowed me a view of the private Leigh Smith that lay beneath or alongside the reluctant public figure of the explorer.

This research was supported by generous help from several sources at my college at Penn State. These included a Research Development Grant, a Faculty Travel Grant, the Associate Dean's Research and Development Fund, a Faculty Summer Fellowship, and the Anthropology Fund. At Penn State Abington, I wish to thank especially the remarkable Dr. Peter P. Johnstone, now of the University of North Texas, as well as my exemplary Division Heads, Dr. James F. Smith and Dr. Gary Calore, as well as Dr. Samir Ouzomgi, Dr. Norah Shultz, Dr. Hannah Klieger, the late Mr. George Simon, our excellent library staff, especially Ms. Jeannette Ullrich, and our computer folks, most especially Mr. Joe Varghese. At Scott Polar Research Institute, the author thanks Dr. Julian Dowdeswell, Dr. Beau Riffenburgh, Ms. Naomi Boneham, and Ms. Heather Lane. Magnus Forsberg, my colleague and boon companion on a 2006 voyage to the North Pole that explored Cape Flora en route, was an immeasurable help with both Arctic wildlife (in particular with discussions of bird life on Moffen and elsewhere in Svalbard) and translations from Swedish. My colleague and friend Dr. Huw Lewis-Jones traveled with me on my first visit to Hancox and Scalands – and appropriately slapped me for not knowing, before our visit, that Nightingale Sound was named for Florence Nightingale and that she was Leigh Smith's cousin. Many thanks to both Huw and to his great lady, Kari Herbert. Additional thanks go to Jan Turner and the staff of the Foyle Reading Room of the Royal Geographic Society; to Isobel Cassidy at Henry Gore-Booth's estate Lissadell; to

Robert Prys-Jones of the Bird Group, Department of Zoology, National History Museum at Tring; to the historian Arthur Credland, to William Barr, and to the anonymous reviewers for the University of Calgary Press whose insights were greatly and gratefully appreciated. As always, my debts to Dr. Susan Barr of Riksantikvaren in Oslo are too large to ever be repaid. Finally, to my family: C.L. and Jeremy and Jenny and my mother, I owe everything.

NOTES

PROLOGUE: *TWILIGHT*

1 Letter from Benjamin Leigh Smith (BLS) to Amy Leigh Smith, June 9, 1871, Hancox Archive.

2 Anonymous, "Arctic discovery," *Saturday Review of Politics, Literature, Science and Art* 35, no. 919 (1873): 741–42.

3 Charlotte Moore, *Hancox: A House and a Family* (London: Penguin, 2010), 99.

4 Norman Moore examination of Benjamin Leigh Smith, December 24, 1909, Hancox Archive, 2.

5 Ibid., 3.

6 Ibid., 4.

7 Ibid.

8 Ibid., Continuation: 4.

9 Ibid.

10 Ibid., Continuation: 7.

11 *The Times*, Dec. 27, 1882, 3.

12 John C. Wells, *The Gateway to Polynia: A Voyage to Spitzbergen from the journal of John C. Wells.* (London: Henry S. King, 1873), 53.

13 *The Times*, op. cit.

1: BENJAMIN LEIGH SMITH AND HIS TIMES, 1828–71

1 Constantine John Phipps, *A Voyage towards the North Pole.* (London: J. Nourse, 1774), 11.

2 Daines Barrington, *The Probability of Reaching the North Pole Discussed.* (London: C. Heydinger, 1775), 4.

3 Ibid., 20.

4 Phipps, *Voyage towards the North Pole*, 27. Every time he uses the device he kindly mentions that he is using 'Lord Charles Cavendish's thermometer'; one could almost suspect Phipps had an investment in it.

5 Ibid., 35–36.

6 Ibid., 38.

7 Ibid., 41.

8 Ibid., 53.

9 Ibid., 185.

10 Moore, *Hancox*, 17.

11 Jenny Handley and Hazel Lake, *Progress by Persuasion: The Life of William Smith, 1756–1835.* (Hazel Lake, 2007), 3.

12 Moore, *Hancox*, 17.

13 Ibid., 18.

14 Handley and Lake, *Progress by Persuasion*, 3.

15 Ibid., 24.

16 Fergus Fleming, *Barrow's Boys*. (London: Granta Books, 1998), 12.

17 William Edward Parry, *Narrative of an Attempt to Reach the North Pole*. (London: John Murray, 1828), x.

18 Ibid.

19 Ibid., 12.

20 Ibid., 20.

21 Ibid., 50.

22 Ibid., 52–53.

23 Ibid., 60.

24 Ibid., 103.

25 *The Times*, June 14, 1838, 5.

26 Handley and Lake, *Progress by Persuasion*, 378.

27 Moore, *Hancox*, 18.

28 Ibid., 19.

29 Brochure, "School for Girls and Boys at Portman Hall," Hancox Archive.

30 Ibid.

31 Letter from Barbara Leigh Smith to BLS, Dec. 7, 1852, Hancox Archive.

32 A.G.E. Jones, "Benjamin Leigh Smith: Arctic Yachtsman," *The Musk-Ox* 16 (1975): 24–31, 24.

33 Helena Wojtczak, *Women of Victorian Hastings, 1830–1870*. (Hastings: Hastings Press, 2002), 22.

34 Letter from Barbara Leigh Smith to BLS, Dec. 7, 1852, Hancox Archive.

35 Ibid.

36 Leigh Smith maintained his interest in the Franklin search throughout his life. An extensive bundle of notes located in the archives of the Royal Geographic Society in London was sent to Leigh Smith by his old captain Alex Fairweather on board *Diana* in November of 1883. These contain records, reports and lists of stores left at Beechey Island by Franklin searchers Edward Belcher, Leopold McClintock, and Allen Young in the years 1851–58, along with a report on the state of the Beechey Island depot by Allen Young while exploring on board *Pandora* in the summer of 1875. Fairweather had come across them while laying at the floe edge near Prince Regent Inlet on board the steamer *Terra Nova* in the summer of 1883. Inuit on sledges appeared and Fairweather stopped them when he noted that their clothing and supplies matched the cache of supplies he knew to exist at Beechey Island. The natives also had a cylinder with records contained in it, which Fairweather reports they were about to use as wadding for their guns. Fairweather sent the records to Leigh Smith asking him if he would forward them to the correct authorities in London. See: Alex Fairweather to Benjamin Leigh Smith, RGS/A2A/LMS/S/20, 1854–75.

37 My children and I spent several rainy hours tracking and eventually locating the Kane family crypt in the Laurel Hill Cemetery in Philadelphia. My son Jeremy memorialized the event in a short film that can be seen at: http://www.youtube.com/watch?v=bksB0aA7_2k&-feature=share&list=UU9-uLp4bZm-j1RNe0RyxV5eg

38 Elisha Kent Kane, *Arctic Explorations*. (Philadelphia: Childs & Peterson, 1856), 37.

39 Frederick Hamilton-Temple-Blackwood, 1st Marquess of Dufferin and Ava,

Letters from High Latitudes. (London: John Murray, 1857), 24–25.

40 Ibid., 43.

41 Ibid., 53.

42 Ibid., 56.

43 Ibid., 59.

44 Ibid., 66.

45 Ibid., 113.

46 Ibid., 159.

47 Ibid., 160.

48 My colleague Dr. Susan Barr attempted to relocate these artifacts during extensive ethnological explorations of the island but they had long since vanished. See: Susan Barr, *Jan Mayen Land*, 222.

49 Dufferin, *Letters from High Latitudes*, 302.

50 James Lamont, *Seasons with the Sea-horses: Sporting Adventures in the Northern Seas*. (London: Hurst & Blackett, 1861), dedication page.

51 Anonymous, "Obituary: Sir James Lamont." *Geographical Journal* 42, no. 3 (Sept. 1913): 301–2.

52 Lamont, *Seasons with the Sea-horses*, 273–74.

53 Charles Darwin to James Lamont, Feb. 25, 1861, Darwin Correspondence Database, http://www.darwinproject.ac.uk/entry-3071, accessed June 19, 2012.

54 Lamont, *Seasons with the Sea-horses*, 13.

55 Ibid., 28.

56 Ibid., 129.

57 Ibid., 170.

58 Ibid., 181.

59 Ibid., 192.

60 Ibid., 198–99.

61 Ibid., 272; italics from the original text.

62 James Lamont, *Yachting in the Arctic Seas*. (London: Chatto & Windus, 1876), 4.

63 Ibid., 5.

64 Ibid., 6.

65 Ibid., 13.

66 Ibid., 231.

67 Norsk Polarinstitutt, *The Place Names of Svalbard*. (Oslo: Norsk Polarinstitutt, 1991 [Skrifter Nr. 80 and 112; Ny-Trykk], 451.

68 Lamont, *Yachting in the Arctic Seas*, 296.

69 Ibid., 371.

70 Charlotte Moore, personal communication, Aug. 17, 2010.

71 Moore, *Hancox*, 21.

72 Ibid., 16.

73 Ludlow diary, April 12, 1863, Hancox Archive.

74 Ibid., July 9, 1869.

75 Ibid., April 28, 1871.

2: EXPEDITION ONE: SVALBARD, 1871

1 Expedition One: Svalbard, 1871 Benjamin Leigh Smith, *Journal of the Schooner Sampson* ([1871], unpublished). Edinburgh University Library, Special Collections, Gen 76–77. This 'journal' is a typescript of an undated, unnumbered, unpublished logbook from the 1871 voyage of *Sampson*. Furthermore, there is some confusion over the name of the vessel in which Leigh Smith first journeyed to the Arctic. Jones (1975) uses *Samson*, while others (Credland 1980; Cromack and Riffenburg 2000 employ *Sampson*. The cover of this typescript journal uses *Samson*, which is then penciled over with *Sampson*, and *Sampson* is

then used throughout the remainder of the typescript. It is so used here.

2 August Petermann, "Geographie und Erforschung der Polar-Regionen, Nr. 58: Die Englisch-Norwegischen Entdeckungen im Nordosten von Spitzbergen, Nordfahrten von Smyth, Ulve, Torkildsen, 19. Juni–27 Sept. 1871." *Mittheilungen aus Justus Perthes' Geographischer Anstalt über wichtige neue Erforschungen auf dem Gesammtgebiete der Geographie von Dr. A. Petermann, 18. Band: 101–106.* (Gotha: Justus Perthes, 1872), 101.

3 Benjamin Leigh Smith, *Journal*, May 19, 1871.

4 Ibid., May 24, 1871.

5 Ibid., May 27, 1871.

6 Ibid., May 28, 1871.

7 Ibid., May 29, 1871.

8 Ibid., May 30, 1871.

9 Ibid., June 3, 1871.

10 Ibid., June 4, 1871.

11 See, for example, August Petermann, "Geographie und Erforschung der Polar-Regionen, Nr. 59: Gillis-Land, König Karl-Land und das Seeboden-Relief um Spitzbergen, nach dem Standpunkte der Kenntniss im Jahre 1872." *Mittheilungen aus Justus Perthes' Geographischer Anstalt über wichtige neue Erforschungen auf dem Gesammtgebiete der Geographie von Dr. A. Petermann, 18. Band: 111–112.* (Gotha: Justus Perthes, 1872). See also: August Petermann, "Smyth' & Ulve's Reise im Nordosten von Spitzbergen und ihre Aufnahmen im Nord-Ost-Lande, Aug. & Sept, 1871." *Mittheilungen aus Justus Perthes' Geographischer Anstalt über wichtige neue Erforschungen auf dem Gesammtgebiete der Geographie von Dr. A.*

Petermann, 18. Band: Tafel 6. (Gotha: Justus Perthes, 1872).

12 David Thomas Murphy, *German Exploration of the Polar World, A History, 1870–1940.* (Lincoln: University of Nebraska Press, 2002), 29.

13 Norsk Polarinstitutt, *Place Names*, 152–53.

14 Ibid., 242–43.

15 Benjamin Leigh Smith, *Journal*, June 8, 1871.

16 Ibid.

17 Cited in Susan Barr, "The History of Western Activity in Franz Josef Land," in: *Franz Josef Land*, ed. Susan Barr (Oslo: Norsk Polarinstitutt, 1872), 61. See also: W.J.A. Grant, "Cruise of the Yacht *Eira*, and Discovery of New Lands in the Far North," *The Leisure Hour.* (London, 1881): 213–20.

18 Benjamin Leigh Smith, *Journal*, June 15, 1871.

19 Ibid., June 21, 1871.

20 Ibid., June 25, 1871.

21 Ibid.

22 Ibid., July 6, 1871.

23 John Murray and Johan Hjort, *The Depths of the Ocean.* (London: Macmillan, 1912 (reprinted in 1965 by J. Cramer, Weinheim, Germany), 11.

24 This almost certainly was a Miller-Casella pressure-protected thermometer, introduced by the British Hydrographic Office in 1869 (see: Anita McConnell, *No Sea Too Deep: The History of Oceanographic Instruments.* (Bristol: Adam Hilger, 1982), 97–98), and testifies to Leigh Smith's employment of the latest in oceanographic recording technology.

25 Benjamin Leigh Smith, *Journal*, July 12, 1871.

26 Ibid., July 13, 1871.

27 Ibid., July 16, 1871.

28 Ibid., July 17, 1871.

29 Ibid., July 18, 1871. These were most likely the ruins of the Dutch whaling station on Ytre Norskøya, dating from 1617, which contain the remains of train-oil boilers and about 180 graves (Susan Barr, personal communication, July 9, 2005). And the most likely point Leigh Smith ascended was the same as that used by Lamont, the hill above the blubber cookeries called Utkiken.

30 Ibid., July 21, 1871.

31 Ibid.

32 Ibid. The yellow flower was either mountain avens (*Dryas octopetala*) or the Svalbard poppy (*Papaver dahlianum*). Leigh Smith probably also observed carpets of purple saxifrage (*Saxifraga oppositifolia*) (see, for example, Vidar Hisdal *Svalbard: Nature and History*. (Oslo: Norsk Polarinstitutt, 1998], 70–77).

33 Ibid., July 27, 1871.

34 Ibid., July 28, 1871.

35 Ibid., July 29, 1871. This was most likely Sørfjellet (596 m/1,955′ high), a precipice that stands astride three major glaciers.

36 Ibid. This spectacular view would take in the north-south lying Åsgårdfonna; the Valhallfonna that runs into Hinlopenstretet; and Dunérbreen that runs north toward Sorgfjorden.

37 Ibid., July 30, 1871.

38 Ibid.

39 Ibid., July 31, 1871.

40 Ibid.

41 See: Norsk Polarinstitutt, *Place Names*, 418. See also: Vilhelm Carlheim-Gyllensköld, *På Åttionde Breddgraden*. (Stockholm: Albert Bonniers förlag, 1900), 46.

42 Benjamin Leigh Smith, *Journal*, August 6, 1871.

43 For a discussion of this confusion, which endured for decades, see Norsk Polarinstitutt, *Place Names*, 242–43.

44 Benjamin Leigh Smith, *Journal*, August 9, 1871.

45 Murphy, *German Exploration*, 27–31.

46 Benjamin Leigh Smith, *Journal*, August 12, 1871.

47 Norsk Polarinstitutt, *Place Names*, 475.

48 Benjamin Leigh Smith, *Journal*, August 19, 1871.

49 Norsk Polarinstitutt, *Place Names*, 445. Neither Leigh Smith nor *Sampson* is mentioned in this note; neither is Leigh Smith cited in the comprehensive list of expeditions to Svalbard from the eighteenth to the twentieth centuries (see: Norsk Polarinstitutt, *Place Names*, 530–34), his place taken by a brief mention of Ulve. On the other side of the ledger, nowhere in Leigh Smith's journal does he mention Captain Ulve by name, evidence of a possible clash between the two?

50 Benjamin Leigh Smith, *Journal*, September 1, 1871.

51 See: Petermann, "Geographie und Erforschung der Polar-Regionen, Nr. 58," "Geographie und Erforschung der Polar-Regionen, Nr. 59," "Smyth' & Ulve's Reise im Nordosten von Spitzbergen," and "Originalkarte zur übersicht der Reisen von Smyth, Ulve, Torkildsen, 1871." *Mittheilungen aus Justus Perthes'*

Geographischer Anstalt über wichtige neue Erforschungen auf dem Gesammtgebiete der Geographie von Dr. A. Petermann, 18. Band: Tafel 5 (Gotha: Justus Perthes).

52 See: Norsk Polarinstitutt, *Place Names*, 82, 142, 378.

53 Benjamin Leigh Smith, *Journal*, September 6, 1871.

54 Evidently, Mohn and/or Petermann decided against this nomenclature because the only substantial island in this area is Raschøya, and it was named not for *Sampson* but for a Norwegian zoologist named Halvor Heyerdahl Rasch (see Petermann, "Geographie und Erforschung der Polar-Regionen, Nr. 58," 106).

55 Benjamin Leigh Smith, *Journal*, September 9, 1871.

56 Ibid.

57 Ibid., September 14, 1871.

58 Ibid., September 20, 1871.

59 Ibid.

60 Ibid., September 27, 1871.

61 See, for example, Joanna Gyory, Arthur J. Mariano, and Edward H. Ryan, "The Spitsbergen Current," *Ocean Surface Currents*. http://oceancurrents.rsmas.miami.edu/atlantic/spitsbergen.html, accessed August 2005.

3: EXPEDITION TWO: JAN MAYEN AND SVALBARD, 1872

1 Ludlow diary, September 26, 1871, Hancox Archive.

2 Ibid., November 23, 1871.

3 Ibid., December 24, 1871.

4 Ibid., May 4, 1872.

5 H. C. Chermside, "Recent Explorations in the Spitsbergen Seas by Leigh Smith," (unpublished manuscript, [1873]). Edinburgh University Library, Special Collections, MS Gen 77.

6 Anonymous, "Arctic Exploration," *The Sussex Advertiser*, September 3, 1872.

7 Wells *The Gateway to Polynia*, 57.

8 Ibid., 58.

9 Clive Holland, ed., *Farthest North: A History of North Polar Exploration in Eye-Witness Accounts*. (New York: Carroll & Graf, 1994), 29–30.

10 Wells, *Polynia*, 2.

11 Ibid., 67.

12 Ibid., 73.

13 Chermside, "Recent Explorations," puts the date at June 5th.

14 Wells, *Polynia*, 94.

15 Ibid., 95.

16 William Scoresby, *An Account of the Arctic Regions*. (Edinburgh: A. Constable, 1820), 6.

17 Wells, *Polynia*, 96.

18 Chermside, "Recent Explorations," puts the date at June 6th.

19 Wells, *Polynia*, 97. These were possibly the Vogt and Berna craters explored by Georg Berna and Carl Vogt in 1861. Wordie ("An Expedition to Jan Mayen Island," *Geographical Journal* 59, no. 3 [1922]: 185) made the case that Scoresby originally explored Vogt Crater, and that Scoresby's name for it – Esk Crater (Eskkrateret) – should have priority. But Wordie also confuses Leigh Smith's visit to the island, writing that it came after that of the Austrian-Hungarian IGY expedition, rather than ten years before it.

20 Wells, *Polynia*, 98. This was either the Palffy Crater (Palffykrateret) of the Austro-Hungarians, or the unnamed

"old and much-eroded crater" noted by Wordie ("Expedition to Jan Mayen Island": 187) in 1921 at an elevation of 610 m/2,000′ in a wide dry valley between the Vogt (Eskkrateret) and Berna (Bernakrateret) craters.

21 Wells, *Polynia*, 162 [approximately £5.70 or $11.50 in 2007].

22 Ibid., 155.

23 Ibid., 188.

24 Ibid., 190.

25 Ibid., 191.

26 Ibid.

27 Ibid., 186.

28 Ibid., 196.

29 Such a find of a Terek sandpiper "would still today be regarded as a first-class rarity to Svalbard" (Magnus Forsberg, personal communication, October 12, 2007) and this – along with Wells's later claim to have found snow-geese in Svalbard – is not considered credible.

30 The entire archipelago is rising steadily due to the removal of the weight of ice sheet that covered it during the Pleistocene (see, for example, W. Blake, Jr., "Radiocarbon dating of raised beaches in Nordaustlandet, Spitsbergen," In: G.O. Raasch, ed. *Geology of the Arctic*. [Toronto: University of Toronto Press, 1961], 133–45; see also: I.U. Olsson and W. Blake, Jr., "Problems of radiocarbon dating of raised beaches, based on experience in Spitsbergen." *Norsk Geografisk Tidsskrift* 18 [1962]: 47–64).

31 Wells, *Polynia*, 204.

32 Herman Melville, *Moby-Dick or The Whale*. (New York: Penguin 1851 [1992]), 491.

33 Ibid., 496.

34 Arthur Credland, personal communication, Oct. 1, 2007.

35 Arthur Credland, "Foreword," in Nicholas Redman, *Whales' Bones of the British Isles*. (England: Redman Publishing, 2004).

36 Wells called it Albert Dirke's Bay – it is actually named after a Dutch whaling skipper Aldert Dirksz (see: Norsk Polarinstitutt, *Place Names*, 112).

37 Wells, *Polynia*, 216–17.

38 Ibid.

39 Ibid., 218.

40 This is perhaps the hut at Elvetangen on the west side of Wijdefjorden about five miles from Dirksbukta and designated as an important cultural monument by Norwegian authorities (see: Sysselmannen på Svalbard 2000, 74).

41 Wells, *Polynia*, 227.

42 Ibid., 303.

43 Alexander Leslie, *The Arctic Voyages of Adolf Erik Nordenskiöld, 1858–1879*. (London: Macmillan, 1879), 190.

44 George Kish, *North-east Passage: Adolf Erik Nordenskiöld, his life and times*. (Amsterdam: Nico Israel, 1973), 101.

45 Leslie, *Arctic Voyages*, 190.

46 Wells, *Polynia*, 304–5.

47 Ibid., 324.

4: EXPEDITION THREE: SVALBARD, 1873

1 Ludlow Diary, October 3, 1872, Hancox Archive.

2 Ibid., October 26, 1872.

3 Ibid., April 12, 1873.

4 Chermside, "Recent Explorations".

5   Anonymous, *Memoir to Illustrate the Origin and Foundation of the Pollock Medal.* (Woolwich: Boddy and Co. 1875).

6   Anthony Bruce, *The Purchase System in the British Army, 1660–1871.* (London: Royal Historical Society, 1980).

7   Paul D. Wilson, "Chermside, Sir Herbert Charles (1850–1929)." *Australian Dictionary of Biography,* vol. 7. (Melbourne: Melbourne University Press, 1979), 631–32.

8   See: Petermann, "Geographie und Erforschung der Polar-Regionen, Nr. 58," "Geographie und Erforschung der Polar-Regionen, Nr. 59," "Smyth' & Ulve's Reise im Nordosten von Spitzbergen," and "Originalkarte zur übersicht der Reisen von Smyth, Ulve, Torkildsen, 1871"; see also P.J. Capelotti, "Benjamin Leigh Smith's first Arctic expedition, Svalbard, 1871," *Polar Record* 42, no. 220 (2006): 1–14.

9   Wells, *The Gateway to Polynia*; see also P.J. Capelotti, "Benjamin Leigh Smith's second Arctic expedition: Svalbard and Jan Mayen Land, 1872," *Polar Record* 44, no. 3 (2008): 255–64.

10 See: Chermside, "Recent Explorations." See also: Henry C. Rawlinson, "First Meeting, 10th November, 1874: Opening Address," *Proceedings of the Royal Geographical Society of London* 19, no. 1 (1874), 5.

11 H. C. Chermside, *Journal on board of the SS Diana.* SPRI (Scott Polar Research Institute Archives), MS 300/4/1. All quotes from this unnumbered journal are from herein cited by their volume and entry date.

12 These letters are stored at the Royal Geographic Society Foyle Reading Room, record group RGS/A2A/LMS/P/30.

13 Norsk Polarinstitutt, *Place Names,* 111.

14 See: "Obituary: Sir James Lamont," *Geographic Journal* 42, no. 3 (1913): 301–2; see also Chermside, "Recent Explorations", 6.

15 Chermside, *Journal,* May 10.

16 Ibid.

17 Ibid.

18 R.E. Potter to his father, May 12, 1873, RGS/A2A/LMS/30.

19 Chermside, *Journal,* May 12.

20 Ibid., May 23.

21 Ibid., May 26. At the time of this expedition, the 'blue ensign' flag was authorized to be flown by British vessels engaged in public service or commanded by an officer of the Royal Naval Reserve.

22 Ibid., May 31.

23 Ibid.

24 Ibid., June 7.

25 William Walker, "Log book of the yacht *Sampson,* kept by Capt. William Walker, 29 April–5 October 1873." SPRI MS 300/3 SL, June 21, 1873.

26 Chermside, *Journal,* June 13.

27 Chermside, "Recent Explorations," 8.

28 Chermside, *Journal,* June 13.

29 Ibid.

30 R.E. Potter to his father, June 13, 1873, RGS/A2A/LMS/P/30.

31 Benjamin Leigh Smith, "To the Editor of the Times," *The Times* (27538): col E, Nov. 19, 1872.

32 Ibid.

33 *New York Times,* "The Spitzbergen Drama," August 3, 1873, 5.

34 Kish, *North-east Passage*, 111–12.

35 August Wijkander, "Letter," June 22, 1873. This was published in a Stockholm newspaper on July 18, 1873. From "Translated excerpts from newspapers re: 1872–1873 Swedish expedition." SPRI MS 301/36/1-2.

36 P. M. Krusenstjerna, "Letter published in the *Official Gazette of Sweden*, July 28, 1873." From "Translated excerpts from newspapers re: 1872–1873 Swedish expedition." SPRI MS 301/36/1-2.

37 Anonymous, "Private letter written on board *Polhem* at Mossel Bay, June 19, 1873, and published in Stockholm newspapers, July 21, 1873." From "Translated excerpts from newspapers re: 1872–1873 Swedish expedition." SPRI MS 301/36/1-2.

38 Alexander Leslie, *Arctic Voyages*, 406.

39 Chermside, *Journal*, June 13.

40 Ibid., June 14.

41 Alfred E. Eaton to Barbara Bodichon, Shrove Tuesday 1873, SPRI MS 300/9 D.

42 R.E. Potter to his father, June 13, 1873, RGS/A2A/LMS/P/30.

43 Chermside, *Journal*, June 22.

44 Ibid., June 28.

45 Ibid.

46 Ibid., June 29.

47 Walker, "Log book of the yacht *Sampson*," June 20, 1873.

48 Chermside, *Journal*, July 2.

49 Ibid., July 6.

50 George Kish, "Adolf Erik Nordenskiöld (1832–1901): Polar Explorer and Historian of Cartography." *Geographical Journal* 134, no. 4 (1968): 487–500.

51 See: "Mr. Leigh Smith's Arctic Expedition," *The Times*, August 26, 1873, 12.

52 Norsk Polarinstitutt, *Place Names*, 140.

53 Chermside, *Journal*, July 11.

54 Norsk Polarinstitutt, *Place Names*, 277.

55 Chermside, *Journal*, July 14.

56 F. C. Mack, Letter to Leigh Smith, February 3, 1876, SPRI MS 301/17/1-3.

57 Chermside, *Journal*, July 15.

58 Ibid., July 21.

59 Ibid.

60 Ibid., July 27.

61 Ibid., July 28.

62 Ibid., July 29.

63 Ibid., August 4.

64 Ibid., August 5.

65 Ibid.

66 Ibid., August 10.

67 See, for example, the description of harbor whaling by British whalers in the 1660s by Martin Conway, *No Man's Land: A History of Spitsbergen from its Discovery in 1596 to the Beginning of Scientific Exploration of the Country*. (Cambridge: Cambridge University Press, 1906), 205. Chermside's estimate of a death date of 100 years earlier seems to be confirmed by later geological research. Using an uplift rate of approximately 1 cm per year, posited for a Russian hunting hut in Nordaustlandet (see: Olsson and Blake, "Problems of radiocarbon dating of raised beaches," 16), Chermside's whale skeletons, resting between six and ten feet above sea level in 1873, would have died or been killed between 182 and 304 years earlier, or at some point between the

years 1569 and1691, an acceptable range
that brackets the discovery and shore-
based exploitation of Greenland whales
around Svalbard and its transition into
pelagic whaling. The greater the annual
uplift, such as the 2.99 cm per year
reported by Alfred Jahn ("The Raised
Shore Lines and Beaches in Hornsund
and the Problem of Postglacial Vertical
Movements of Spitsbergen," *Polish
Geographical Review* 31, Supplement
(1959): 157) from Hornsund in southern
Svalbard, the more recent the death
of the whales. Jahn's Hornsund data
applied to Augustabukta would produce
a death range of 1764 to 1807, with a
median year of 1786 – and very close
to Chermside's supposition. Of course,
the beach matrix itself is not an absolute
dating of the whale since, as Blake
("Radiocarbon dating of raised beaches
in Nordaustlandet, Spitsbergen,",
137) points out, such whales did not
necessarily die right at the shore. Blake's
radiocarbon dating of whalebone
fragments found at an elevation of 7.8
m asl (25.59´) produced dates of more
than 6,000 BP (ibid., 141). A host of
other factors, from storm surge to human
agency, could also factor into the timing,
location, and elevation of the remains.
The only certainties are that the higher
the whale's elevation and/or the slower
the rate of uplift, the more likely such
skeletons predate human activity on
Svalbard.

68 Chermside, *Journal*, August 10.

69 Ibid., August 29.

70 Norsk Polarinstitutt, *Place Names*,
96. See also: F.R. Kjellman, *Svenska
Polarexpedition År 1872 + 1873 under
ledning af A.E. Nordenskiöld*. (Stockholm:
P.A. Norstedt + Söner, 1875).

71 Chermside, "Recent Explorations," 19.

72 Ibid., 21.

73 Ibid., 22.

74 Ibid., 23.

75 Ibid., 23–24.

76 Chermside, *Journal*, August 10. This
a very similar description to that in
Leslie's expeditionary biography of
Nordenskiöld, wherein Leslie describes
Nordenskiöld's landing on August 5,
1861, at Phippsøya, "several isolated
mountains about 1,800 feet high,
connected by a low land covered with
driftwood and fragments of ships"
together with remains of whale skeletons
found lying high above the present
level of the sea both on the east side
of Parryøya and on the promontory of
Martensøya (see: Leslie, *Arctic Voyages*,
79).

77 Walker, "Log book of the yacht
Sampson," October 5, 1873, SPRI MS
300/3 SL.

78 C.V. Owen, "Chermside, Sir Herbert
Charles (1850–1929)," in *Oxford
Dictionary of National Biography*.
(Oxford: Oxford University Press, 2004).
Online edition: http://www.oxforddnb.
com/view/article/32390, accessed 6 July
2009.

79 Wilson "Chermside, Sir Herbert Charles
(1850–1929)," 631–32.

80 Norsk Polarinstitutt, *Place Names*, 96.

81 R.E. Potter to his father, September 30,
1873, RGS/A2A/LMS/P/30.

82 R. Collinson, "Referee report by R.
Collinson," Nov. 12, 1874, RGS/A2A/
JMS/17/76.

5: THE AWAKENING TO A NEW LIFE, 1874–1879

1 Ludlow diary, September 29, 1873, Hancox Archive.

2 Moore, *Hancox*, 50–51.

3 Ludlow diary, December 2, 1874.

4 Swedish Legation in London. Letter to Leigh Smith, May 6, 1874, SPRI MS 301/35.

5 Anonymous, "Arctic Exploration," *Edinburgh Review*, 141, no. 288 (1875), 447–81.

6 Ludlow diary, April 28, 1875.

7 Chauncey C. Loomis, *Weird and Tragic Shores*. (New York: Knopf, 1971).

8 Julius Payer, *New Lands within the Arctic Circle*. (New York: D. Appleton, 1877), 174.

9 See, for example, Susan Barr "Norwegian use of the polar oceans as occupational arenas and exploration routes," *Polar Record* 37, no. 201 (2001), 99–110.

10 See: E. Tammiksaar, et al., "Hypothesis versus Fact: August Petermann and Polar Research," *Arctic* 52, no. 3 (1999): 237–44.

11 Kane, *Arctic Explorations*, 305.

12 Payer, *New Lands within the Arctic Circle*, 49–50.

13 Ibid., 54.

14 Ibid., 56.

15 Ibid.

16 Ibid., 59.

17 Ibid., 77.

18 Ibid., 123.

19 Ibid., 136.

20 Ibid., 175.

21 Ibid., 181.

22 Ibid., 182.

23 Ibid., 289.

24 Ibid., 312.

25 Ibid., 314.

26 Ibid., 339.

27 Admiralty Arctic Committee *Papers and Correspondence relating to the Equipment and Fitting Out of the Arctic Expedition of 1875*. (London: HMSO,1875), A2.

28 Ibid., 5.

29 Ibid., 5–6.

30 Ibid., 12.

31 Ibid., 14.

32 Lamont, *Yachting in the Arctic Seas*, v.

33 Ibid., 91.

34 Fleming, *Barrow's Boys*, 374.

35 Lamont, *Yachting in the Arctic Seas*, 92.

36 David Gray to Leigh Smith, September 23, 1876, SPRI MS 301/13/2.

37 Letter to Leigh Smith, June 28, 1876, SPRI MS 301/9/1.

38 Ludlow diary, June 10, 1876.

39 Ibid., July 3, 1876.

40 David Gray to Leigh Smith, January 19, 1877, SPRI MS 301/13/2.

41 Ludlow diary, April 15, 1878.

42 Ibid., August 9, 1878.

43 Ibid., March 3, 1879.

44 Ibid., September 16, 1879.

45 Ibid., November 9, 1879.

46 Ibid., November 24, 1879.

47 Ibid., December 31, 1879.

6: EXPEDITION FOUR: FRANZ JOSEF LAND, 1880

1 C. R. Markham, "The Voyage of the 'Eira' and Mr. Leigh Smith's Arctic Discoveries in 1880." *Proceedings of the Royal Geographic Society* 3, no. 3 (March 1881):130.

2 Alex R. Buchan, "SS *Windward* – whaler and Arctic exploration ship," *Polar Record* 24, no. 151 (1988): 213.

3 Ibid., 214.

4 The origins of the name *Eira* have been lost. It could refer to the Gaelic spelling for Ireland, but this seems an unlikely connection for Leigh Smith. An interesting and plausible notion comes from an article in *Aftenposten* (Susan Barr, personal communication, June 7, 2012) about the Norwegian river Eira, and its fame as the favorite salmon-fishing place for English lords in the nineteenth century, though there is no direct evidence of Leigh Smith visiting the river (see: Hans Kristian Krogh-Hanssen, "Lakselordenes gjemmested," *Aftenposten*, June 6, 2012, Reise, 8). My colleague Magnus Forsberg suggests a Welsh version of the Linnaean nomenclature for the Snow Goose: Snow Goose *Anser caerulescens* (Linnaeus, 1758), in Welsh: Gwydd yr Eira. This idea is supported by an amusing note written by Mabel to Amy in 1880: "Uncle Ben sent me a LINE the other day – REALLY a line – 'The name is to be the *Wild Goose*' – we suppose this is serious – if so he is bound to find the Pole when he attempts it next or the amount of criticism which will be the result will be simply awful." Letter from Mabel Leigh Smith to Amy Leigh Smith, February 20, 1880, Hancox Archive.

5 Basil Lubbock, *The Arctic Whalers*. (Glasgow, 1937), 412.

6 Conversions carried out using the National Archives (UK) currency converter at: http://www.nationalarchives.gov.uk/currency/

7 William Baxter to Leigh Smith, April 1, 1881, SPRI MS 301/3/1-31.

8 Ludlow diary, May 4, 1880.

9 Ibid., May 9, 1880.

10 Ibid., May 27, 1880

11 Ibid.

12 Ibid., May 31, 1880.

13 Ibid., June 12, 1880.

14 Moore, *Hancox*, 144.

15 Grant, "Cruise of the Yacht *Eira*, 213.

16 Ibid., 213.

17 Ibid., 215.

18 Ibid.

19 See: C. R. Markham, "W.W. May," *Proceedings of the Royal Geographic Society* 7, no. 3 (March 1896), 324.

20 Markham, "The Voyage of the 'Eira' and Mr. Leigh Smith's Arctic Discoveries in 1880," 131.

21 Ibid., 143.

22 See: *The Times*, "Mr. Leigh Smith's Arctic Expedition," October 19, 1880, 10; see also: Moore, *Hancox*, 152.

23 A margin note written by George Nares in Clements Markham's original article explains that "It was named Bell Island from the shape of a hill on it." See: Sir George Nares, "Referee report," 11, RGS/A2A/JMS/17/104.

24 W.J.A. Grant, "Cruise of the Yacht *Eira*, and Discovery of New Lands in the Far North," *The Leisure Hour* (an illustrated

magazine for home reading), (London, 1881), 218.

25 Markham, "The Voyage of the 'Eira' and Mr. Leigh Smith's Arctic Discoveries in 1880," 133.

26 It is probable that all of these place names were a post-expedition collaboration between Leigh Smith and Markham, with Leigh Smith providing the names of favored relatives, or colleagues and scientists who had either been with him in 1880 or on one of his earlier expeditions, with Markham (and Sir George Nares) adding in particularly influential individuals in geographical circles in England or as a small reward to the museum curators who identified the collections returned by the expedition. An example of the latter is the waterway on the eastern side of Bruce Island that was named Miers Channel, for Edward J. Miers (1851–1930), curator of the crustacean collection at the Natural History Museum, a young biologist who would describe the marine invertebrates Leigh Smith delivered to the Natural History Museum in London after the expedition.

27 A margin note written by George Nares in Clements Markham's original article explains: "The channel was named after Captain *De Bruyne*, the leader of the Dutch Expedition of 1879; and the large island received the name of *Northbrook*, in honor of the late President of our Society, and present First Lord of the Admiralty [italics in original]." See: Nares, "Referee report," 13, RGS/A2A/JMS/17/104.

28 Markham, "The Voyage of the 'Eira' and Mr. Leigh Smith's Arctic Discoveries in 1880," 134.

29 Ibid., 144.

30 A margin note written by Sir George Nares in Clements Markham's original article explains that it was "now called Cape Grant." See: Nares, "Referee report," 17, RGS/A2A/JMS/17/104.

31 A margin note written by Sir George Nares in Clements Markham's original article explains that it was "named Cape Crowther after the mate of the *Eira*." See: Nares, "Referee report," 17, RGS/A2A/JMS/17/104.

32 Ibid., 17.

33 Ibid. An expedition to search for the wreck of the *Eira*, as well as survey other areas of historical and scientific interest in Franz Josef Land, has been proposed by the explorer Milko Vuille. See: http://acarsa.com/.

34 *The Times*, "Mr. Leigh Smith's Arctic Expedition," October 19, 1880,10.

35 Markham, "The Voyage of the 'Eira' and Mr. Leigh Smith's Arctic Discoveries in 1880,"145.

36 C. R. Markham to Bates, September 26, 1880, RGS/A2A/CB6/15-31.

37 Ibid.

38 *The Times*, "Mr. Leigh Smith's Arctic Expedition," October 19, 1880, p. 10.

39 Markham, "The Voyage of the 'Eira' and Mr. Leigh Smith's Arctic Discoveries in 1880,"139.

40 Clements Markham, "Memorandum on Future Polar Discovery," October 11, 1880, RGS/A2A/RGS/CB6/15-31.

41 Ludlow diary, October 17, 1880.

42 *The Times*, "Mr. Leigh Smith's Arctic Expedition," October 19, 1880, p. 10.

43 A. H. Markham to Benjamin Leigh Smith, Nov. 7, 1880, SPRI MS 301/18 D.

44 Nares, "Referee report," Jan. 19, 1881, RGS/A2A/JMS/17/104).

45 C. R. Markham to Benjamin Leigh Smith, Nov. 17, 1880, SPRI MS 301/19/1 D.

46 Ibid.

47 C. R. Markham to Benjamin Leigh Smith, April 11, 1881, SPRI MS 301/19/3 D.

7: EXPEDITION FIVE: FRANZ JOSEF LAND, 1881–1882

1 Markham, "The Voyage of the 'Eira' and Mr. Leigh Smith's Arctic Discoveries in 1880,"146.

2 Ibid., 146.

3 Ibid., 147.

4 Ibid., 150.

5 A. H. Markham to Benjamin Leigh Smight, Nov. 7, 1880. SPRI MS 301/18 D.

6 C. R. Markham, "The Voyage of the 'Eira' and Mr. Leigh Smith's Arctic Discoveries in 1880,"150.

7 William Baxter to Benjamin Leigh Smith, Oct. 18, 1880, SPRI MS 301/3/1-31.

8 William Baxter to Benjamin Leigh Smith, Nov. 6, 1880, SPRI MS 301/3/1-31.

9 William Baxter to Benjamin Leigh Smith, Jan. 12, 1881, SPRI MS 301/3/1-31.

10 William Baxter to Benjamin Leigh Smith, Dec. 16, 1880, SPRI MS 301/3/1-31.

11 William Baxter to Benjamin Leigh Smith, Jan. 10, 1881, SPRI MS 301/3/1-31.

12 Ludlow diary, April 2, 1881, Hancox Archive.

13 W.J.A. Grant to Benjamin Leigh Smith, February 24, 1881, SPRI MS 301/12/3 D.

14 Ibid.

15 *The Times*, May 24, 1881, p. 10.

16 William Lofley to Benjamin Leigh Smith, Nov. 16, 1880, SPRI <MS #?>.

17 William Lofley to Benjamin Leigh Smith, Nov. 22, 1880, SPRI <MS #?>.

18 William Lofley to Benjamin Leigh Smith, April 11, 1881, SPRI MS 301/16/1-16.

19 T. Cromack and B. Riffenburgh, "William Robertson's account of Benjamin Leigh Smith's second expedition to Franz Josef Land in *Eira*." *Polar Record* 36, no. 199 (2000): 305–16.

20 Ibid., 308.

21 Ludlow diary, June 6, 1881.

22 Cromack and Riffenburgh, "William Robertson's account," 308.

23 A later chart of Franz Josef Land produced after the Jackson expedition names the bay between capes Lofley and Ludlow 'Weyprecht Bay.' The deeper bay between Cape Ludlow and Cape Neale to the southeast was later named Cambridge Bay, and it is possible that Leigh Smith was the one who named it after his alma mater, or asked Frederick Jackson to do so after his expedition fifteen years later. This 'bay' would eventually be revealed as Cambridge Sound, separating Alexandra Island to the northwest with Prince George Island to the southeast.

24 "Notes on animals & birds, 1881–82," SPRI MS 301/33.

25   Cromack and Riffenburgh, "William Robertson's account," 309.

26   Ibid.

27   Ibid.

28   Log of *Eira*, 1881–1882, SPRI MS 300/6 SL.

29   Ibid.

30   Cromack and Riffenburgh, "William Robertson's account," 309.

31   Ibid., 310.

32   Ibid.

33   C. R. Markham, "Second Voyage of the *Eira* to Franz Josef Land," *Proceedings of the Royal Geographic Society* 5, no. 4 (April 1883), 206.

34   Moore, *Hancox*, 153.

35   Cromack and Riffenburgh, "William Robertson's account," 310.

36   Benjamin Leigh Smith. 1881–82. "Notes and draft account, 1881–82," SPRI MS 301/32 BJ.

37   Cromack and Riffenburgh, "William Robertson's account," 310.

38   See: "Stores save from *Eira*, 1881," SPRI 301/34 D.

39   Cromack and Riffenburgh, "William Robertson's account," 310.

40   Ibid., 311.

41   Benjamin Leigh Smith. 1881–82. "Notes and draft account, 1881–82," SPRI MS 301/32 BJ.

42   See: Benjamin Leigh Smith, "Diary," 1881, SPRI MS 301/2 BJ.

43   Ibid.

44   Cromack and Riffenburgh, "William Robertson's account," 311.

45   Log of *Eira* after the shipwreck, SPRI MS 300/5-6 SL.

46   Ludlow diary, September 29, 1881.

47   Ibid., October 11, 1881.

48   Ibid., November 4, 1881.

49   Giæver to Gore-Booth, November 26, 1881, Hancox Archive; see also LTR from A.E. Nordenskiold to Sir Allen Young, May 13, 1882, RGS/CB7/65.

50   Ludlow diary, November 28, 1881.

51   Ibid., December 1, 1881.

52   Log of *Eira* after the shipwreck, SPRI MS 300/5-6 SL.

53   Cromack and Riffenburgh, "William Robertson's account," 312.

54   Ibid., 310.

55   Log of *Eira* after the shipwreck, SPRI MS 300/5-6 SL.

56   Cromack and Riffenburgh, "William Robertson's account," 312.

57   Log of *Eira* after the shipwreck, SPRI MS 300/5-6 SL.

58   Cromack and Riffenburgh, "William Robertson's account," 312.

59   Log of *Eira* after the shipwreck, SPRI MS 300/5-6 SL.

60   Cromack and Riffenburgh, "William Robertson's account," 313.

61   Log of *Eira* after the shipwreck, SPRI MS 300/5-6 SL.

62   Cromack and Riffenburgh, "Robertson's account," 313.

63   Ibid.

64   Ibid.

65   Log of *Eira* after the shipwreck, SPRI MS 300/5-6 SL.

66   Cromack and Riffenburgh, "William Robertson's account," 314.

67   Ibid.

68   Ludlow diary, February 15, 1882.

69 *The Times*, June 1, 1882, 10.

70 Ibid.

71 *The Times*, June 1, 1882, 10.

72 Ibid.

73 Ludlow diary, June 19, 1882.

74 Log of *Eira* after the shipwreck, SPRI MS 300/5-6 SL.

75 Ibid.

76 Ibid.

77 Ibid.

78 Ibid.

79 Cromack and Riffenburgh, "William Robertson's account," 314.

80 Ibid., 315

81 Ibid., 316.

82 *The Times*, August 22, 1882, 4.

83 See: Nares, "Referee report," RGS/A2A/JMS/17/107.

84 *The Times*, August 22, 1882, 4.

8: BENJAMIN LEIGH SMITH AND HIS TIMES, 1883–1913

1 Milicent Ludlow diary, August 21, 1882, Hancox Archive.

2 Ibid.

3 *The Times*, August 21, 1882, 7.

4 Moore, *Hancox*, 155.

5 Ibid., 130.

6 *The Times*, January 19, 1883, 3.

7 *The Times*, February 13, 1883, 6.

8 *The Times*, April 4, 1883, 5.

9 *The Times*, June 20, 1883, 7.

10 Moore, *Hancox*, 178.

11 Norman Moore, "Benjamin Leigh Smith," June 10, 1887, Hancox Archive.

12 See: B. Leigh Smith, "Referee report," RGS/A2A/JMS/15/95.

13 Arthur G. Credland, "Benjamin Leigh Smith: A Forgotten Pioneer," *Polar Record* 20, no. 125 (1980): 131; A.G.E. Jones, "Benjamin Leigh Smith: Arctic Yachtsman," *The Musk-Ox* 16 (1975): 24–31.

14 Murray and Hjort, *The Depths of the Ocean*, 11.

15 Petermann, "Geographie und Erforschung der Polar-Regionen, Nr. 58, 105.

16 Jonathan M. Karpoff, "Public versus Private Initiative in Arctic exploration: the Effects of Incentives and Organizational Structures." Independent Institute Working Paper 23 (2000): 2.

17 Benjamin Leigh Smith to H.R. Hill, written from Scalands, November 6, 1892, SPRI MS100/60/3.

18 Benjamin Leigh Smith to H.R. Hill, Chateau Clerant, March 9, 1893, SPRI MS100/60/3.

19 Even the simple wooden plank on his grave disappeared for a time before it was recently rediscovered near the church where he is buried in Brightling. His descendants placed a replacement marker on the centenary of his death in 2013.

20 Benjamin Leigh Smith to H. R. Hill, Chateau Clerant, March 9, 1893, SPRI MS100/60/3.

21 Benjamin Leigh Smith to Amy Moore, July 26, 1899, Hancox Archive.

APPENDICES

APPENDIX 1: CREW OF *EIRA* DURING THE 1881–82 EXPEDITION, FROM *THE TIMES*, AUGUST 22, 1882.

Benjamin Leigh Smith, commander
W. H. Neale, M.B.B.S., medical officer
William Lofley, ice master
J. Crowther, first mate
T. Fenton, second mate
G. Byers, harpooner
A. Valentine, harpooner
C. Marshall, harpooner
J. Harvey, boatswain
W. Masson, cook
J. Johnson, carpenter
J. M'Millan, A.B.
R. Crooks, A.B.
D. Milne, A.B.
G. Alexander, A.B.
A. Robertson, A.B.
D. Walker, A.B.
A. Gray, A.B.
J. Allan, A.B.
J. Gill, steward
T. Clarke, cook's mate
William Robertson, chief engineer
G. Pert, second engineer
J. Thompson, blacksmith
William Laing, fireman

APPENDIX 2: *NOTES ON ANIMALS & BIRDS 1881–82* [LIKELY WRITTEN BY W.H. NEALE], SPRI MS 301/33

On July 25th, 1881, we reached Gray Bay at Cape Grant + Cape Crowther there are large loomeries; a short distance up the bay on the W side many rotgies had their young among the basaltic columns of the lofty cliffs.

Other birds seen were:

Snowbird
Mobley
Boatswain
Arctic tern
Dovekies
Eider duck
Burgomeister
Kittiwake
Sandling
Brent goose
Snowy owl
Falcon

On E side near head of Gray Bay there were a good number of snow birds and dovekies [indistinct], but too high up for one to obtain the eggs. At C Stephen there was a large loomery & at C Forbes there were a few looms, a good number of rotges & dovekies & some snow birds.

At Bell Is the same species of birds were seen and on the S side there was a large loomery and nests of Kittiwakes, Dovekies, Rotges, snowbirds & burgomeisters. Rain geese & brent geese were seen & [indistinct] on the cliffs 700 ft high but no nests were seen.

At C Flora there was a very large loomery, and also many Rotges, Dovekies, Kittiwakes, & snowbirds. In the low land several snow buntings & [indistinct] were seen, no nests were found. The looms lay their eggs on the bare rocks & the dovekies & rotges lay them in the crevices of the rocks. The kittiwake makes a nest of [indistinct] and moss. The snow bird makes a rudimentary nest of moss & feathers, but of no definite shape. Each species seen occupies a separate part of the cliff.

The rotgees & dovekies left about the first wek in Sep. Looms were very scarce after Sep. 10th. On Sept 22nd journal says a few Burgomeisters, Snow birds, molloys, kittiwakes, Eider Duck & Brent geese seen but getting very scarce.

On Oct 13 3 or 4 snow birds & occasionally a Burgomeister or molloy seen hovering around the meat outside house. On Oct. 28 whilst killing some walrus, 2 snow birds, 2 or 3 molloys, & Burgomeisters were seen and remained for 2 or 3 days eating the refuse of the carcass.

On Feb. 8 a snowy owl was seen, the first bird to arrive. On Feb. 18th 2 or 3 flocks of dovekies were seen flying to the NW and on the 20th there were a great number seen in the water. March 9th the first loom was seen but it was not until the end of March that they began to settle on the rocks and then they would only stop on the cliffs for a few hours & go away for 4 or 5 days. We were not aboe to get up the hill and shoot any until the 16th of April.

APPENDIX 3: *STORES SAVED FROM EIRA 1881* [LIKELY RECORDED BY W. H. NEALE], SPRI MS 301/34; D

* Stores marked thus were saved for the boat journey. Also 16 gallons of rum, 12 lbs of tea and 50 tins of milk; about 800 lbs of cooked walrus meat added to the above, completed our stock of provisions for the boat journey.

Corn beef 516*
Libby cooked beef 856 lbs*
Compressed mutton 50 lbs*
Salt meat 1 ½ casks
Cooked meats in 2 lb tins 180 lbs*
Chicken in 1 lb tins 13 lbs*
Ox tongues in 2 lb tins 20 lbs*
Soup & boulli in 6 lb tins 570 lbs*
110 two lb tins of soup 220 lbs*
Ox tongues 23*

Spirits
Rum 75 gallons
Whiskey 18 bottles
Gin 12 bottles
Sherry 18 bottles
Champagne 72 bottles
Beer 60 bottles
Brandy 12 bottles

Milk 200 tins
Cocoa milk 60 tins*
Coffee & milk*
Van Houtens Cocoa 6 lbs

Cabin biscuits 80 lbs
Flour 6 casks
Tea 80 lbs
Sugar 1 cask
Molasses ½ cask
Tapioca 14 lbs
Cornflour 14 lbs

Vegetables, etc
Carrots & potatoes in 6 lb tins 2268 lbs
Carrots in 4 lb tins 160 lbs
Turnips in 2 lb tins 96 lbs
Dutch vegetables in 10 lb tins 360 lbs
Goward's dried potatoes 194 lbs
One lb tins of vegetables such as peas, beans, brussel sprouts, apricots, macedonie [sic] 200 lbs
Apples in 2 lb tins 50 lbs
Prunes 40 lbs
Jams in 1 lb tins 90 lbs
Morris compressed vegetables 24 tins
Kopps consolidated soups (each box containing 144 tins) 2 boxes
Pickles 15 bottles
[Knorr's?] sauces 18 bottles

APPENDIX 4: *SUPPLIES LOADED ONTO THE FOUR ESCAPE BOATS, JUNE 1882, FROM THE "LOG OF EIRA AFTER THE SHIPWRECK, 28 NOV 1881–31 MARCH 1882,"* SPRI MS 300/5-6 SL

NO. 1 WHALE BOAT

Corned beef
3–14 lbs
5–7 lbs
31–2 lbs
Libby
10–6 lbs
13–4 lbs
Compressed mutton
2–6 lbs
1–4 lbs
Total 267 lbs
Ave: 38 and 1/7 lbs.

26 Soups Boulli
24 small soups
1 chicken
21 two lbs meat
3 one lb meat
2 tongues
Total: 256 lbs
Ave: 36 and 2/7 lbs.

NO 2. WHALE BOAT

Corned beef
3–14 lbs
6–7 lbs

15–2 lbs
Libby
9–6 lbs
11–4 lbs
Compressed mutton
2–6 lbs
Total 224 lbs
Ave: 37 and 1/3 lbs.

23 Soups Boulli
23 small soups
4 chickens
18 two lbs meat
Total: 224 lbs
Ave: 37 and 1/3 lbs.

NOS. 3 & 4 WALRUS BOATS

Corned beef
4–14 lbs
4–7 lbs
15–2 lbs
Libby
9–6 lbs
11–4 lbs
Compressed mutton
1–6 lbs
Total 218 lbs
Ave: 36 and 1/3 lbs.

23 Soups Boulli
23 small soups
4 chickens
18 two lbs meat
4 tongues
Total: 232 lbs
Ave: 38 and 2/3 lbs.

SELECT BIBLIOGRAPHY

Admiralty Arctic Committee. *Papers and Correspondence relating to the Equipment and Fitting Out of the Arctic Expedition of 1875*. London: HMSO, 1875.

Anonymous. "Arctic Exploration." *Sussex Advertiser*, September 3, 1872.

———. "Arctic Exploration." *Edinburgh Review* 141, no. 288 (1875): 447–81.

———. "Arctic discovery." *Saturday Review of Politics, Literature, Science and Art*, 35, no. 919 (1873): 741–42.

———. *Memoir to Illustrate the Origin and Foundation of the Pollock Medal*. Woolwich: Boddy and Co., 1875.

———. "Obituary: Sir James Lamont." *Geographical Journal* 42, no. 3 (1913): 301–2.

———. "Private letter written on board *Polhem* at Mossel Bay, June 19, 1873, and published in Stockholm newspapers, July 21, 1873." From "Translated excerpts from newspapers re: 1872–1873 Swedish expedition." Cambridge: Scott Polar Research Institute Archives, 1873, MS 301/36/1-2.

Baldwin, Evelyn B. *The Search for the North Pole*. Chicago: privately printed, 1896.

Barr, Susan. "The History of Western Activity in Franz Josef Land," In: *Franz Josef Land*, ed. Susan Barr. Oslo: Norsk Polarinstitutt, 1995.

———. *Jan Mayen*. Oslo: Norskpolarinsitutt, 1991.

———. "Norwegian use of the polar oceans as occupational arenas and exploration routes." *Polar Record* 37, no. 201 (2001): 99–110.

Barrington, Daines. *The probability of reaching the North Pole discussed*. London: C. Heydinger, 1775.

Berton, Pierre. *The Arctic Grail*. New York: Viking, 1988.

Blake, W. Jr. "Radiocarbon dating of raised beaches in Nordaustlandet, Spitsbergen." In: G.O. Raasch, ed. *Geology of the Arctic*. Toronto: University of Toronto Press, 1961, 133–45.

Bruce, Anthony. *The Purchase System in the British Army, 1660–1871*. London: Royal Historical Society, 1980.

Buchan, Alex R. "SS *Windward* – whaler and Arctic exploration ship." *Polar Record* 24, no. 151 (1988): 213–22.

Capelotti, P.J. "Benjamin Leigh Smith's first Arctic expedition, Svalbard, 1871." *Polar Record* 42, no. 220 (2006): 1–14.

—. "Benjamin Leigh Smith's second Arctic expedition: Svalbard and Jan Mayen Land, 1872." *Polar Record* 44, no. 3 (2008): 255–64.

—. "Benjamin Leigh Smith's third Arctic expedition: Svalbard, 1873." *Polar Record* 46, no. 4 (2010): 359–71.

Capelotti, P.J., editor. *The Franz Josef Land Archipelago: E.B. Baldwin's Journal of the Wellman Expedition to Franz Josef Land, 1898–1899.* Jefferson, North Carolina: McFarland Publishers, 2004.

Carlheim-Gyllensköld, V. *På Åttionde Breddgraden.* Stockholm: Albert Bonniers förlag, 1900.

Chermside, H. C. *Journal on board of the SS Diana.* 3 vols., 1873. Cambridge: Scott Polar Research Institute Archives, MS 300/4/1.

—. "Recent Explorations in the Spitsbergen Seas by Leigh Smith" (unpublished manuscript, n.d. [1873]). Edinburgh University Library, Special Collections, MS Gen 77.

Conway, William Martin. *No Man's Land: A History of Spitsbergen from its Discovery in 1596 to the beginning of Scientific Exploration of the Country.* Cambridge: Cambridge University Press, 1906.

Credland, Arthur G. "Benjamin Leigh Smith: A Forgotten Pioneer." *Polar Record* 20, no. 125 (1980): 127–45.

—. "Foreword." In: Nicholas Redman, *Whale' Bones of the British Isles.* England: Redman Publishing, 2004.

Cromack, T., and B. Riffenburgh. "William Robertson's account of Benjamin Leigh Smith's second expedition to Franz Josef Land in *Eira.*" *Polar Record* 36, no. 199 (2000): 305–16.

Dahle, Kolbein. *Kulturminneplan for Svalbard 2000–2010.* Sysselmannens rapportserie Nr. 2/2000. Longyearbyen: Sysselmannen for Svalbard, 2000.

Dufferin, and Ava, F., Marquis of. 1857. *Letters from High Latitudes.* London: John Murray.

Eaton, Richard E. "Mr. Leigh Smith's Arctic Expedition." *The Times,* August 26, 1873, p. 12.

Fleming, Fergus. *Barrow's Boys.* London: Granta Books, 1998.

Forsius, Henrik. "Medical Problems Connected with Wintering in the Arctic during A.E. Nordenskiöld's Expeditions in 1872–73 and 1878–79." *Arctic Medical History* 52 (1993): 131–36.

Grant, W.J.A. "Cruise of the Yacht *Eira,* and Discovery of New Lands in the Far North." *The Leisure Hour* (an illustrated magazine for home reading), London, 1881, 213–20.

Gyory, Joanna, Arthur J. Mariano, and Edward H. Ryan. "The Spitsbergen Current." *Ocean Surface Currents.* http://oceancurrents.rsmas.miami.edu/atlantic/spitsbergen.html (August 2005).

Handley, Jenny, and Hazel Lake. *Progress by Persuasion: The Life of William Smith, 1756–1835.* Hazel Lake, 2007.

Hisdal, Vidar. *Svalbard: Nature and History.* Oslo: Norsk Polarinstitutt, 1998.

Holland, Clive, editor. 1994. *Farthest North: A History of North Polar Exploration in Eye-Witness Accounts.* New York: Carroll & Graf.

Horn, Gunnar. *Franz Josef Land: Natural History, Discovery, Exploration, and Hunting.* Oslo: NSIU Skrifter 29, 1930.

Jahn, Alfred. "The Raised Shore Lines and Beaches in Hornsund and the Problem of Postglacial Vertical Movements of Spitsbergen." *Polish Geographical Review* 31, Supplement, 1959.

James, Dermot. *The Gore-Booths of Lissadell.* Dublin: Woodfield Press, 2004.

Jones, A.G.E. "Benjamin Leigh Smith: Arctic Yachtsman." *The Musk-Ox* 16 (1975): 24–31.

Kane, Elisha Kent. *Arctic Explorations.* Philadelphia: Childs & Peterson, 1856.

Karpoff, Jonathan M. "Public versus Private Initiative in Arctic Exploration: The Effects of Incentives and Organizational Structures." *Independent Institute Working Paper Nr. 23* (2000). http://www.independent.org/pdf/working_papers/23_arctic.pdf.

Kish, George. "Adolf Erik Nordenskiöld (1832–1901): Polar Explorer and Historian of Cartography." *Geographical Journal* 134, no. 4 (1968): 487–500.

————. *North-east Passage: Adolf Erik Nordenskiöld, His Life and Times.* Amsterdam: Nico Israel, 1973.

Kjellman, F.R. *Svenska Polarexpedition År 1872 + 1873 under ledning af A.E. Nordenskiöld.* Stockholm: P.A. Norstedt + Söner, 1875.

Krogh-Hansen, Hans Kristian. "Lakselordenes gjemmested." *Aftenposten,* June 6, 2012, Reise, 8.

Krusenstjerna, P.M. "Letter published in the *Official Gazette of Sweden,* July 28, 1873." From "Translated excerpts from newspapers re: 1872–1873 Swedish expedition." Cambridge: Scott Polar Research Institute Archives, MS 301/36/1–2.

Lamont, James. *Seasons with the Sea Horses.* London: Hurst & Blackett, 1861.

————. *Yachting in the Arctic Seas.* London: Chatto & Windus, 1876.

Leigh Smith, Benjamin. "To the Editor of the Times." *The Times* (27538): col E, Nov. 19, 1872.

————. *Journal of the Schooner Sampson* (unpublished, [1871]). Edinburgh University Library, Special Collections, Gen 76–77.

Leslie, Alexander. 1879. *The Arctic Voyages of Adolf Erik Nordenskiöld, 1858–1879.* London: Macmillan.

Loomis, Chauncey C. 1971. *Weird and Tragic Shores.* New York: Knopf.

Lubbock, Basil. *The Arctic Whalers.* Glasgow: Brown, Son & Ferguson, 1937.

Markham, C. R. "Second Voyage of the *Eira* to Franz Josef Land," *Proceedings of the Royal Geographic Society* 5, no. 4, (April 1883).

————. *The Threshold of the Unknown Regions.* London: Samson Low, 1875.

Markham, C. R. "The Voyage of the 'Eira' and Mr. Leigh Smith's Arctic Discoveries in 1880." *Proceedings of the Royal Geographic Society*, 3 no. 3 (March 1881).

———. "W. W. May." *Proceedings of the Royal Geographic Society*, 7, no. 3 (March 1896).

McConnell, Anita. *No Sea Too Deep: The History of Oceanographic Instruments*. Bristol: Adam Hilger., 1982.

Melville, Herman. *Moby-Dick; or, The Whale*. New York: Penguin, 1851 [1992].

Moore, Charlotte. *Hancox: A House and a Family*. London: Penguin, 2010.

Murphy, David Thomas. *German Exploration of the Polar World, A History, 1870–1940*. Lincoln: University of Nebraska Press, 2002.

Murray, John, and Johan Hjort. *The Depths of the Ocean*. London: Macmillan, 1912. (Reprinted in 1965 by J. Cramer, Weinheim, Germany.)

Nordenskiöld, Adolf Erik. "Redogörelse för den Svenska Polarexpeditionen år 1872–73." *Kgl. Vetenskaps, Akad.* 2, no. 18 (1875).

Norsk Polarinstitutt. *The Place Names of Svalbard*. Oslo: Norsk Polarinstitutt, 1991. Skrifter Nr. 80 and 112; Ny-Trykk.

Nugent, Frank. *Seek the Frozen Lands: Irish Polar Explorers, 1740–1922*. Cork: Collins Press, 2004.

Olsson, I.U., and W. Blake, Jr. "Problems of radiocarbon dating of raised beaches, based on experience in Spitsbergen." *Norsk Geografisk Tidsskrift* 18 (1962): 47–64.

Owen, C.V. "Chermside, Sir Herbert Charles (1850–1929)." In: *Oxford Dictionary of National Biography*. Oxford: Oxford University Press, 2004. Online edition: http://www.oxforddnb.com/view/article/32390, accessed 6 July 2009.

Parry, William Edward. *Narrative of an Attempt to Reach the North Pole*. London: John Murray, 1828.

Payer, Julius. *New Lands within the Arctic Circle*. New York: D. Appleton, 1876.

Petermann, August. "Geographie und Erforschung der Polar-Regionen, Nr. 58: Die Englisch-Norwegischen Entdeckungen im Nordosten von Spitzbergen, Nordfahrten von Smyth, Ulve, Torkildsen, 19. Juni–27. Sept. 1871." *Mittheilungen aus Justus Perthes' Geographischer Anstalt über wichtige neue Erforschungen auf dem Gesammtgebiete der Geographie von Dr. A. Petermann*, 18. Band: 101–6. Gotha: Justus Perthes, 1872.

———. "Geographie und Erforschung der Polar-Regionen, Nr. 59: Gillis-Land, König Karl-Land und das Seeboden-Relief um Spitzbergen, nach dem Standpunkte der Kenntniss im Jahre 1872." *Mittheilungen aus Justus Perthes' Geographischer Anstalt über wichtige neue Erforschungen auf dem Gesammtgebiete der Geographie von Dr. A. Petermann*, 18. Band: 111–12. Gotha: Justus Perthes, 1872.

———. "Originalkarte zur Übersicht der Reisen von Smyth, Ulve, Torkildsen, 1871." *Mittheilungen aus Justus Perthes' Geographischer Anstalt über wichtige neue Erforschungen auf dem Gesammtgebiete der Geographie von Dr. A. Petermann*, 18. Band: Tafel 5. Gotha: Justus Perthes, 1872.

————. "Smyth' & Ulve's Reise im Nordosten von Spitzbergen und ihre Aufnahmen im Nord-Ost-Lande, Aug. & Sept, 1871." *Mittheilungen aus Justus Perthes' Geographischer Anstalt über wichtige neue Erforschungen auf dem Gesammtgebiete der Geographie von Dr. A. Petermann*, 18. Band: Tafel 6. Gotha: Justus Perthes, 1872.

Phipps, Constantine John. *A Voyage towards the North Pole*. London: J. Nourse, 1774.

Rawlinson, Henry C. "First Meeting, 10th November, 1874: Opening Address," *Proceedings of the Royal Geographical Society of London* 19, no. 1 (1874): 1–17.

Ritter, Jürgen, and Ulrich Schacht. *Von Spitzbergen nach Franz-Josef-Land*. Dortmund: Harenberg Kommunikation, 1993.

Scoresby, William. *An Account of the Arctic Regions*. Edinburgh: A. Constable, 1820.

Slupetzky, Heinz. *"A History of the Austrian Discovery of Franz Josef Land: The Austro-Hungarian Tegetthoff Expedition, 1872–1874."* In: *Franz Josef Land*, ed. Susan Barr. Oslo: Norsk Polarinstitutt, 1995.

"The Spitzbergen Drama." *New York Times*, August 3, 1873.

Tammiksaar, E., with N.G. Sukhova and I.R. Stone. "Hypothesis versus Fact: August Petermann and Polar Research," *Arctic* 52, no. 3 (1999): 237–44.

Walker, William. "Log book of the yacht *Sampson*, kept by Capt. William Walker, 29 April–5 October 1873." Cambridge: Scott Polar Research Institute Archives, MS 300/3.

Wells, John C. *The Gateway to Polynia: A Voyage to Spitzbergen from the Journal of John C. Wells*. London: Henry S. King, 1873.

Wijkander, August. "Letter." June 22, 1873 (published in a Stockholm newspaper on July 18, 1873). From "Translated excerpts from newspapers re: 1872–1873 Swedish expedition." Cambridge: Scott Polar Research Institute Archives, MS 301/36/1–2.

Wilson, Paul D. "Chermside, Sir Herbert Charles (1850–1929)." In: *Australian Dictionary of Biography*, vol. 7, 631–32. Melbourne: Melbourne University Press, 1979.

Wojtczak, Helena. *Women of Victorian Hastings, 1830–1870*. Hastings: Hastings Press, 2002.

Wordie, J.M. "An Expedition to Jan Mayen Island," *Geographical Journal* 59, no. 3 (1922): 180–94.

INDEX

birth of, 18, 19
cab injuries, 149–50
control of family, xxii–xxiii, 218–19
decorations, xxi, 177–78
dementia, xvii
expeditions to Franz Josef Land, 153–71, 175–206, 225–26
expeditions to Svalbard, 51–75, 78–95, 97–119, 224–25
family relations, 19, 24, 218
formative years, 1–3, 22
and Franklin expedition, 2–3, 124–25
furthest north of, 71–72, 224
illegitimacy of, 24–25
inability to document expeditions, xxi, 219–20
inheritances, 22, 24, 26, 34
at Jesus College, 22, 26
ocean temperatures controversy, 78, 224–25
reluctance to appear in public, 177
and sinking of *Eira*, 184–86
wealth of, xi, 22
writings at Cape Flora, 189–92
Leigh Smith, Benjamin Valentine, 221
Leigh Smith, Isabella (Bella), 19, 21, 46, 123, 162
Leigh Smith, Mabel, 123, 149, 154, 218
Leigh Smith, Millicent, 217, 218, 220
Leigh Smith, Philip, 221
Leigh Smith, Willy, xix, 19, 21, 46, 153, 197
Lerwick, 81–82, 101, 154, 169
Lewis-Jones, Huw, *230*
Little Table Island (Vesle Tavleøya), 15, 18
Livesay, William, 42
Lofley, William (captain of *Eira*), 154, 159, 166, 176, 178, 179
sinking of *Eira*, 183
Longden, Anne (mother of Leigh Smith), 19, 21
Loomis, Chauncey, 126
Low Island (Lågøya), 15, 16, 67, 114
Ludlow, John, xxv, 46, 77, 97, 123, 124, 149, 165–66, 180, 194–95, 197, 204
death, 218
diary of, 46–48, 177
Lutwidge, Skeffington, 4, 6, 12, 13
Lyell, Charles, 34

M

Mabel Island, 162, 182
Mack, Frederick Christian, 112–13
Magdalena Bay (Magdalenafjorden), 5, 45, 110, 119, 155
Markham, Albert, 145, 156, 171, 175, 176
Markham, Clements, xxvii, 138, 142–43, 145, 151, *152*, 158, 163, 164, 168, 194, 196, 214, 225
accepts medal on behalf of Leigh Smith, 178
praises Leigh Smith, xxvii, 169–70
reads Franz Josef Land paper, 171, 175
Martens Island (Martensøya), 119
Mawson, Douglas, xix
May, Walter W., 158
May Island, 158–59, 160, 162
McClintock, Leopold, 2, 138, 178, 196, 220
McClure, Robert, 125, 178
Miers, Edward, J., 170
Mikkelsen, Ejnar, xix
Moffen Island, 6, 44, 73, 81, 88–90, 115–16
whale skeleton on, 88, *89*
Mohn, Henrik, 70
Moore, Charlotte, xxiii, 10, 20, 24, 220, *230*
Moore, Norman, xxii–xxix, 46, 218
competency examination of Leigh Smith, xxii–xxix
poem about Leigh Smith, 220–21
Mussel Bay (Mosselbukta), 26, 94, 103–8, 110, 206

N

Nansen, Fridtjof, 87, 171, 175–76, 227
Nares, George, 145, 171, 173, 220
Neale, William, xxiv, xxv, 154, *156*, 159, 160–70, 175, 193, 198, 214, 220
Nelson, Horatio, 3, 7–8
Nelson Island (Nelsonøya), 8, 108
Nightingale, Florence, 11, 27, 149, 162, 217
Nightingale, William, 11
Nightingale Sound, 25, 162, 164
Nordaustlandet, 45, 65, 75, 79, 86, 110, 117, 166, 224
Nordenskiöld, Adolf Erik, xxi, xxii, 26, 81, 92–95, 100, 110–11, 117, 119, 138, 148, 178, 205, 225
rescue by Leigh Smith, 103–7
Northwest Passage, 1, 2, 8, 11